The
Acoustic
Guitar
Handbook

How to Buy, Maintain, Set Up, Troubleshoot, and Repair Your Guitar

Paul Balmer

Voyageur Press

First published in 2011 by Voyageur Press, an imprint of MBI
Publishing Company, 400 First Avenue North, Suite 300,
Minneapolis, MN 55401 USA

Voyageur Press titles are also available at discounts in bulk
quantity for industrial or sales-promotional use. For details write
to Special Sales Manager at MBI Publishing Company, 400 First
Avenue North, Suite 300, Minneapolis, MN 55401 USA.

To find out more about our books, visit us online at www.
voyageurpress.com.

ISBN-13: 978-0-7603-4022-6

Cover designed by: Karl Laun

Printed in the USA

The
Acoustic
Guitar
Handbook

**How to Buy,
Maintain, Set Up,
Troubleshoot,
and Repair
Your Guitar**

Paul Balmer

Contents

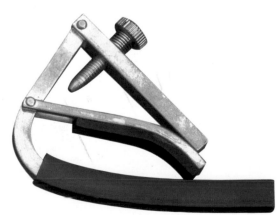

Introduction

'The Acoustic Guitar' – were ever three words loaded with so many possibilities?

Strictly speaking, any guitar can be played 'acoustically', even a Fender Strat! But, what I think we guitarists tend to mean by an acoustic guitar is guitars designed to be *heard* acoustically. However, with the ambient noise levels of the average modern music venue, even these are now amplified – either with a microphone, piezo-electric or moving-coil transducer, magnetic pickup, or all four!

I remember a time in the mid-20th century when many guitarists expected the 'new' electric guitar to supplant the 'old' acoustic. The new electric Fenders and Gibsons were full of adolescent sparkle, looked cool and could be heard over the loudest band. It's a testament to the beauty, range and sensitivity of the acoustic guitar that the opposite has happened, and the acoustic is more popular than ever.

'The quest to be heard'

Nevertheless, the design and development of the acoustic guitar in all its variants is the story of 'the quest to be heard'. In the early 21st century, that quest has been realised, and the acoustic guitarist can now take centre stage at any major amphitheatre, knowing that, PA crew permitting, he will be heard.

A small Torres 1888 guitar (reproduction by Victor Payne).

A little history – some key players and their instruments

The 'classic' guitar has a repertoire rooted in the tablature for the lute-like Vihuela, and the first mention of 'Guittara' itself occurs in 1621 in a Masque by Ben Jonson, with the oldest surviving instrument dating from around 1590. The Stradivarius five-course 'Baroque' guitar is one of only two known surviving examples from a lost epoch.

By 1860, after thousands of years of evolution, guitar development had settled down, and a familiar shape emerged, with six strings tuned EADGBE, still smaller than many current guitars, and often played in a domestic parlour for musical evenings, or perhaps a song at the local tavern. No real problem, as yet, for the guitars 'small' voice to be heard.

The 'Spanish' Guitar

The newer 'six-course' repertoire developed by Fernando Sor (1778–1839) in Spain, and Mauro Giuliani (1781–1829) for the Italians, coincides with the emerging concept of 'Concert' performance. The quest to be heard in larger venues had begun.

Virtuoso player Francisco Tarrega (1852–1909) encouraged the great Spanish luthier Antonio Torres (1817–1892) to help, and the result was the bigger guitar we now recognise as the standard 'Spanish' instrument, with gut strings. Torres even patented an internal metal 'reflector', or Tornavoz, designed to further improve projection. This concept returns again and again to this day.

From 1912, the nineteen-year-old Spanish virtuoso Andres Segovia (1893–1987) took the audacious step of playing his acoustic Ramirez and Hauser guitars to Philharmonic halls unamplified. I and millions of others sat as he waited for silence and insisted; "The audience, must come to the guitar." Eventually, in 1945 he worked with Albert Augustine to

Brendan McCormack playing Emilio Pujol's Vihuela.

Andres Segovia.

The innovative
Yamaha NX electro-
acoustic 'classic'.

Paul Balmer helps Julian Bream
(with Hauser 1) tell his story; 'My
Life In Music'.

Prince of the guitar." Williams, with his dazzling technique and projection, has pushed luthiers to new levels, initially working with Ignacio Fleta and latterly the innovative Greg Smallman. David Russell and Sharon Isbin keep the classic guitar alive into the 21st Century.

Throughout the late 20th century, Laurindo Almeida and Charlie Byrd had kept nylon-string guitars alive in popular music, and the new Yamaha NX series has helped Antonio Forcione in jazz, and Rodrigo Y Gabriela in a fantastic new hybrid, take 'nylon strings' to the world's great arenas.

develop more robust nylon strings and perhaps a few more decibels. Segovia was by no means the first in the concert hall, it was the scale of his ambition that set him apart.

In South America, Augustin Barrios Mangore (1885–1944) was the first 'classic' guitarist to make commercial recordings. Interestingly, he experimented with steel strings. But Segovia had opened the door, and soon virtuoso players would appear internationally – Alirio Diaz (b1923) in Paraguay, Narciso Yepes (1927–1997) in Spain, Ida Presti (1924–1967) in France and Luise Walker (1910–1998) in Vienna. In 1955, armed with the now established Augustine strings, Spaniard Narciso Yepes made the first stereo recording of Rodrigo's Concierto de Aranjuez (1939) – a turning point for public recognition of this 'new' instrument.

Julian Bream (b1933) may be the greatest musician ever to take the guitar as his first instrument, and that has inspired composers such as Benjamin Britten, Malcolm Arnold, William Walton and Richard Rodney Bennett to produce a startling new repertoire.

Then, in 1952, Segovia heard the eleven-year-old Australian guitarist John Williams and declared him "a

Steel-string acoustics and the USA

The first American guitars were probably the gut-strung Vihuelas of the Spanish conquistadors and, up until 1900, American guitars largely followed the standard European Hispanic tradition. This tradition was bolstered by first-generation Americans like CF Martin (1796–1873) who, arriving in New York from Saxony, initially made gut-strung guitars in the Viennese style of his employer, Johann Georg Stauffer (1778–1853).

But the great American revolution has to be steel strings on a Spanish design, a trend which can be traced in the USA back to the 1880s. One reason for this change was the problem of now metal frets wearing out expensive gut strings – up until the early 19th century the guitar had movable gut frets. Nickel frets were more robust, but bit into expensive gut strings. From the 1880s on, there had been experiments with even more robust steel strings, then in common use by the fashionable mandolin orchestras of the time. Carl and August Larsen of Chicago may have been the first to standardise steel strings on the American guitar, circa 1900, and composer WC Handy certainly claims to have heard 'a knife-edged guitar wail' at the Mississippi Delta's Tutwiler station in 1903. The change was certainly consolidated with the 'Hawaiian guitar' craze, which swept the USA in the early 20th century.

A 1912 Broadway musical, 'Bird of Paradise'*, had brought guitarist Joseph Kekuku's (1874–1932) Hawaiian glissandi slide styles to popular

A Gibson L5 archtop guitar.

music, and steel strings sustain glissandi far better than gut. Hawaiian groups were also a big hit at the 1915 Panama-Pacific International Exposition in San Francisco. With both coasts swept by an Hawaiian wave, it's no surprise that the first 'louder' Martin/Ditson 'Hawaiian' Dreadnoughts of 1916 had steel strings, though were still fan braced! Interestingly, from 1928–30, Kekuku taught guitar in Chicago!

Some makers were more radical in the search for volume; Lloyd Loar (1886–1943) developed the earlier experiments of Orville Gibson (1856–1918), returning to the violoncello model for his carved archtop L5 guitars of 1922. These were designed to emphasise the guitar's mid-frequencies and cut through the brass sections of the newly emerging jazz and dance-band 'orchestras'. Early versions included an internal 'Virzi Tone Producer', a wooden disc mounted inside the body directly under the bridge, also designed to increase power.

A National Reso Phonic Style 3 single resonator.

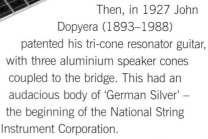

Then, in 1927 John Dopyera (1893–1988) patented his tri-cone resonator guitar, with three aluminium speaker cones coupled to the bridge. This had an audacious body of 'German Silver' – the beginning of the National String Instrument Corporation.

In Europe, driven by the newly imported Jazz, Mario Maccaferri (1900–1993), for his 1931 'Selmer' guitar, favoured laminated wood sides and back, and a solid top with a gentle arch or pliage. This, sometimes combined with another wooden variant of the internal resonator, plus a sound-reflecting varnished interior, was almost loud enough for Django Rheinhardt (1910–1953). However, the gypsy genius Rheinhardt would soon discover the benefits of borrowing the vocalist's microphone, and

* 'Bird of Paradise' featured Hawaiian music and musicians, and would tour the USA firing not only the Hawaiian guitar craze, but also launching the Ukulele into popular culture. Leo Fender and others later devised an electric 'lap' steel, and the rest is history!

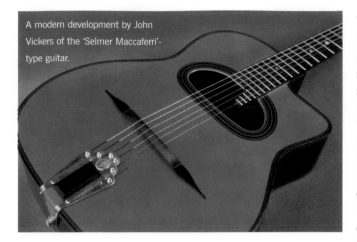

A modern development by John Vickers of the 'Selmer Maccaferri'-type guitar.

would return from a 1946 USA gig with Duke Ellington, armed with a magnetic pickup. It all sort of worked.

The Gibson CF100E of 1951, and the J160 of 1954 with single-coil P90's built into the bridge, began a revolution that sparked the piezoelectric innovations of Ovation and Fishman in the 1960s and 70s, and the continuing developments of Bob Taylor, Yamaha and L.R. Baggs.

Birth of the 'Dreadnought'

"My great grandfather, working with my grandfather and his son, went out and talked to players. The parlour guitars couldn't be heard in banjo and Mandolin orchestras – there was plenty of treble but no bass, so that led to the 12-fret Dreadnought. And then banjo players came to us and said; 'It's difficult for us to play', so we redesigned with a narrower neck and 14 frets to the body, and it's stayed the same since 1916." *CF Martin IV*

A 1929 Ditson model 111 HR – 12 frets to the body.

The Rural Blues Guitars

In the early 20th century, many rural blues musicians of the Mississippi Delta seem to have adopted the 'Hawaiian' slide glissandi and open tunings. They mostly turned the guitar back to the 'Spanish' playing position and curiously referred to open-G tuning D-G-D-G-B-D as 'Spanish'. According to Don Kent in 'Before the Blues', the glissandi effect, which produces the distinctive blues 'moan', had been so missed by early fretless banjo players, that when the banjo started to be commonly fretted, the blues players covered the frets with copper sheeting. Steel strings and knives and bottlenecks would soon give the emergent blues guitars all the 'moan' they could handle.

A ladder-braced Kalamazoo, with Michigan Maple back and sides.

Many blues players are photographed using high-end studio-prop guitars belonging to the photographer, as in Big Bill Broonzy (1898–1958) with an elaborate Gibson. Consequently, though Hooks Bros of Memphis took a shot of Robert Johnson (1911–1938) with a Gibson L1, we don't really know that he ever owned one! His playing partner, Johnny Shines, told an interviewer that Robert's favourite was 'a Kalamazoo'. This was Gibson's budget 'survive the depression' guitar, and a cheap photo-booth shot of Johnson certainly shows him with that type of guitar. Significantly, this had ladder bracing (as do most Stellas – see page 8). In 1935, this type of guitar was sold as a package, including a '107' case, a set of strings some polish and cloth, a leather pick case and a 'guitar instructor', all for $9.50 (sometimes discounted to $6!)

These cheaper guitars have a distinctive sound – low on bass and general sustain, the strings are usually worn and dull. Fittingly, they

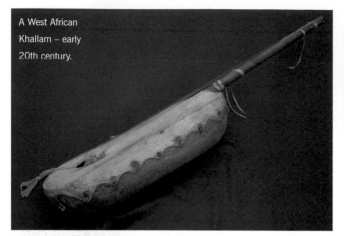

A West African Khallam – early 20th century.

A 1910 Stella Sovereign.

often have the same dry earthy timbre as the West African Khallam or Konting**, as played by some of the blues players' ill-fated ancestors. These players adapted to their instruments' limitations, developing a percussive driving insistence that didn't require sustain, the handy broken bottleneck blunted in a candle flame provided 'the blues'.

Most blues players bought 'Stellas' (Latin; Star) and occasionally 'Sovereigns' made by Oscar Schmidt at his Ferry St factory in Jersey City. Like CF Martin, Oscar was another immigrant from Saxony Germany, and established his factory in 1879. His guitars were distributed by catalogue and through furniture and 'dry goods' outlets for as little as $2! Virtually all Stellas use the older 'European' ladder bracing for both top and back and, interestingly, the few 'X-braced' examples don't have that distinctive blues sound. The company suffered hard in the depression, and in 1940 the Stella assets were acquired by the growing Harmony Guitar Company. The favourite

strings for many blues players were Black Diamonds made in Sarasota Florida since 1890. Josh White insisted on these for his battered Martin, a guitar I was fortunate enough to have at my studio for a while.

In the 21st century, Keb Mo, Chris Thomas King and Eric Bibb have all breathed new life into the acoustic blues, playing Nationals, Martins and Fylde.

The steel-strung 12-string

The key blues and ballad player of the 12-string has to be black American singer Leadbelly. Legend has it that sometime around 1912, a young Huddie ('Leadbelly') Ledbetter, then travelling with an even younger Blind Lemon Jefferson, purchased a used Stella 12-string in a Dallas pawnshop. Stellas were larger than the other 12-strings being made at the time, measuring 16 inches across the lower bout – 'the quest to be heard'. Leadbelly's own 12-string had a non-standard retro-fit floating pickguard and a standard tailpiece. By 1954, the by-then famous (Harmony-made) Stella 12-string cost $36.

Leadbelly preachin' the Blues in the 1940s.

**Khallam (Wollof), Konting (Mandinka) – the example shown is a Wollof bought by the author in Gambia, West Africa, in 1987.

One Hispanic artist always associated with the 12-string, and supporting the possible Vihuela/Spanish origin of the instrument, is the legendary Mexican singer Lydia Mendoza, born in 1916.

Folk Legend Pete Seeger worked with Leadbelly in New York, and said he considered his role in spreading the 12-string as, "One of the most important jobs I ever did." 'We Shall Overcome', which was recorded live at Carnegie Hall on June 8, 1963, featured Seeger using a 12-string on what became the anthem of the civil rights movement.

Another 12-string aficionado is legendary singer Judy Collins; "After listening to a lot of Pete Seeger and Jim McGuinn – those guys that play the 12-string really well – I loved that big sound. It sounded like a little orchestra, so I started to hanker after a 12-string. Dick Boak at Martin did some great work on that – I'm a soprano and I need the depth of that sound."

In the latter half of the 20th century, Leo Kottke, from Athens Georgia invented a whole new 12-string technique for the modern era.

The first guitarist 'singer-songwriters'

Switching from banjo, Nick Lucas (Dominic Nicholas Anthony Lucanese) was perhaps the first of the modern guitarist 'singer-songwriters'. His hit 'Tiptoe Through The Tulips' (No.1 for 10 weeks in 1929) was played on his 1928 'signature' steel-strung Gibson. Nick had earlier recorded the first guitar instrumentals; 'Pickin' the Guitar' and 'Teasin' the Frets' in 1922.

The 'Four Aristocrats' Vitaphone recording artists had a very early Ditson 111 Dreadnought, most likely used 'Hawaiian-style' alongside two ukuleles.

In the forties and fifties, country legend Hank Williams, with his 1941 Martin D28, would define the accompanying role of the Dreadnought, and in the 21st century, that steel-strung flat-top still takes centre stage in the country singer-songwriter arena.

Woody Guthrie – "This Machine Kills Fascists."

Emmylou Harris has long championed the Gibson J200, and the electro-acoustic revolution means many players now use Grand Auditoriums and Dreadnoughts live.

The American 'folk' guitarists

Woody Guthrie declared 'This Land is Your Land', and with his dustbowl ballads gave a voice to 'the regular guy'. He had several guitars, all variously labelled 'This Machine Kills Fascists', amongst them are Gibson L2s, Martin Koas and an unidentified Gibson Jumbo. Woody's use of the simple guitar accompaniment to a heartfelt lyric would be the archetype for a whole generation, based initially around the clubs of New York's Greenwich Village.

His most famous disciple is naturally Robert Zimmerman, renamed Bob Dylan (b1941), for the romantic Welsh bard Dylan Thomas. Switching from electric guitar in 1960, Dylan's erratic acoustic style seems to have started with a 1949 Martin 00-17. In 1961 he changed to a Gibson J50.

Nick Lucas with an upmarket Stella/'Galiano'.

Bob Dylan declares "The times they are a changin'" on his Gibson J50.

The Greenwich Village folk writers and interpreters of the early and mid-sixties included Joan Baez, who had earlier startled the 1958 Newport Folk festival, accompanied by a very small, rare Martin 0.45. Soon, the Gaslight and Kettle of Fish clubs would reverberate to the Martins and Gibsons of Judy Collins, Peter, Paul, and Mary, Simon & Garfunkel, The Kingston Trio, Tom Paxton, Phil Ochs, Joni Mitchell, Ramblin' Jack Elliot and Laura Nyro. Their influence would encircle the globe throughout the sixties, giving huge impetus to the original US luthiers, but also spawning a plethora of imitations from Europe to Japan. Perhaps the most successful Martin and Gibson emulators being the Swedish Levin and Hagstrom brands. These were excellent guitars, and Levin was eventually acquired by Martin. Hagstrom made excellent affordable copies of the Gibson B45, but with 12 frets to the body rather than 14.

The British folk and blues guitarists

The American folk revival had gathered its artists from a diverse canvass – Rock n' Roll, Country, Appalachian and 'Broadway', with Tin Pan Alley joining in once the major label CBS had unexpected success with both Dylan and Paul Simon.

In England, the mix was just as rich, with vestiges of the Victorian 'English Folk Song and Dance Society' meeting music hall, jazz, blues and skiffle – usually in a spare room over a pub.

In 1950, Josh White became the first black bluesman to visit Britain. He played the folk and variety circuit with a battered Martin, which he had to sell to pay his air fare home. The guitar remains in London with his radio producer Charles Chilton, and shows considerable wear from Josh's aggressive playing. This guitar marks the popular return of the European 'Martin' guitar to Europe – now steel strung in the manner of the 'English Guitar' or Gittern.

William Lee Conley 'Big Bill' Broonzy was probably born in

1901 and knew all the pain of the blues first hand – his uncle had been lynched for just talking back to a white man;

"Now if you was white, should be all right
If you was brown, could stick around
But if you black, whoa brother,
Git back, git back, git back."

Broonzy's influence on the British scene cannot be overestimated, and encouraged by his success, Sonny Terry and Brownie McGhee would also hit the British jazz club and folk pub circuit. Significantly, in 1948 Brownie had played in a Harlem-based outfit called the Dan Burley Skiffle Group. Though the term had been used as early as 1926 – an authentic 'skiffler' had arrived in Britain armed with another Martin.

Skiffle

British skiffle's aspiration, 'Home made music on home-made instruments', was born out of post-war austerity and inspired by the records of Leadbelly and 'Big Bill'. Tea-chest basses and washboard percussion came from flea markets, and the guitars once more from catalogues and second-hand shops. Tony Donegan, with his wonderful and then very rare Martin 00028, started with an interval guest spot at 'trad jazz' venues, singing Leadbelly songs in a whining, energetic and glorious sprint. Hearing Lonnie Johnston when they shared a bill in 1952 at The Royal Festival Hall, Donegan changed his name as a tribute to his new hero. The record success of the skinny white boy Lonnie Donegan, as Chris Barber's Washboard Wonders, spawned 100s of imitators in towns throughout England. The most successful skifflers produced a guitar boom, and demand was only satisfied by cheap guitar imports from Czechoslovakia and Russia.

'Big Bill' Broonzy

Lonnie Donegan, on Pye records in 1956. He told me if I didn't like it I could eat it!

As the skiffle boom of 1957–8 faded away, it left a legacy that would eventually inspire British rock, as John Lennon's skiffle group The Quarrymen became The Silver Beetles, and Bruce Welch's Railroaders skiffle group (with Hank Marvin) became Cliff Richard's Drifters and then Shadows. Hank had a Hofner 'pressed' archtop, and Bruce somehow had a metal-bodied National! Many skiffle enthusiasts, however, stayed acoustic and became subsumed in a folk revival. This 'new folk' was always a hybrid, drawing on everything from the scholarly A L Lloyd, who recorded 'Skewball' for record label Topic with Steve Benbow (1931–2006) on guitar in 1957 – was it skiffle or folk? – to the Liverpool-based Spinners with their more populist roots.

In turn, the British folk Topic label was also avidly listened to by the New York Greenwich Village fraternity;

"I learned and recorded 'Farewell To Tarwathie' from A L Lloyd on the Topic label. I can still see the sleeve, a black and white drawing of a whaling ship!" Judy Collins

So the songs and guitars started to criss-cross the Atlantic.

Born in 1940, Davey Graham was of Guyanese/Scottish descent, and through Steve Benbow saw greater possibilities in the instrumental art of the guitar. By 1959 he had written 'Anji', a tune he wrote for his girlfriend. This took the flamenco form of Soleares and crossed it with the rhythms and feel of 'Big Bill' Broonzy. This tune was soon being played by every aspirant guitarist in England. Visiting American Paul Simon 'took it all back home' and a new strand entered the guitar repertoire, the acoustic folk guitar 'solo'. If this wasn't enough, Davey saw the potential of DADGAD tuning, and blended the influences of the Arabic U'd and Celtic modality to create a sound world wholly his own. His weapon of choice was usually a Martin or Gibson, though from 2005 he played a wonderful Fylde Falstaff.

Martin Carthy (b1941), the boy Chorister turned skiffler, turned folk interpreter, had the distinct advantage of being able to read Cecil Sharpe's censoriously transcribed melodies and lyrics, and then work out an informed performance. Outside the closed world of 'guitarists' guitarists' Martin Carthy remains a largely unsung genius.

Another British guitarist who had a big influence across genres was Diz Disley (1931–2010). He had played trad jazz and skiffle, and featured on albums with Martin Carthy and Dave Swarbrick, before touring the world with a Maccaferri, accompanying the world's greatest jazz violinist Stephane Grappelli. In the words of Paul Simon; "I've been Walt Disneyed, Diz Disleyed, Rolling Stoned and Beatle'd 'til I'm blind..." ***

In the UK, in the mid-sixties Bert Jansch (b1943) and

*** For more on Diz Disley, see 'Stephane Grappelli – A life in the jazz century' DVD, Decca.

Davey Graham serenades his Anji.

John Renbourn (b1944) defined the new acoustic territory. Renbourn told me; "I started out trying to sound like Bill Broonzy and I'm still tryin!"

A world of acoustics

Australia has Tommy Emmanuel, a man who has taken Merle Travis picking styles to another level. France has Pierre Bensusan, Africa has given us Ali Farka Toure, Baaba Maal and Mansour Seck. Meanwhile, the USA has had the benefit of Stefan Grossman's wisdom for over 50 years, and still the acoustic guitar evolves. As players we can all contribute to that, as the unique acoustic guitar voice is at last able to compete alongside its electric cousin and even the loudest drummer.

Maintaining your acoustic

However, the acoustic guitar still depends for its subtle voice on a delicate resonant frame, and this requires care and attention, as do the mechanics of machine heads, necks and transducers. It's also fun to realise that the acoustic guitar has many voices, with the accents of Spain and America competing with the perfume of Brazilian rosewood and the tang of spruce. The variety and unprecedented quality is intoxicating.

So, this isn't a 'strip-down' manual for enthusiastic guitar builders, more a guide to understanding how your acoustic works, and striving to get the best performance from it.

So, welcome. Let us choose the right acoustic for the music we wish to make, and give it, in the words of Joan Armatrading, some 'Love and Affection'.

Paul Balmer, December 2010

A classic 'Spanish' guitar

The modern 'Spanish' guitar shape and structure was principally defined by the great Spanish luthier Antonio de Torres in around 1860. This example by Amalia Ramírez continues that tradition with some later refinements.

Neck This is often of mahogany and not always in one piece. The better guitars have a very slim flat rear profile ideal for 'classic' hand posture. The bone nut is often a generous 53mm, facilitating complex two- and three-part counterpoint. For reasons of balance, and with much lower string tension, there is no adjustable truss rod.

Fingerboard Usually of ebony, and left unmarked with position indicators. The radius is traditionally flat – ideal for contrapuntal music with very critical intonation between parts. The neck and body join at the 12th fret, and the highest half-fret usually gives a top B on the first string.

The Flamenco variant In the early 20th century Classic and Flamenco guitars were very distinct, with the Flamenco guitar retaining the lighter back and sides of cypress that contribute to its brighter more percussive sound. In the early 21st century these distinctions are blurring, with many players opting for classic rosewood as well as modern machine heads, not wooden pegs. The Ramírez Flamenco guitar, however, retains the parallel back and sides.

Nylon strings tied at the fixed bridge and saddle Since 1945 nylon and silver-plated wire-wound nylon strings have become almost universal and their consistent gauges have encouraged luthiers to offer more finely intonated saddles. The string tie is a variation on the fisherman's knot of Andalucía. The glued bridge is most often of rosewood.

Slotted peghead Now with machine heads. Many Torres guitars originally had wooden friction pegs, and their lighter weights are still preferred by some flamenco players. The machine heads sit in a slotted arrangement to reduce the weight factor and restore balance.

Sides Most often rosewood and usually now from India, not Brazil, as world timber shortages have imposed necessary restrictions. Laminates are often substituted.

Soundhole and rosette Usually a simple circle of approximately 9cm and often decorated with a maker's signature rosette – here the current 'Ramírez roses'.

Top (lower bout 37cm) One-piece spruce or cedar, most often supported with the fan brace system made popular by Torres.

Back Often two-piece rosewood with a decorated central splice usually parallel-braced with three narrow scalloped braces. The back is often not parallel with the top, but converges approx 5mm towards the neck.

A classic small-bodied steel-strung

In New York in the early 20th century the 'American' guitar began to be more commonly strung with steel strings. This was initially a small-bodied European 'parlour'-type guitar, not unlike the 'Spanish' guitar.

Neck Often of mahogany and with a separate headstock, which is still slotted for balance and not always in one piece. The early Martin necks have a marked V profile but the modern 0028 has a slimmer profile. The modern guitars do feature a useful adjustable truss rod, though an original would not. The neck-to-body joint is a traditional dovetail.

Fingerboard Usually of ebony and often marked with elaborate position indicators. The radius is now gently radiused for ease of chordal techniques; in this case 16in (40.6cm). The neck still usually joins the body at the 12th fret, though by 1929 banjo players were asking for 14 frets, slimmer necks and pickguards! This example has an extra full fret, giving a top C on the first string.

Provision for attaching a substantial strap Though the European guitar had most often been played seated – perhaps retained with a ribbon – the new American guitar was played by mobile minstrels, and cloth and leather straps became the norm.

Soundhole and rosette Still most often a simple circle of approximately 9.5cm and often decorated with the maker's signature rosette – here the Martin example has a three-ring 'Style 28' inlay.

Back Two-piece rosewood or mahogany with a decorated central splice, usually parallel-braced with four narrow scalloped braces. The back is usually not parallel with the top but converges as much as 2cm towards the neck – a development from the European model.

Steel strings pinned at the fixed bridge and saddle From 1900 Martin and others offered steel strings, though it was still a custom order. The steel string conversion was largely driven by a fashion for Hawaiian styles, which benefited from a sustained glissandi. The strings were 'pegged' – a technique borrowed from the harp – as steel strings naturally resist a knot.

Slotted peghead Now almost universally fitted with machine heads. The Stauffer tradition from Germany encouraged this approach and it became an American norm. The machine heads sit in a slotted arrangement to reduce the weight factor and restore balance.

An even smaller variant: the Seagull The current fashion for 'parlour' guitars has led to even smaller instruments, such as the Canadian-made Seagull. This has a top bout at only 23.5cm and a lower at 33cm, with an 18.5cm waist. Despite the small dimensions this is a big-sounding guitar very suited to fingerstyle blues, and has the post-1929 14 frets to the body. See more of this guitar on pages 19 and 122.

Sides Most often Indian rosewood or mahogany – world timber shortages have imposed necessary restrictions on Brazilian woods.

Top (lower bout 35.75cm) One-piece Sitka spruce, most often internally supported by the X bracing system adopted by Martin in 1860, giving – fortuitously – more support for the extra tension afforded by steel strings. There is still no pickguard as fingerstyle techniques were still prevalent.

The 0028 'Vintage Series' example pictured here is by C.F. Martin.

The modern Dreadnought

In 1916 the Ditson Company of Boston commissioned the C.F. Martin Company of New York to supply a small run of large-bodied steel-strung guitars, eventually named after the huge British battleship of the time HMS *Dreadnought*.* In 1931 this design was adopted by C.F. Martin as the D2, and since that time almost every guitar manufacturer has produced a similar model. The D2 would evolve into the flagship D28.

The original Dreadnaught Had 12 frets to the neck, and when banjo players asked for 14, the bridge and the X brace had to move closer to the neck – which dramatically affects the sound. This strikes you immediately when you play the 'Judy Collins' 12-fret (see page 138) next to the modern D28. The 12-fret has a much stronger bass and hence more resonant bloom across the entire spectrum – so if you don't need 14 frets, stick with 12!

Solid peghead Now universally with machine heads; the Stauffer tradition from Germany encouraged this approach and it became an American norm. The first Dreadnaught's machine heads sat in a slotted arrangement to reduce the weight factor and restore balance.

Neck Often of mahogany and with a separate headstock that is still slotted for balance and not always in one piece. The early Martin necks have a marked V profile.

Fingerboard Usually of ebony and often marked with elaborate position indicators. The board is now gently radiused for ease of chordal techniques; in this case 16in (40.6cm). The neck originally joined the body at the 12th fret, though by 1934 Martin offered 14 frets to the body. This example has an extra full fret, giving a top C on the first string.

Sides Most often rosewood, now usually from India as world timber shortages have imposed necessary restrictions on Brazilian woods.

Provision for attaching a substantial strap Though the European guitar had most often been played seated this guitar was for Jazz banjo players and standing Hawaiianeers.

Back Two-piece rosewood with a decorated central splice usually parallel-braced with four narrow scalloped braces. The back is usually not parallel with the top but converges as much as 2cm towards the neck – a marked change from the European model.

Top (lower bout 39.75cm) Now one-piece spruce, between 1916 and 1921 the original 'Hawaiian' version was Torres 'fan-strutted' and sometimes made of koa. The modern Dreadnought is internally supported by the X-bracing system – this was needed for the large body and also offered support for the extra tension afforded by the standard steel strings. The D2 still had no pickguard but the D28 would be squarely marketed at the plectrum player and has always had one fitted.

Soundhole and rosette Still most often a simple circle at approximately 9.5cm and often decorated with the maker's signature rosette – here the classic Martin example has a three-ring 'Style 28' inlay.

Steel strings pinned at the fixed bridge and saddle From 1900 Martin and others offered steel strings, though it was still a custom order. The steel string conversion was largely driven by a fashion for Hawaiian styles, which benefited from a sustained glissandi. The strings were 'pegged', as steel strings resist a knot. The 'belly bridge' – a bulge at the back of the bridge – helps support the top and transmits saddle vibration.

* Launched with the words 'Trust in God and dread not'.

The 'archtop' guitar

This response to 'the quest to be heard' harks back to Orville Gibson's carved top and the violoncello tradition, with a floating bridge retained by string tension. The example shown here is a 1950s version of the classic Lloyd Allayre Loar Gibson L5.

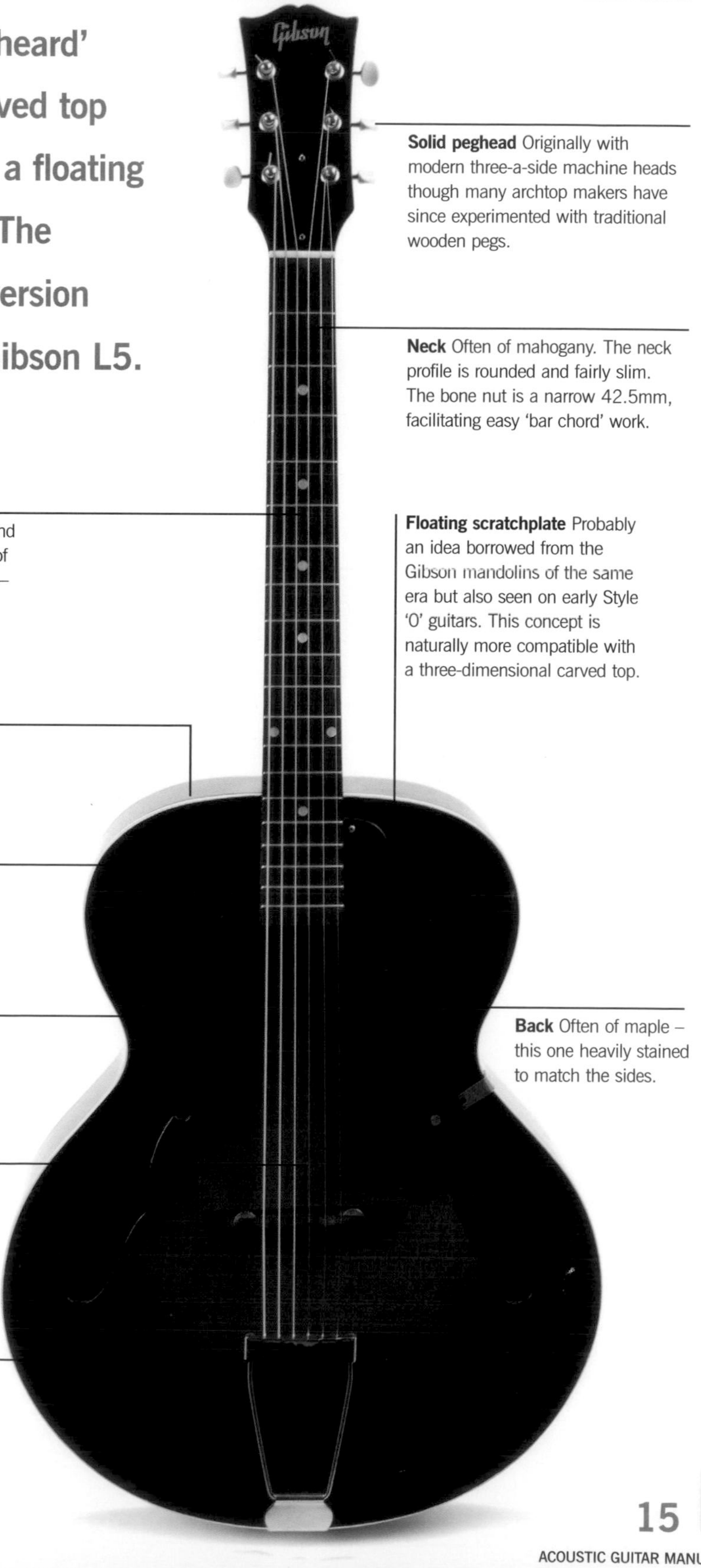

Solid peghead Originally with modern three-a-side machine heads though many archtop makers have since experimented with traditional wooden pegs.

Neck Often of mahogany. The neck profile is rounded and fairly slim. The bone nut is a narrow 42.5mm, facilitating easy 'bar chord' work.

Fingerboard Rosewood with simple dot markers at III, V, VII, IX, XII and XV. Interim models had elaborate block markers but close to the end of production the guitar reverted to basics. The radius is 10in (25.4cm) – not far from a '50s Strat. The neck and body join at the 14th fret and the highest (19th) fret gives a classic top B on the first string.

Floating scratchplate Probably an idea borrowed from the Gibson mandolins of the same era but also seen on early Style 'O' guitars. This concept is naturally more compatible with a three-dimensional carved top.

Sides These have been made of birch, maple and even rosewood, as appears to be the case with this 1953 model.

Top (lower bout 41cm) Bigger even than a Dreadnought and with a radical carved top of spruce supported by two almost parallel braces – a treble bar and a bass bar. Some early Loar models had a Virzi Tone Producer under the bridge.

F holes Two large F holes, designed to inhibit sustain in favour of transient attack and enhanced mid-range projection – just like a violin. We're used to this idea now but in 1922 it was a radical departure.

Back Often of maple – this one heavily stained to match the sides.

The floating bridge This floating bridge marks a radical change in approach from the classic fixed bridge. Whereas the fixed bridge transfers energy to the top in a rocking motion, pulling on the top, the archtop principle 'pumps' the top under downward pressure from the strings – favouring a different harmonic emphasis and creating a totally different timbre.

Trapeze tailpiece Just as on a violin, the strings are secured to the bottom edge of the guitar on a hinged tailpiece – again, many subsequent makers have switched to cello-like wooden tailpieces.

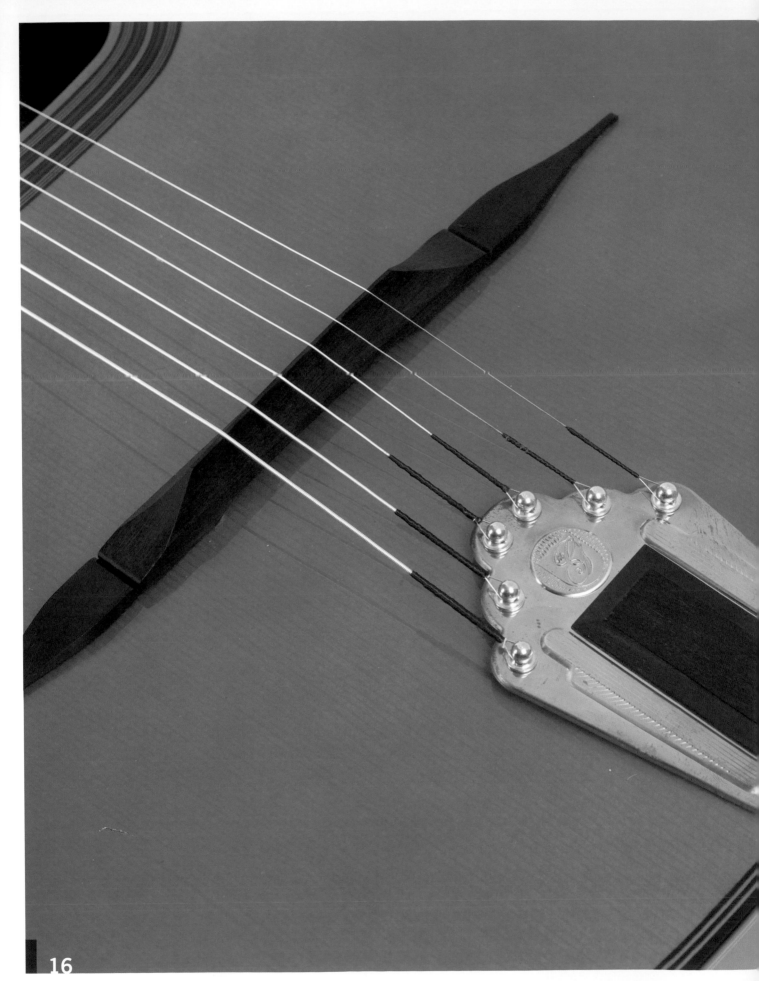

Buying an acoustic guitar

There has never been a better time to buy a new acoustic guitar. Computer-aided CNC machining means that the traditional art of the luthier is enhanced by an unprecedented accuracy of cut. The range of guitars available is also expanding, with everything from a modest 'Spanish' beginner's instrument to accurate reproductions of the most sophisticated diversions, from all-metal 'Nationals' to 'Gypsy Jazz' and classic archtops. The Dreadnought and its copies have become the most popular acoustic guitars in the world, but good Classic and Flamenco instruments are also available as never before.

LEFT A 'Selmer'-type tailpiece from Belleville.

RIGHT A Martin 'Eric Clapton' 00028.

New acoustics

With today's almost bewildering choice, the first question has to be 'What sound do I want from my new acoustic?' It may help to consider what brought you to the acoustic guitar in the first place. Was it a particular artist or style?

USA-made 'Judy Collins' Martin HD 355SJC Dreadnought.

Spanish-made Ramírez 1A Traditional model guitar.

USA-made 'Eric Clapton' Martin 000-28EC 'Orchestral Model'.

USA-made 'Custom Shop' Gibson J200 Super Jumbo.

■ The Dreadnought

The steel-strung Dreadnought has become popular through its versatility as an accompanying guitar in both vocal and instrumental work. It's also the 'singer songwriter's' portable work-station, and in the studio has provided a sympathetic chordal bed on virtually every great pop song and many rock recordings. Though designed as a plectrum guitar it can also been used 'fingerstyle' to great effect.

■ Spanish and Flamenco

These are ideal for solo performance and are the perfect place to start building an understanding of how the guitar works. Modern amplification and a stunning range of hybrid crossover music have brought a whole new audience to this articulate nylon-strung voice. Think Julian Bream to Rodrigo y Gabriela! Though clearly designed as a fingerstyle guitar, George Harrison played his Ramírez with a pick. Listen to the different timbres afforded by cypress and rosewood.

■ The Grand Auditorium

A vintage alternative to the Dreadnought, is becoming increasingly popular with steel string fingerpickers. Brought to the attention of the world via Eric Clapton's MTV *Unplugged*, it's perfect for the adventurous picker reaching for the dusty end of the fingerboard. The Taylor take on the Grand Auditorium has a useful cutaway, an 'NT' neck and 'expression system' electronics.

■ The Jumbo & Super Jumbo

Gibson's response to the Martin Dreadnought, a round-shouldered alternative popular with singer-songwriters. Steel-strung, versatile and BIG! Designed for plectrum and hybrid picking. Country pickers, such as the Everly Brothers, Emmylou Harris and even Bob Dylan, have favoured this particular Nashville Skyline.

Canadian-made Seagull 'Grand' Parlour guitar.

1953 'L5 Professional Special Grand Concert Model' Gibson archtop.

British-made Maccaferri Selmer-style 'Model Orchestre' Gypsy Jazz.

Chinese-made 'Roy Orbison' Epiphone 'Bard' FT-112 12-string.

■ The Parlour guitar

The big-voiced, small-bodied favourite of many Blues singers. Steel-strung but with a clarity harking back to the Spanish tradition. Great for intricate fingerstyle work.

■ The Archtop

A plectrum guitar built for dance bands and jazz in the 1920s, this guitar is finding new friends in the area of Country music, song accompaniment and even Gypsy Jazz. It has a unique middle heavy sound that sticks out in the mix.

■ The Gypsy Jazz

A very specialist plectrum guitar based on the Selmer Maccaferri design. Its distinctive voice is rarely heard outside the Django fraternity.

■ 7-, 9-, 10- and 12-string

These rather specialist instruments have found favour in Folk and Blues contexts. In recording situations the 12-string provides a distinctive chordal pad and some striking intro fills. Not ideal for beginners due to fingering and tuning challenges.

■ Baroque and Renaissance

Four- and five-course guitars are suddenly available again and are popular in early music ensembles seeking authentic continuo textures. They're all very individual and are usually taken up by accomplished players of the more standard Spanish guitar. The strings are arranged in pairs or 'courses' and the frets are made of movable gut. There is also a fantastic solo repertoire for these guitars that remains largely undiscovered.

Electro-acoustic guitars

Since the 1954 Gibson J160, electro-acoustic options have been increasingly available across all genres of acoustic styles.

Unless you're buying a guitar for pure solo classical use, home or studio, then it's really worth considering an 'electric' ready guitar. The early 21st century is a noisy place, and ambient noise levels and ensemble requirements mean the acoustic guitar is rarely heard in public truly unplugged. The increasingly sophisticated onboard electronics offer a minimum hassle hook-up to a PA or acoustic amplifier.

A floor-mounted preamp with a direct feed DI is a good investment if you do a lot of this work. See pages 108 and 116 for more on this.

Cutaways You're unlikely to need cutaways (for the higher octaves) and electrics on your first 'beginner' guitar, but if you're an established electric player branching out these are both desirable and fun.

The amazing Martin X-series guitars have Fishman electronics.

'Previously loved' acoustics

There's a lot of mystique about old guitars and some of it is justified. I've played some great vintage guitars. However, I've also played a lot of old 'dogs'. This is my take on the dilemma, having played and worked with thousands of guitars.

Golden gems

There are still some out there but the good ones have mostly been found. Folk singer Burl Ives let me play his two wonderful Hauser 1s, certainly the best classical guitars I've ever played (they're now in a museum). Eric Clapton has a fabulous 000042 Martin – it's rightly still his favourite acoustic.

If you find a wonderful old guitar and can afford it, buy it (you may need a bank loan). But buy it with your ears, not for its provenance (which needs to be firmly established – see panel).

And of course there are pitfalls to beware. Acoustic guitars are frail, and the good ones get used a lot. Ergo, they wear out. The great virtuoso John Williams has worked his way though Fletas, Kohnos and Smallmans. This is largely due to the 'drumhead' nature of the braced top. It's a mechanical membrane that gets 'floppy', and the timbre changes, usually

for the better, at least in the first ten years; it then reaches an optimal flexibility – and it can be downhill from there on. The Burl Ives Hausers mentioned above make a great exception to that rule.

I have a wonderful late 1930s Kalamazoo (see page 82) but it needs a refret, a neck reset, a top realign, some new machines, a new saddle and bridge repair. Even with all that attention it will never be as useful as the new Fylde on page 156. I would only use the Kalamazoo in a studio for a very specific vintage sound, which it has. For a working stage guitar I would need electrics, which it would be criminal to install – so I wouldn't do that.

So I'd suggest you only buy a great vintage guitar that you can use; otherwise admire them from a distance, like a supermodel.

Pitfalls

■ **Machine heads** wear out.

■ **Necks** bend and need resetting – there's no corrective truss road in most classic guitars!

■ **Frets** need replacing.

■ **Intonation expectations** have risen, and computer-aided engineering aids that on new guitars, which also often have compensated saddles.

Second-hand electro acoustics

Technology has marched on; the simple magnetic pickup of the 1951 CF100E or a piezoelectric device of 1966 cannot compete with modern Fishman piezo/blends, modelling software and the 'expression' systems devised by Taylor and Yamaha.

The built-in preamps on many electro acoustic are virtually sealed units and replacing parts and chips in these would be impractical and certainly not cost-effective. So when they're worn out it's better to replace these units wholesale – and it may actually be cheaper to replace the whole guitar!

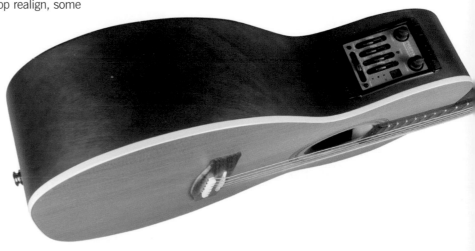

In conclusion

- Of the guitars experienced while writing this book in 2011, the four Martins, the Taylor, the Fylde and three Gibsons are all new and very fine upmarket guitars, and they all have 'character'. Buy the sound you need for your music!
- The Yamaha is one of the finest electro acoustic 'classicals' I've ever played.
- The Yamaha beginner guitars are tremendous value and work well, with accurate intonation at a very affordable price.
- Old acoustics are for collectors and studio use. I would buy new for any contemporary stage-work.
- If you're in the market for an electro acoustic, see page 107 for a survey of the onboard transducers and preamp options and check for developments, as these are computer-chip orientated and upgrades appear every few months! Many new systems feature upgradable software downloads.
- If you need an upmarket-sounding, steel-strung acoustic that works well in a PA and will stand the rigours of the road, check out the Taylors. I believe Bob Taylor is the Leo Fender of the acoustic guitar – he makes practical, easily serviced, good-sounding guitars at an affordable price. The NT neck is a work of genius and the 'expression system' is the equivalent of what Leo Fender did with the Broadcaster – he allowed us to be heard.
- At home and in the studio check out new and vintage Martin, Gibson, Washburn, Fylde and Ramírez guitars – wallow in their glorious and individual voices recorded with the best omni-directional capacitor mikes.
- If you're 'economically challenged' try a Yamaha or any number of Far Eastern variants. There are some fabulous bargains to be had. If you're a beginner take an experienced teacher with you and let him guide you. No two acoustic guitars are the same and that's part of the charm.

Custom acoustics

Consider using a bespoke luthier for a special guitar. The small-scale luthiers are in an enviable position. Roger Bucknall at Fylde tells me he can get all the woods he needs in the small quantities he requires. He can be 'picky' and select timbers for a specific guitar or client. Major manufactures are necessarily denied that privilege as their volume output means that they must use what they can get, and are being very imaginative in meeting the situation square on – they're all finding ways of using different tone woods and getting the best from them.

Verifying authenticity

Confirming authenticity means a thorough examination by an expert. Types of lacquer and glue coupled with construction analysis will all add up to a bigger picture – guitars have already appeared on BBC TV's *Antiques Roadshow* and acoustic experts such as Ivor Mairant's store in London are available for valuations.

Seek provenance just as Sotheby's or any auction house would. Bills of sale, hang tags, 'vintage correct' cases, photos of the instrument from a dateable source are all clues. I would recommend forensic analysis for an alleged 1902 Gibson – before taking out the second mortgage it will cost you!

Ironically it's perfectly possible to buy a great new acoustic these days with lots of vintage mojo and a very convincing image. I personally believe that a great guitar is a great guitar, whether manufactured 50 years ago or last week. It's the sum of the parts that counts and a great piece of timber is a great piece of timber, and a well-crafted new guitar will most likely sound even better when it's 'played in'.

I have been fortunate to play priceless guitars and they weren't necessarily the best, while I own inexpensive guitars that work brilliantly. So 'buy with your ears' and keep an open mind. Good hunting!

1953 'L5 'Professional Special' Grand Concert Model' Gibson archtop

Wood shrinkage will naturally lead to 'crazed' lacquer – it can be as charming as a wrinkle!

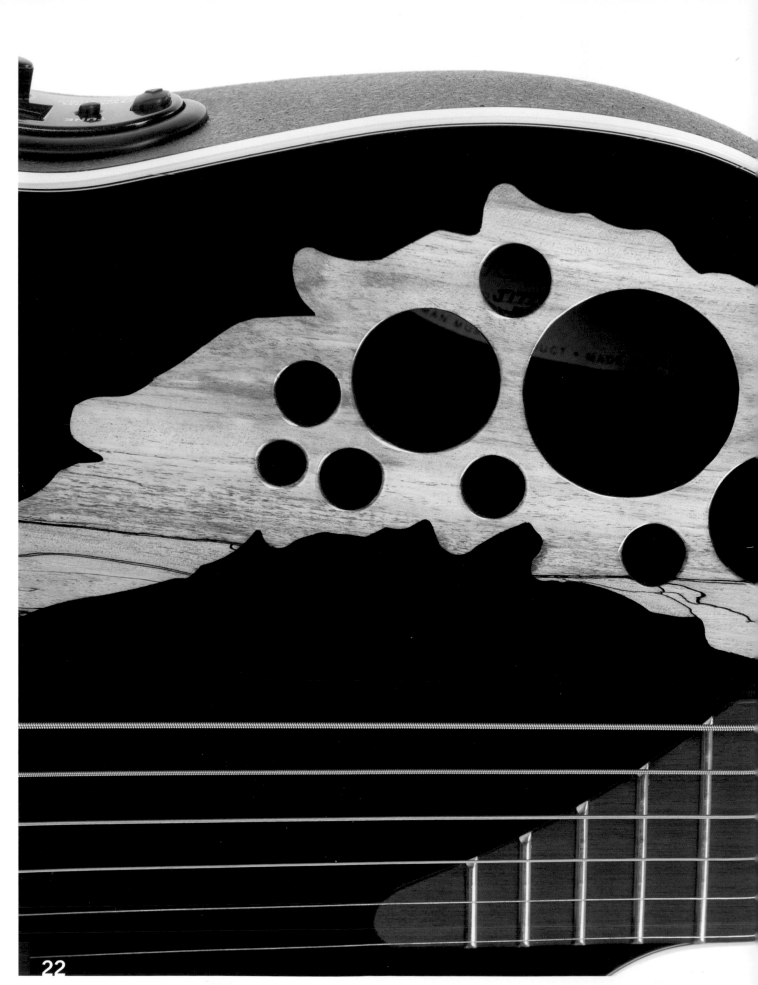

The rich variety

The fabulous variety of types of acoustic guitars is part of the instrument's charm. Whatever you aspire to play there's a guitar to match, with specialist guitars for songwriters, bluesmen, jazzers, flamencos and bluegrass country pickers. There are reasons for each guitar's distinctive voice and your choice can be informed by exploring the options and understanding their evolution.

LEFT An Ovation LX.

RIGHT A Fylde Ariel.

Know your
'Classic' and Flamenco guitar

At the heart of the 'Spanish' sound is its unique stringing.

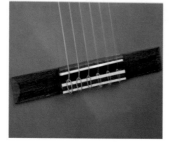

In 1946 the Classic guitar was blessed with American Albert Augustine's development of nylon strings – an innovation that probably saved this wonderful voice from extinction. Previously the Classic guitar had relied on gut strings sourced from double-length violin strings, which were temperamental, frail and extremely sensitive to temperature and humidity; they were a struggle to maintain in a world getting louder and more internationally mobile. The 'new' nylon and silver-wound nylon strings are almost always tied at the fixed bridge, and the bone or plastic saddle is increasingly 'tempered for intonation' as our ears, trained to greater expectation by digital recordings, become more critical of accurate pitch. Interestingly the saddle is a relatively modern innovation – prior to the 1850s many Classic guitars had no saddle, as shown in the accompanying picture.

■ Spruce or cedar tops
These are predominantly fan braced in a tradition consolidated by Antonio de Torres, but with increasing top-end competition from the 'lattice' structure of Greg Smallman and Mathias Dammann. This crucial top, acting acoustically like a drumhead, can have a different character depending on the choice of 'tone wood'; cheaper guitars may even have a laminate, but all serious professional instruments have either cedar or spruce tops.

■ Mahogany neck
Traditionally made in one piece, though this is becoming rare as more frugal use of diminishing timber resources ironically encourages *more stable* laminates.

■ Flat fingerboard
Almost every Classic guitarist prefers a broad, flat, ebony fingerboard. This lends itself to fingering intricate counterpoint, giving the left hand room to manoeuvre and aiding accurate pitch between parts. The slab of hard ebony also lends rigidity and stability to the neck – a major contributor to good tone.

■ Bone nut

Once ivory and now often plastic, a well-cut accurate nut is at the heart of good tone and accurate intonation. On a student economy guitar always consider replacing a cheap hollow plastic nut. A bone nut has the added advantage of being self-lubricating.

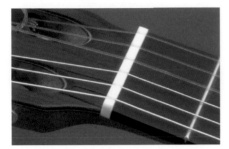

■ Rosewood back and sides

The predominant choice. However, the Flamenco guitar often follows an older, lighter cypress tradition, seen here on my Baroque guitar made by Peter Sensier. This fine new Yamaha NX guitar is also crafted in maple.

■ Slotted headstock or (increasingly rarely) wooden pegs

Machine heads were rare in the 19th century, and their 20th-century popularity has led to the slotted headstock, which restores balance by reducing the headstock weight. A diminishing number of flamenco players and baroque specialists still favour wooden pegs and they can be remarkably stable – more so than machine heads once settled. Definitely worth a try!

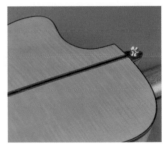

■ Optional cutaway

It was once thought unnecessary to have a cutaway on the Classic guitar, as 19th century repertoires rarely employed the higher octave. However, 20th- and 21st-century composers have pushed the boundaries. Also, guitarists coming from popular music idioms expect access to the top octave, and the cutaway Classic is very popular with players of jazz and Brazilian music, as well as Nuevo Flamenco.

■ Electric preamp

As the world gets louder and the Classic guitarists reach out to more diverse audiences, many Classics have become available with onboard preamps, microphones and piezo and dynamic transducers. The sophistication of these units varies largely according to budget, but at best they can sound very like an acoustic Classic guitar. See page 154 for three-quarter and one-eighth size Classic guitars for younger students.

Know your
Dreadnought

The Dreadnaught *style*, though yet unnamed, first appeared in 1916, when it was manufactured by Martin as the 'Ditson Hawaiian' for music dealer Oliver Ditson, and sold in very small numbers. In 1931 it reappeared – christened 'Dreadnaught' in allusion to the huge HMS *Dreadnought* battleship – as the Martin D1 and D2. In the catalogue for 1935 it was still referred to as a 'Bass' guitar, and sold for $100! In the 1960s it became the Dreadnought, more accurately spelt with an 'o'.

■ Steel strings

At the heart of the Dreadnought's appeal are those high tension steel and bronze-wound strings literally trying to tear the bridge off the lightly braced top. That tension and its singing sustain provide a gorgeous backdrop

to any voice, male or female. The extra bass, suitably balanced with a singing treble, provides the perfect guitar for chord or arpeggio accompaniment, vocal or instrumental. The current popular scale length is 64.5cm.

■ Classic oversize body

Shown here is the Martin HD28, which first appeared in 1932 and is the standard-bearer of the class. The current size is upper bout 29cm, lower bout 39.5cm, with a waist of 27.5cm and a body length of 50.5cm. The 'square' shoulders are part of the defining shape.

■ Tone wood top

Often Sitka spruce as here, though even laminates can perform surprisingly well, especially when amplification is introduced. Lightly X-braced for that classic sound. **NB:** This top needs repair to the displaced string cavities.

■ Pickguard

Most commonly fixed to the top, though floating guards have been known. The Dreadnought is designed as a plectrum guitar though the best ones also respond well to a lighter fingerstyle touch.

■ Rosewood sides and back

Again, laminates are becoming common and other sustainable timbers are proving acceptable.

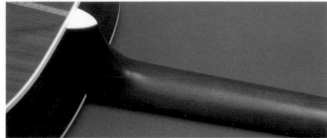

■ 14 frets to the body

The first Martin-made Ditson Dreadnaughts had been '12 frets to the body', a tradition established with the Torres and Panormo guitars of the 19th century. As the early Dreadnaughts largely provided accompaniment or unfretted Hawaiian solos this was not a problem, but as banjo players switched to guitar and took to soloing they wanted better high fret access. Following a custom order in 1929 a Martin '14-fret access' was introduced on its 'OM' model in 1930 and on the Dreadnaught in 1934, though 12-fret models remained available.

From 1920 some Martins had 20 frets total, giving a top C in the useful 'folk' key of C Major.

■ Neck

A hardwood neck – the timber varies and Martin and others are taking the business of sustainable forestry very seriously, so it's not always mahogany. Stratobond, a distinctive patented laminate, provides a good eco-friendly solution.

■ X-bracing

Not applied on the Dreadnaught until 1921, though attributed to C.F. Martin in the 1850s, this alternative to fan bracing (also consolidated circa 1850) provided a more substantial top brace that would come into its own with the introduction of steel strings. Variants on this bracing system are now standard in virtually all wooden steel string guitars. Scalloping the braces can fine-tune a top for specific resonant frequencies. Martin's X-bracing moved closer to the bridge in 1938 to help with the extra tension of heavier gauge steel strings.

■ Hardwood fingerboard

Ebony in this case, aiding the stability of the neck – a great contributor to tone, but rosewood is a cheaper and viable alternative. A mild radius, typically 16in (40.6cm), breaks from the classical flat profile.

■ Position markers

Simple dots at III, V, VII, IX and XII are a relatively modern innovation (circa 1900) and Martin's are famous for their more elaborate mother of pearl blocks, stars and snowflakes. They're usually duplicated on the fingerboard edge.

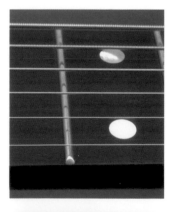

■ Dovetail neck joint and mahogany block

The traditional approach; but simpler joints and even bolt-on necks are being used with great success.

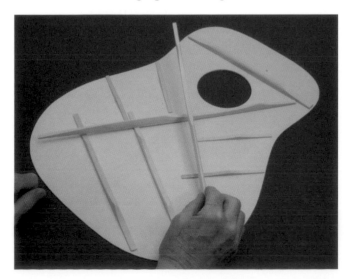

Solid headstock

The classical 'slotted' headstock is rarely seen on a Dreadnought, and single rather than 'three-in-a-row' machines make for easier maintenance.

Nut

Preferably bone though plastics are increasingly being used. Since 1939 $1^{11}/_{16}$in has been Martin's width.

Adjustable truss rod

Has only appeared on Martins since 1985! Traditionally accessed through the soundhole as here, though many other manufacturers' Dreadnoughts have a headstock access. Modern D28s require a very long 5mm specialised Allen wrench as shown. Early Dreadnaughts often have non-adjustable neck reinforcements or no truss rod at all!

Minimal ornamentation

The classic Dreadnought has a clean, frill-free line, but when requested the Martin company and others have set the mother of pearl to stun! 'Herringbone' binding is another established favourite.

Electric preamp

Since the 1950s many rock and pop musicians have preferred the acoustic Dreadnought as a *studio* rhythm guitar. However, the evolving technology of the '60s to the present has also made the Dreadnought a very viable instrument in even the largest stadiums. See page 106.

Bridge and saddle

A fixed rosewood – or in this case ebony – bridge. The separate slot-fixed saddle has increasingly complex intonation filing, this quest for accuracy being driven by the more prevalent use of higher playing positions where intonation becomes more critical. Also the studio 'microscope' is more revealing, as is error-exposing stage amplification.

Optional cutaway

It was once thought unnecessary to have an upper bout cutaway on the Dreadnought – many players confined themselves to positions I–V. However, John Renbourn and others pushed the expectations of the acoustic guitar to the point where today the cutaway is commonplace even on a Martin.

Pin string retainers

A system borrowed from the harp. Works well with ball-end steel strings but their seating and shape are critical to tone.

The eco-friendly Martin X-series.

Know your
Jumbo and Super Jumbo

As 'the quest to be heard' continued into the 1930s Gibson responded with their 1934 'Jumbo' guitar. This slightly larger version of their L2 guitar was sometimes ladder-braced like a 'Stella' but had Gibson's distinctive round shoulders and 14 frets to the body.

■ Steel strings
Gibson had advocated steel strings from 1902 and these Jumbo guitars would stand up well next to Dreadnaughts in terms of volume and projection. Gibson were early to supply the 'singer songwriters', and Nick Lucas had accompanied his hit *Tip Toe through the Tulips* on a slightly smaller L0.

■ Classic 16in body and sloping shoulders
Shown here is the Gibson J160, a favourite songwriting machine with the Beatles' John and George from 1962 (Paul McCartney still favours his Epiphone Texan).

■ The Super Jumbo
The Super Jumbo of 1938 took the big body to extremes.

■ A variety of tone woods and most often a distinctive sunburst finish

■ Mahogany sides and back

■ Pickguard
This is fixed to the top, as the Jumbo was conceived as a plectrum guitar.

■ The J160 has an unusual 15 frets to the body and a P90 pickup

■ Ladder bracing
The 1960s J160E was still ladder-braced – possibly to inhibit acoustic feedback.

■ Rosewood fingerboard
Rosewood is a cheaper and viable alternative to ebony. A gentle radius typically breaks from the classical flat profile.

■ Position markers
Trapeze inlays at I / III / V / VII / IX / XII / XV / XVII are unusual and duplicated on the fingerboard edge.

■ Mahogany neck
Dovetail neck joint and mahogany block – the traditional approach. But simpler joints and even bolt-on necks are being used with some success.

■ Solid headstock
'Three-in-a-row' Kluson machines make for easier maintenance.

■ Electrics
The 1954 J160E was one of the very first 'designed' acoustic electrics, with a simple single-coil magnetic P90 pickup built into the last fret and a front-mounted volume and tone control just like a regular 1950s electric guitar.

29

Know your
Grand Auditorium

'Back to the Future'...

In 1990 Robert Johnson's Grammy for 'Best Historical Album' showed Johnson playing a Gibson L1, a relatively small, narrow-waisted guitar that was neither Jumbo nor Dreadnought.

Then in 1992 Eric Clapton recorded MTV's *Unplugged* and featured a slightly larger but similar-shaped 1939 Martin 00042. The recording won six Grammys and revived the fortunes of Martin and the acoustic guitar beyond anyone's wildest dreams. Soon there were shops named after the concept and *Acoustic Guitar* Magazine carried the headline 'The Return of Acoustic Rock!'

The synergy achieved by these two events has led to a resurgence of interest in guitars of this approximate shape and helped inspire the development of a new electro acoustic. Significantly, the Grand Auditorium was the first guitar shape designed from scratch by Bob Taylor. Unveiled to commemorate the Taylor company's 20th Anniversary in 1994, the GA has the width and depth of a Dreadnought but its narrower waist gives it the appearance of a smaller instrument. This also adds treble 'zing' across the guitar's tonal spectrum, sharpens the definition of individual notes, and enables the guitar to rest comfortably in the lap. With mass removed from the width of the GA's braces the guitar top moves faster, resulting in a snappy, bell-like tone.

USA-made 'Eric Clapton' Martin 000-28EC 'Orchestral Model'

■ Classic 'hourglass' figure

The *term* 'Grand Auditorium' seems to have first been used by C.F. Martin in 1977, when it was applied to the M38. A similar cutaway version from 1981 is known as the MC28. The Taylor 614CE featured on page 168 has a similar profile but with a cutaway.

This guitar has a classic square-shouldered shape and size – specifically a 38.5cm lower bout, 29cm upper bout, with a narrow 24cm waist.

USA-made Taylor 614 CE Grand Auditorium electro acoustic

The Taylor has a similar 40cm lower bout and the same 29cm upper bout, with a 24cm waist.

The slightly smaller size lends itself to fingerstyle as well as plectrum playing – and therein, probably, lies its attraction.

■ Sides and back

Rosewood on the Martin and big-leaf maple in the case of the Taylor.

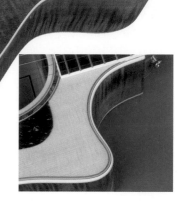

■ Frets

The 'Robert Johnson' guitar had 12 frets to the body but both 'modern' takes have 14. Both guitars have 20 frets total, giving a top C, and they share a similar 15–16° radius.

■ Optional cutaway

It was once thought unnecessary to have an upper bout cutaway on the Grand Auditorium. However, today the cutaway is commonplace even on a Martin.

■ Hardwood neck

The actual timber varies. Martin and others are taking the business of sustainable forestry very seriously, so the neck is not always mahogany. The Taylor has a detachable NT neck. See page 170 for more on this.

■ Electric preamp

The Taylor version features extremely sophisticated electrics, but tastefully accessed. See page 173.

In late 2010, Martin introduced the OMCPA1 as a direct response to the Taylor, with a modern neck and Fishman Aura electronics.

Know your Resonator

Designed in 1927 by John Dopyera, the Resonator guitar comes in several versions, some with a wooden body and some of all-metal construction. They all have a loudspeaker cone-like resonator connected to the bridge, some versions having as many as three – The Tricone. The National Style 3 pictured here has a body of plated brass.

■ Bridge
The Resonator is a single-cone type with a small wooden bridge acting directly into the centre of the cone.

■ Headstock
The headstock is of the old-style slotted type with an elaborate ivoroid veneer.

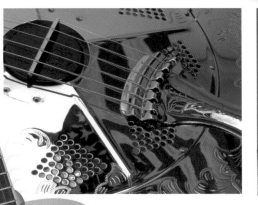

■ F holes
The guitar has elaborate F holes cut directly through the brass.

■ Neck and bracing
The neck and internal bracing are wooden.

■ Frets
There are 12 frets to the body.

Know your
Gypsy Jazz

Designed for the Selmer company of Paris by classical guitarist Mario Maccaferri in 1931, the Gypsy Jazz guitar has become an art deco icon for a whole branch of jazz. A real Selmer such as Django Reinhardt's 'Petit Bouche' is clearly out of reach of most people, but many makers are now producing accurate copies.

■ Body
Everything about the Selmer is outrageous – the body is eccentric but was very early in providing a useful cutaway. A significant contributor to its characteristic sound is the interior varnish, intended to make a bright brash arc through Louis Armstrong's trumpet or Stephane Grappelli's violin.

■ Fingerboard
The fingerboard extension reaches for the fourth octave and the soundhole speaks for itself!

■ Headstock
The slotted headstock has the most elaborate enclosed brass tuners ever seen – Selmer, famous for their saxophones, knew how to work brass and the zero fret keeps the open strings and the fretted notes in the same tone world.

■ Back and sides
The back and sides are laminates *by design*. The top has a gentle pliage – a nod to Lloyd Loar's archtop and perhaps mandolin roots.

■ Bridge
The bridge is the biggest on any guitar ever made and the tailpiece with its looped strings is one of a kind – modern versions allow conventional ball-end strings, but purists would never do that!

Know your
12-string

The 12-string guitar has six courses
or pairs of strings. The 'standard tuning'
is with the first and second strings in
unison and the bottom four strings in
octaves. In the octave pairs on the acoustic
version the high octave usually sits above
the low octave from a players' perspective
(Rickenbacker do the opposite on their electrics).

In the 1950s the 12-string was often
tuned down to C pitch rather than E, this to
better accommodate the extra tension inherent in
a doubling of strings. During the 1960s lighter-gauge
strings encouraged players to use standard pitch – generally
12-string guitars don't cope with this and there are many
otherwise fine instruments out there with belied tops and warped
necks. The bonus effect of tuning down to D or even C pitch
is the extra bass this produces, making up for the 12-string's
naturally 'toppy' sound. The greatest 12-string exponent
Leadbelly always tuned down, resulting in that rich sound
he's famous for. See page 197 for more on Leadbelly tunings.

■ Body
Usually a Dreadnought shape,
though Grand Auditorium is
also common. The top needs to
be substantially braced to cope
with the extra string tension.
Leadbelly's Stella 12s had
ladder bracing. The Gibsons
and Martins are 'X' braced.

■ Neck
Mahogany with a truss rod
and an extended headstock
to accommodate the
doubled-up machines.

■ Bridge
The usual Dreadnought
fixed bridge with 12 pins
and, these days, a heavily
compensated saddle.

■ Back and sides
Mahogany and rosewood
are the favourites though
laminates work well.

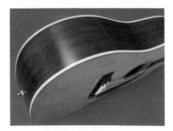

Know your
Bowlback

The Bowlback guitar, with a 'plastic' back and sides, became popular from the late 1960s when new, rugged fibreglass plastics first became available. The market leader and chief innovator is the Ovation company founded by Bill Kaman, who use 'Lyrachord' and 'Lyrachord GS' – a lighter, stronger formula. The first Bowlback guitar to be introduced was the Balladeer in 1969.

■ Top

Available in a range of sizes, though the most common is broadly Grand Auditorium size with or without a cutaway. Some Adamas guitars have unusual graphite tops though conventional spruce is often used. These guitars feel smaller than they are due to their less bulky and less angular shape – a plus for many female guitarists.

■ Neck

Hardwood with a truss rod and a distinctive headstock.

■ Electrics

Ovation were industry leaders in the field of piezo-electric undersaddle transducers, and the electro acoustic arena is the Bowlback guitar's most successful application. Ovation were amongst the first to introduce handy onboard preamps.

■ Bridge

The usual classic fixed bridge, though in this case 'through strung'.

■ Distinctive soundholes

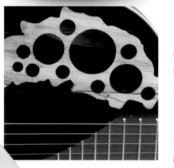

Many bowlbacks have conventional round soundholes though Ovation and particularly the Adamas range are famous for intricate multiple array holes. These may further contribute to the guitars anti-feedback qualities.

■ Back and sides

Of Lyrachord on Ovation's guitar and of similar plastic and fibreglass formulations on the many 'copies'. The concept is to exploit the different reflective properties inherent in a bowlback shape. The inhibition of acoustic 'standing waves' within the guitar body may contribute to less acoustic feedback in the electro acoustic models.

Setting up and tuning

Our perception of 'good tone' on an acoustic guitar is heavily dependent on the traditional 'organic' synergy of wood and bone, and therefore most experiments with high-tech adjustable bridges, saddles and nuts have failed at the first hurdle. However, the careful application of traditional cutting and filing techniques coupled with strobe tuners and compensated saddles has made acoustic intonation more of a science in the 21st century. If you have an older acoustic guitar you may want to consider some modern non-destructive set-up techniques and simple maintenance to help with demanding performance situations.

LEFT L.R. Baggs preamp, DI and tuner.

RIGHT An Ovation Bowlback guitar.

Electronic tuners and sweeteners

Tuning your guitar was once a long apprenticeship, and many bands had only one individual who could tackle the job. Digital technology has stepped in and now offers a plethora of exotic possibilities.

A Peterson strobe tuner in acoustic sweetened mode.

One lump or two?

Tuning an acoustic guitar has never been easier than in the early 21st century.

The bluesmen of the Mississippi delta and the Merseybeat musicians of my misspent youth would only have a neglected piano for reference. Other options included a faintly out of tune set of 'pitch pipes' and a wonky tuning fork.

The introduction of electronic tuners since the early 1980s has offered guitarists an increasingly accurate reference tool. The key word here is 'reference'. The open strings of a guitar tuned to correspond with an accurate electronic tuner provide a great starting point for accurate tuning. However, it is essential to remember that the guitar, like the piano, is a 'tempered' instrument. Even the most accurately fretted and set up guitar is built on a tempered tuning system that compromises the science of pitch by considering 'enharmonic' notes such as C# and Db as the same note, which they are not!

■ Tempered tuning

If we all played fretless guitars this would not be an issue. However, there are very few fretless guitars and even less fretless guitarists.

■ Tempered tuning in practice

In the real world a tuning compromise has been reached, referred to as 'equal temperament', and most rock and pop musicians will happily accept the faint 'out of tuneness' associated with certain chords in certain keys and positions on the fingerboard.

In fact in single-string solo playing many players consciously or unconsciously 'temper' certain notes slightly sharp or flat by a combination of listening and microtonally 'bending' notes as they play. This technique, combined with pitch-dependent vibrato, is so indigenous to the guitar as to be second nature.

This factor even contributes to the guitar's expressive 'human' quality – keyboards, for instance, can never really do this.

For accurate rhythm playing which naturally incorporates chords many guitarists will 'tune to key', using an electronic tuner for reference and then 'tempering' the relevant notes within the pivotal chords of a song to reach an acceptable compromise that 'sounds' musical.

Sweetening

The Peterson brand of tuners are very popular with guitar techs as they offer not just pre-programmed tempered tuning and 'sweetened' tunings but also programmable tunings. This means the tech can set up a *specific guitar* for a *particular number* in a live set tempered to the key of the song to be performed – this is why Mark Knopfler's National is so brilliantly in tune for the opening of *Romeo & Juliet* every night on a 50-date world tour.

The Strobo Flip tuner shown has special sweetenings for 12-string, Baroque guitar, lute, open-string slide tunings DADGAD etc.

This is how Peterson themselves express the benefits:

'If we choose wisely, we can make the most important chords in a given key be the perfect ones. This is the concept behind Just Intonation (JST in the Temperament Menu of Peterson tuners). In the key of C, the chords of C major, F major, and G major can each have perfectly harmonious tuning intervals. Unfortunately, other chords, especially those in more remote keys like C# and F#, sound much worse than they would in equal temperament. If an instrument like a piano is tuned in Just Major temperament for the key of C, notes and chords that fall in the C Major scale sound wonderful. Modulating to the key of G, most chords sound good, some not quite as good. If one takes a more adventurous trek into the key of E, say, some real "ear-sores" start to develop in certain chords and intervals. Historically, the clinkers are dubbed "wolf tones", which gives some indication of their "charm".

'Between the extremes given above, there are countless compromises. Why not settle for some nearly perfect chords in the most popular key signatures, while keeping the "wolves" at bay in the less travelled ones? There are about as many such "well tempered" scales as there have been minds conceiving of them. Every temperament generally takes the name of its earliest inventor or biggest proponent. Some of the more successful ones, like Werkmeister (WRK), Young (YNG), Kirnberger (KRN), and Kellner (KLN), are included in current models of Peterson tuners. Besides stock historic

The Peterson is also available in a useful pedal-board version as the 'StroboStomp'.

temperaments, Peterson Virtual Strobe Tuners also feature unique instrument-specific temperaments such as GTR for guitar, BAS for bass, and (VS-II/V-SAM only) E9 & C6 tempered tuning for pedal steel guitar. The VS-S StroboStomp pedal tuner/DI also features four optimized Buzz Feiten Tuning System presets for electric guitar, acoustic guitar, bass guitar and 12-string guitar. All Peterson tuners (except the VS-1) are user-programmable, allowing the saving of up to 244 user temperaments to memory. The V-SAM allows you to adjust any temperament to any one of 12 roots, making these temperaments available in any specific key.'

■ The bottom line

Tune your guitar to EADGBE (or whatever exotic tuning you favour) using a tuner for reference, then 'temper' by ear or using a strobe as required.

Professional practice

Tuning discrepancies that are sometimes acceptable in a stage situation with its visual distractions can become all too obvious when transferred to the analytical environment of the recording studio. Most pro guitarists will confer with their guitar techs prior to a recording and agree which guitars are required. The tech will then set up these guitars with new strings and an intonation check. Many an hour of valuable session time is saved this way. It's always worth checking your set-up before an important recording session.

Repairs maintenance and adjustments

A well set-up acoustic guitar is a delight – harder to play perhaps than any electric, but not a strain. With good strings, a well-shaped nut and saddle, and properly lubricated machines, the guitar should stay in tune and sound great. The acoustic is more fragile, and needs more attention paid to the temperature and humidity of any storage or transport. The modern electro-acoustic needs some very specific maintenance and perhaps a software upgrade.

LEFT Fitting a pre-amp.

RIGHT A Ramirez 1A classic.

Safety first

As far as I know nobody has died in an incident involving the acoustic guitar. However, the electro acoustic does present some issues – enough to have Bob Taylor wisely install an earth leakage fuse on his guitars. *Working* on purely acoustic guitars also presents the expected issues of sharp tools and solvents.

Electric shock

Many electric guitarists have either been killed or badly burned through accidental exposure to mains current, and the electro acoustic guitarist now faces similar risks. Often the strings are part of the earth path, so a fuse that blows when dangerous currents are detected is a wise precaution. Though the UK's adoption of 240V may seem to present a greater risk than the USA's 110V, it's actually the amperes that are the killer not the volts! Amperes are the measure of current, and high currents are the ones to avoid.

Acoustic amplifiers run happily on domestic supplies at relatively low current ratings, so the situation of one guitarist one amp is a pretty safe scenario, especially if we observe a few precautions:

■ Always ensure a good earth or ground connection. This allows a safer path to earth for any stray current, which always flows along the easiest path. The earth or ground offers a quicker route to earth than through you, and therein lies its safety potential. Taylor guitars carry their own patented fused string ground, which seems likely to become standard equipment in the near future (see page 111).

■ Never replace fuses with the wrong value *eg* a 5-amp fuse in a 3-amp socket. Fuses are there to protect us and our equipment from power surges. A higher value means less protection. Never replace a fuse with a bodge such as silver foil or similar. This offers no protection at all.

■ Consider using an external earth leakage trip or similar circuit-breaker in any situation where you have no control or knowledge of the mains power.

■ Maintain your mains leads. Check them regularly for damage and strained wires. If fitted the earth wire *must* be in place.

■ Never operate an amplifier with the safety cover removed, especially valve amplifiers known for their HT circuits.

■ Never put drinks on or near amplifiers.

■ Never touch a stage lighting circuit or lamp. Apart from mains electricity issues they are often also dangerously hot. Leave stage lamps to qualified electricians.

Beware of

■ Multi amp/multi PA scenarios that aren't professionally administered. Professional PA and lighting supervisors are very safety-conscious and trained in health and safety to a legal minimum requirement. The danger comes with 'semi pro' and amateur rigs which are not closely scrutinised. If you're in any doubt don't plug in until you've talked to the on site supervisor and feel you can trust his assurances.

■ Unknown stage situations, especially those which feature big lighting rigs. This is easily said but hard to adhere to. Even the most modest gigs nowadays have quite sophisticated lights and sound. The crucial issue is that all the audio equipment is connected to the same PHASE. Danger particularly arises when microphones are connected to one PHASE and guitars and basses to another. A bass/vocalist could find himself as the 'bridge' between 30 amps of current! If in any doubt be rude and ask.

Hearing damage

Leo Fender's first amplifiers knocked out a feverish 4W of audio. The Vox AC30 was OK for most of us but by the early 1960s Paul McCartney had a T60. By 1964 The Beatles had the first 100W VOX amps, specifically made to cope with concerts in vast football stadiums and the noise of immense screaming crowds.

By 1970 100W was the norm for a guitar 'head' in a small club and the first 10,000W PA systems had rocked Woodstock.

Pete Townshend of The Who first complained of the hearing impairment tinnitus in the mid '70s and for many years refused to tour with a band as his hearing worsened.

Consider using earplugs when working in noisy environments.

Chemical Hazards

Paints and solvents

Traditionally guitars are finished with nitrocellulose lacquer and this practice continues on many guitars, especially vintage types. Nitrocellulose lacquers produce a very hard yet flexible, durable finish that can be polished to a high gloss. The drawbacks of these lacquers include the hazardous nature of the solvent, which is flammable, volatile and toxic. The dangers inherent in the inhalation of spray paints are serious enough to be covered by legal statutes in the USA, UK, and Europe.

Masks can provide some protection against solvents and paint.

Symptoms

- **Acute and chronic ingestion:** Large doses may cause nausea, narcosis, weakness, drowsiness, and unconsciousness.
- **Inhalation:** Irritation to nose and throat. At high concentrations, same effects as ingestion.
- **Skin:** Cracking of skin, dermatitis, and secondary infections.
- **Eyes:** Irritation.
- **Symptoms of overexposure:** Repeated skin contact may cause dermatitis, while the skin defatting properties of this material may aggravate an existing dermatitis. (Source: Material Safety Data Sheet.)

Polyurethane

Vapours may accumulate in inadequately ventilated/confined areas. Vapours may form explosive mixtures with air. Vapours may travel long distances and flashback may occur. Closed containers may explode when exposed to extreme heat.

Symptoms

- **Ingestion:** May be similar to inhalation symptoms – drowsiness, dizziness, nausea, irritation of digestive tract, depression, aspiration hazard.

- **Inhalation:** Dizziness, drowsiness, fatigue, weakness, headache, unconsciousness.
- **Skin:** Drying, cracking, dermatitis.
- **Eyes:** Burning, tearing, reddening. Possible transient corneal injury or swelling of conjunctiva. (Source: Carbon Black Carcinogen by IARC, Symptoms of Overexposure.)

Recommended precautions

Always wear goggles/full face shield and other protective equipment. Avoid skin contact by wearing protective clothing. Take a shower and bathe your eyes after exposure. Wash contaminated clothing thoroughly before reusing it.

... So, with all this in mind, remember that the addresses of recommended guitar repair men and spray shops can be found in your local *Yellow Pages*.

If you really feel you want to customise your guitar finish then you must take extreme precautions, particularly to avoid inhalation of the dangerous mist created by the spray process.

A passive mask available from DIY stores will only offer the most minimal protection. If in any doubt consult the paint manufacturer for detailed precautions specific to the paint type you've chosen.

The key to saving your hearing is 'dose' figures. Research has shown that you risk damage if exposed to sound 'dose' levels of 90dB or above for extended periods. Health and safety limits for recording studios now recommend no more than 90dBA ('A' standing for average) per eight-hour day, these levels to be reduced dramatically if the period is longer or the dBA higher.

Transient peaks, as in those produced by a loud snare drum or hi-hat, can easily push levels beyond these figures. Be careful where you stand in relation to drums and amplifiers – a small movement can effect a dramatic change in transient sound level. Don't be afraid to ask about peak and average levels. Your ears are your greatest asset as a musician, so don't be embarrassed into thinking you can't question sound levels.

Repetitive strain injury

Guitarists need to think about posture, warm-up routines and avoiding over-practising. RSI is not funny and affects millions of players. Generate good habits early and stick to them.

Tools and working facilities

Many acoustic guitar adjustments can be done using regular domestic workshop tools. However, some specialist tools can make 'nut work' and lubrication a lot easier.

Necessary workshop tools

Some of the tools listed below can double up as your essential gig bag wrap, but as you don't have to carry all the workshop tools around we can be less concerned about weight and portability. It's very convenient, for instance, to have separate screwdrivers rather than the interchangeable-bit variety. More substantial wire cutters also make string changing a little easier.

■ **Set of Phillips-type screwdrivers sizes No.0, No.1, No.2**
It may seem a small point, but I recommend using the correct size and type of screwdriver. Many valuable guitars have survived 30 years on the road but often have a selection of odd screws and 'stripped' screw heads. These look unsightly, slow down maintenance, and make the simplest job a chore. The correct 'point' size will reduce screw stripping and is also less likely to skate across your prized paintwork.

■ Use type No.0 Phillips for some Kluson machine heads.
■ Use type No.1 Phillips for pickguard, rear access covers, jack socket, some machine head screws and strap buttons.
■ Use type No.2 Phillips for neck bolts.

A screwdriver with interchangeable heads is an alternative option. However, you will often need several heads at the same time, which means a lot of changing around. This option is nevertheless useful on the road, when a compact toolkit is more practical.

Sometimes an electric screwdriver can take the strain out of repetitive tasks. However, be sure to protect the guitar as the screwdriver 'torques out'. *Never* do this on plastic parts, as old plastics become brittle and easily crack under sudden pressure.

The tools used in our case studies.

■ **Set of car feeler gauges
(.002–.025) (0.05–1mm)**
These are used for assessing
and setting the nut height.

■ **12in (150mm) ruler with ¹⁄₃₂in
and ¹⁄₆₄in increments (0.5mm increments)**
Used for setting and assessing the string action.

■ **4mm straight-slot screwdriver**
Useful for many applications.

■ **Screw extractor HSS drills and tap wrenches**
For removing broken screws.

Useful tools for
'action setting'.

■ **Zap-It electric
screwdriver attachment**
Makes light work of
de-stringing guitars.

■ **Portable suction fixing vice**
This ingenious device is
terrific if you have no suitable
permanent workbench. Ideal
for nut filing.

■ **Stewmac jack socket fixer**
The 'Jack The Gripper' tool is
great for securing loose jack
sockets without a lot of string
removal and fiddling around
inside the soundhole. An
expanding cam on the 'driver'
grips the internal jack whilst
you tighten the nut with a
standard ³⁄₈in socket wrench.

⚡ Tech Tip

**When working on vintage brittle plastics
consider using a fixed torque screwdriver
– set to avoid over-tensioning.**

■ **Gauged nut files**
A set of gauged nut files make optimising the parameters
on this simple but vital component 100% easier.

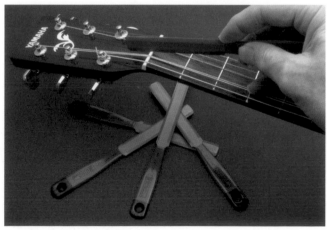

Consider also having a set of bench drawers and tidies for
all those often misplaced odds and sods that are essential
for guitar maintenance!

■ Electronic tuner

An accurate electronic tuner with a jack socket as well as an external clip-on microphone will make short work of adjusting the intonation of individual string lengths. The strobe types are the most accurate.

■ Wire cutters

Useful for cutting strings to length. Overlong strings at the headstock are a safety hazard and tear up your gig bag.

■ Peg winder and bridge pin remover

Time saving, and avoids RSI when changing strings.
Fit one to your electric screwdriver.

■ Polish and cloth

A soft duster for body and back of the neck, a lint-free cotton hankie for strings & fingerboard. Proprietary guitar polishes differ from household furniture polishes, which often contain silicone. The wax used in guitar polish is emulsified to avoid any sticky residue, especially under the heat from stage lighting – Dunlop make a good 'two-stage' system. The handy Planet Waves cloths come ready impregnated with just enough polish.

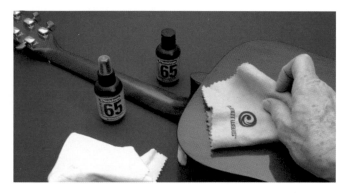

✎ Tech Tip

The worst-case scenario with soldering is melting the plastic on interior wires – so be quick! But also keep the components steady: a wire moved while solder is setting may cause a 'dry joint' and poor conductivity.

John Diggins – Luthier

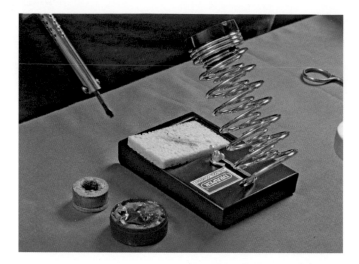

Soldering tips

When soldering heat-sensitive parts such as pickups and potentiometers, it's quicker and safer to tin all the components (*ie* apply a little solder) and *then* join them together for the minimum amount of time whilst applying heat from the iron.

■ Soldering iron

This should be at least 25W with a penlight tip. The iron is essential when repairing electro acoustic wiring. It's worth investing in a stand with a sponge cleaner attached (Draper components 23554 or similar). A crocodile clip multi-arm is also useful for holding small components in place.

■ A tube of solder

Multicore-type non-acid resin.

■ Tweezers

For rescuing dropped screws from awkward cavities and removing hot wires during soldering.

■ Crocodile clips

Can be used as isolating 'heat sinks' – but not too close to the joins, as they'll hamper the operation by drawing away too much heat.

■ Solder syringe

Makes light work of drawing old solder from previous electrical joints.

■ A small penlight torch

Useful for closer examination of details. Useful any time but especially in a stageside emergency.

Useful accessories

- Vaseline or ChapStick for lubrication.
- Silicone or graphite locksmiths' nut lubricant. The Planet Waves 'Lubrikit' is an alternative neat and convenient solution, applying a precise amount of lube via an adapted syringe. The supplied tiny swabs are for the hard-to-reach spots – I suspect there may be questions at Customs, however!

- Matchsticks or cocktail sticks for lubrication application and 'rawlplugging' screws.
- Pipe cleaners and cotton buds for cleaning awkward spots; an old electric toothbrush can also be useful.
- Radius gauges for determining the shape of bridge saddles.
- An electronic multimeter for testing electro circuits.
- A set of socket spanners is good for removing and tightening pot nuts, jack sockets and some modern machine heads.

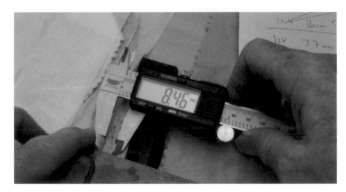

- Mechanical and digital callipers, great for all sorts of detailed measurements.
- Loctite or similar multi-purpose superglue.
- Craft knife for some nut work.
- Thread gauges, useful for checking for correct threads on replacement screws etc.
- Rubber hammer, safer in many situations on valuable instruments.
- Wire stripper.
- Lemon oil for rosewood fingerboards.
- Fingerboard wax for ebony.
- Spare jack socket and batteries.
- Dental abrasives and/or abrasive cord for fine-tuning a nut slot.

The insulated handles on these tools are soft rubber – less likely to scratch the guitar.

Working environment

Many guitar repairs and much maintenance can be safely carried out with the guitar resting in its hard shell case on a normal kitchen table or on a Workmate-type DIY bench, suitably padded. The photographs in this book are 80% of work done at home on a Draper Workmate. However, see page 43 on paint repairs for precautions regarding the inhalation of cellulose etc.

Outside the guitar case environment, a small 1m square of carpet sample bluetacked to a workbench can avoid a lot of inadvertent damage to guitar paintwork. An alternative is a proprietary roll-up guitar mat and neck rest.

All the guitar techs and luthiers consulted for this book seemed to have their own ingenious home-made tools for very specific jobs.

Essential gig bag accessories

Carrying a few spares can save you a long walk, but you have enough to carry to a gig without hauling your whole toolkit around. The mere essentials compactly stowed in a tool wrap will potentially save a lot of pre-gig hassle, and should fit in your gig bag zip compartment.

We suggest...

A multipoint screwdriver with Phillips '0', '1' and '2' point bits and small and medium point conventional straight heads. The Cruz Tools gig bag kit has '1' and '2' point Phillips and 3mm and 6mm straight-slots. A straight-slot screwdriver is useful to have around for dealing with broken mains plugs and blown fuses. Also:

- A small pair of wire snips for emergency string changes.
- Small 'emergency only' soldering iron and 6in of solder (not included in the Cruz Tools kit at present).
- Some 13-amp and 5-amp (UK) fuses as well as any specific to your area of touring (ie USA and European equivalents, etc).
- A PP3 battery (for FX).
- A penlight torch.
- Spare plectrums and or finger picks.
- Allen or hex keys for truss rod, etc.

- A nail file.
- A Leatherman or similar multitool – useful for a sharp blade and decent pliers.
- Insulating tape.
- Feeler gauges.
- 6in rule.
- An electronic tuner.
- Spare strings.
- Plumbers' PTFE tape – useful for securing loose control knobs.
- Bridge pin lever (usually found on most peg winders).

As we go to press the Cruz Tools kit doesn't include a mini Haynes manual – but I'm working on it!

Unfortunately, by having this kit with you you'll acquire a reputation as Mr Ever Ready, and before long everybody in the band will come to depend on your tools!

It's worth doing a little maintenance

...Or getting an expert to do it for you. The acoustic guitar is a frail piece of craftsmanship easily broken, but even the rigours of the world tour have been surmounted with the help of a good flight case and a little loving care. Clearly few of us would risk taking a vintage Ramírez on the road, but barring abuse and given a few careful tweaks it would undoubtedly acquit itself well. The '53 Gibson in our case studies is still being gigged.

Vintage antiques

If you're lucky enough to own a Vintage acoustic then what you have in your possession is not just a good instrument but a piece of popular music history. Given its rarity, you must regard the guitar as you would any other valuable 'antique'.

Whilst such guitars are considered a valuable investment, I personally share the view of many antique furniture collectors that design and function are part of the charm of such items and therefore they are best kept in use. I wonder about the 'investor' who thinks an instrument is best consigned to a bank vault. For me this seems a waste, like the owner who never actually drives his Ferrari. Researching in the world's museums I've observed that unplayed instruments simply wilt and die.

So I recommend you enjoy your guitar whilst observing a few cautions:

- Never subject the instrument to any extremes of change in temperature and humidity. The chief victim here is the finish, which can crack or 'pave' as the underlying wood shrinks or expands. Vintage guitars are more prone to this as their paints and glazes are pervious – which may contribute to the character of their sound as the wood continues to 'breathe'.

- Give the guitar a good wipe down with a lint-free cloth after playing. This will reduce any damage to metal parts and finish caused by perspiration – the main cause of rust to the machine heads. This, of course, also preserves the strings, often doubling their useful life.

- Keep all the moving parts suitably lubricated.

- Use a good stable guitar stand. This sounds so obvious, but many once fabulous instruments turn up on the repair bench having been accidentally knocked off some precarious perch. Luthier John Diggins repairs one broken neck a month. Two of the case study guitars had broken headstock joints on arrival.

This wonderful 1833 Martin – probably the first made in the USA – is kept at a constant temperature of 22-25 degrees and humidity of 45-55%, exactly the same as the Martin factory. *(Courtesy of Guitar Junction UK)*

Authenticity

Many true 'relics' of the last 100 years have defective parts, particularly machine heads. It's perfectly natural to want to replace these. However, it is almost a custodial responsibility to replace them tastefully. These guitars will outlive us and carry on being worthwhile instruments for centuries. I predict the authentic 'early music' enthusiasts of 2050 will include people performing Robert Johnson licks on authentic Gibson L1s and Kalamazoos. So seek out the most authentic replacement parts possible. It's relatively easy to buy 'aged' parts with a suitable patina that ooze an atmosphere of smoky bars and long years on the chitlin circuit (see *Useful contacts* appendix). Do, however, make a careful note of any changes, as this will save arguments over authenticity at a later date.

Hangtags and inventory cards are useful sources of 'provenance'.

■ Keep the originals parts

Authenticity remains an issue 'under the hood', and with an old instrument it is extremely prudent to conserve any original bits. This may sound over the top at present but the collectors and players of the next century will remember you warmly for taking that extra bit of trouble.

Over the years I have personally accumulated a small collection of bits from previous guitars, including a couple of bridge parts from a '62 Fiesta Red Strat, my first proper guitar. Now in 1969 when I sold the guitar, these seemed to be scrap metal and it never occurred to me to pass them on. But if the guitar still exists, and it probably does (serial no 87827 – let me know if you have it!), these old parts are an important piece of what antiquarians call 'provenance'. A dealer may spot the 'new' saddle pieces I obtained with great difficulty in 1966, and wonder if the guitar really is a '62 Fiesta Red, but if the present owner had the old parts it completes a part of that story which supports the authenticity of the overall instrument.

So put those old parts in a safe place and label them with any information you have.

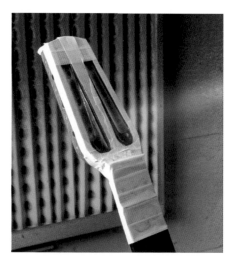

When not to respray

Never be tempted to respray a Vintage Martin. However tatty it may have become *it's worth more in its original state*. Again it's like the 'bruises' on a piece of Chippendale furniture – they are a testimony to the artefact's history. The same, of course, applies to younger guitars, but somehow they don't resonate with quite the same history (yet!).

Do-it-yourself versus calling in an expert

We all have varying levels of competency in carpentry, electronics and painting. I personally made some silly mistakes as a teenager – I stripped down an Archtop guitar with Nitromors paint stripper; it never recovered and sounded terrible! I put a tailpiece on a 12-string to save its bulging belly, and with too little downward pressure on the saddle it sounded very thin. This book is part driven by the desire to help others avoid my youthful errors.

So bottom line is, if you're good with tools and prepared to be diligent and extremely careful, you can probably do most of what this manual expounds and either maintain a lovely instrument in peak performance or radically improve a budget Yamaha. However, if you have *any doubts at all* about your abilities call an expert.

In 1965 there were no guitar techs (not even for Eric Clapton), only luthiers, who all regarded my guitars as a bit of a joke. Today there are at least half a dozen skilled techs in every major city in the world and they all have a sneaking regard for the old warhorses that keep bouncing back.

USA-made National 'Reso Phonic' Style 3.

Gibson L2 Centennial Edition.

Never

- Practice refretting on a vintage instrument. Buy a budget acoustic and learn the craft first.
- Attempt a respray unless you have all the required tools and skills and a dust-free environment. Always wear a protective mask and protective clothing.

- Force the wrong size screw in a body or component. Consider using fixed-torque screwdrivers on vintage instruments.
- Always protect the guitar's surfaces during any maintenance or lubrication.

But whatever else you do, enjoy that special piece of popular music history by playing it every day and trying very hard to wear it out!

I have seen and played a lot of guitars in the last 40 years and I have this thought to pass on:

A well set-up budget Yamaha is a better working instrument than a poorly set-up custom order Martin. In crude terms a good working guitar is about 70% set-up and 20% the synergy of the parts – all pieces of wood are different and even machined metal parts vary in their composition and microscopic detail. The last 10% is alchemy. A good guitar is a good guitar whether old or new. As my late great teacher Brendan John McCormack often said, 'It's just a plank of wood – *you* have to make the music.'

Does a guitar respond to being played well? Does the prevalent temperature and humidity affect a guitar's sound? Yes. But *great guitars* still have a certain mystery about them – long may it remain.

> ### ✎ Tech Tip
>
> There is no such thing as one perfect set-up – what's right for Mark Knopfler is not right for Eric Clapton – so seek your own ideal set-up.
>
> *Glenn Saggers – Mark Knopfler's guitar tech*

Stageside repairs

Given that you're likely to be using amplification and there are perhaps issues of rigging an amp, tuning up and checking of leads etc, it's worth arriving at a gig at least one hour before show time. This also allows for sound-checks and time for the things that inevitably go wrong to be put right. Sound-checks also give the PA engineers a chance to serve your needs better – to understand the likely combinations of instruments and any instrument changes during your set. Sound-checks are also great for finding solutions to the inevitable hiccups that arise in an unfamiliar venue.

No sound from your electro acoustic? – Step 1

- Don't panic! Work systematically through the cable chain starting at the guitar, as the whole system is very unlikely to have failed.
- Where fitted, try changing the preamp balance selector to another pickup, eg from piezo to mike. Are the volume controls turned up? Is the battery OK? Most preamps have a PP3-type battery – is the tuner working (they usually share a battery)? Try changing the battery.
- Still no sound? Try replacing the cable between the guitar and the amplifier with a new cable (one you're sure is working – for instance, the one another guitar player is already successfully using).
- In the above step you should bypass and eliminate any effects chain.
- If you then have sound, try reinserting the effects chain. (Still no sound? Go to Step 2).
- If you have sound then you merely had a faulty cable, the most common cause of onstage sound failure. *Never* be tempted to the false economy of cheap cables – they always let you down by failing at critical moments and can also affect your sound by introducing higher capacitance at certain frequencies. Buy reputable rugged cables – the switched types from Planet Waves in the picture are useful for onstage cable switching *without* deafening your audience. A simple button on the jack mutes the output.

- If a faulty cable is *not* the culprit then it would seem that some component of the effects chain is faulty – work through the chain replacing one cable at a time and hopefully isolating the fault.
- If cable replacement doesn't solve the problem try systematically removing one effect at a time from the chain.
- If you find a 'dead' component of the chain try replacing its associated battery or power supply.

No sound from your electro acoustic? – Step 2

- Still no sound, even though you're now plugged directly into the amplifier with a 'new' cable?
- The likely scenario is a 'failed' amplifier, so try checking the obvious causes such as:

  - Has the volume been inadvertently turned down to zero?
  - Check the master volume and all channel gains.
  - Is the standby switch in the ON position?
  - Does the mains light (if fitted) show 'ON'?
  - Is the amplifier plugged to the mains? Is the mains switched on? Does the stage have a separate fuse?
  - Are other amplifiers on the same circuit working?

- If yours is the only failed amp then look to the fuses. There are likely to be fuses on the amplifier (usually a screw-type fuse cartridge near the mains switch). There may also be fuses in the mains plug. Try replacements.
- If all of this fails then you must assume the amplifier has a major fault and try a 'work around' – eg sharing an amplifier with the other musicians etc. Any band should carry at least one spare amp.
- The crucial thing here is to be systematic – work through the chain logically, eliminating elements of the chain until the fault is isolated.

The guitar won't stay in tune?

Strings!

The most likely cause of tuning difficulties on an otherwise well-maintained guitar is poor or worn strings. The bad news is that changing strings one hour before a gig is also a formula for disaster, as the strings really need time to settle. In an emergency try replacing any individual strings that seem particularly troublesome – rusty or damaged strings inevitably cause severe tuning problems.

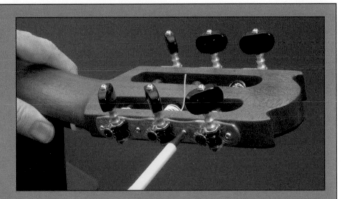

Loose components?

- Have the neck-securing screws worked loose (Taylor, Fender and other bolt-on neck guitars)? A quarter-turn can improve the neck stability, but don't go mad – beware of cracking the surrounding lacquer by overtightening.

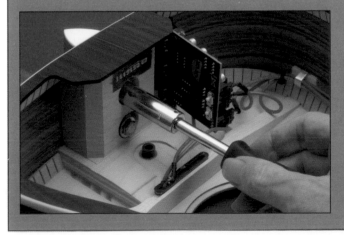

- Are the machine heads loose?

NB: A machine head that is securely fitted but turns without altering pitch needs replacement. In practice this is unlikely to happen suddenly and should be picked up during routine maintenance.

- Are the strings well secured? A good fisherman's knot at both ends of a monofilament nylon string will prevent tuning slippage. The bottom three wound strings are usually sufficiently held with a single loop.

In practice any loose component in the string path will cause instability and hence tuning problems – examine the guitar for loose nut and saddle. If the strings are OK and there are no obvious loose components then perhaps you've changed string gauges without adjusting the saddle and nut?

Three-monthly checks

It's worth giving your acoustic guitar a regular check over. Screws come loose, strings rust and pegs work their way out of their sockets. Woods deserve a little TLC to prevent drying out and shrinkage. A small investment of time will pay dividends in a more dependable instrument.

Strings and stringing

Change these according to use, at least weekly if you're a gigging professional and at least every three months for students. Use the same brand consistently and use the same gauge and metal type, as this will save time-consuming adjustments to the action and intonation. Different strings have different tensions and gauges can vary from heavy to extra light. Cheap strings are a generally a false economy – they're inconsistent and wear out quicker. Consider using 'coated' strings for their resistance to perspiration – some people (including Bruce Springsteen) have very acid sweat that can play havoc with guitar strings, and the coated types may last longer.

New strings are consistent in their profile and hence more 'harmonically correct' along their length – this makes them easier to tune. Old strings are worn by fret contact, are inconsistent and above all sound dull.

Keep new strings sounding good longer by wiping them after every use with a lint-free cloth. This removes corrosive perspiration and prevents premature rusting. Planet Waves

offer a simple string-cleaning tool that may be of benefit if there is some debris build-up on the strings. The felt pads are lubricated with an alcohol cleaning solution.

Early Gibson L5s came fitted with burnished strings and some players even fitted flatwound strings of a type now associated with mainstream jazz styles. Today's fashionable guitar sounds tend to be bright and crisp and this is best achieved with conventional roundwound strings.

Always use acoustic guitar strings. This sounds obvious but acoustic guitar strings are different from electric strings – particularly the basses, which tend to use bronze and phosphor bronze alloys. Specialist strings made of brass and copper err towards a vintage early 20th-century sound. Other specialist strings include Gypsy Jazz formulations for Maccaferri-type guitars and Hybrid gauge strings with a lighter treble and a heavier bass.

For classic Spanish guitar the 'normal' arrangement is often three monofilament trebles and three silver-plated wound basses on nylon filament. These are available in three tensions – low, medium and high – chosen to suit individual player's preferences. Few Classic players are aware of the many options available for third strings. The monofilament third can often be a little flabby due to its thickness to length ratio. D'Addario offer a very good alternative with their 'composite' thirds, which despite their off-putting brown colour do have a brighter tone. Savarez the French manufacturer offer a light gauge wound third which has an excellent sound, though short-lived, as the very fine windings quickly break – I feel it's worth the hassle, however.

Stick to one brand as these will be balanced across the gauges for equal tension. To reduce string breakage lightly lubricate any contact points at nut and saddle with a small amount of graphite. Do this every time you change your strings. The lubricant acts as an insulator against moisture, and reduces friction and metal fatigue.

Small guitars such as the one-eighth and three-quarter size instruments used by children need appropriate gauge strings if they're to tune correctly – the German Dr Junger company can supply these. See *Useful contacts* appendix.

Stringing a modern steel-string acoustic with a solid headstock

If possible change one string at a time to avoid the sudden change in tension caused by a complete destringing of the guitar body.

1 Where fitted, loosen the machine head tension screw.

2 De-tension the old string using a peg winder or Zap-It attachment.

Don't skimp on strings.

3 Carefully unpick the old string from the barrel and, pushing the string into the bridge, ease the bridge pin loose a little – 'jiggling' and sometimes a little leverage may be required (the end of many string winders is notched for just this purpose). In difficult situations the peg can be pushed out by reaching inside the soundhole and pushing it up with a short dowel.

4 Push the new string ball end through the bridge pin hole and ease the pin on top. Any slot in the bridge pin should face the guitar soundhole.

5 Pull the string up to contact the bridge pin – with luck the pin will hold its position (keep checking!).

6 Thread the other end of the string through the posthole and wrap the string back on itself, forming a simple knot – note how the bass strings wrap to the right of the barrel and the treble strings to the left.

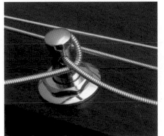

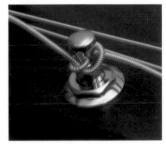

7 Tighten the string whilst maintaining it under tension. You don't need a lot of turns on the barrel. Always manoeuvre the string to wind down the barrel, thus improving the break angle to the nut.

8 Tune to pitch. You may sometimes find the bridge pin rides up in the bridge and needs reseating.

9 Trim the excess string with some wire cutters.

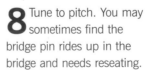

Stringing a 'classic' Spanish acoustic with a slotted headstock

If possible change one string at a time to avoid the sudden change in tension caused by a complete destringing of the guitar body.

1 De-tension the old string using a peg winder or Zap-It attachment.

2 Carefully unpick the old string from the barrel and the bridge.

3 Push the new string through the bridge pin hole and tie this in a Fisherman's knot for the treble strings, two turns on the third string, three on the second and four on the first. The bass strings are usually fine with a single turn.

4 Pull the string up to the headstock string barrel and do a similar knot.

5 Tighten the string whilst maintaining it under tension. You don't need a lot of turns on the barrel – perhaps two or three. Try to manoeuvre the string for the straightest possible pull at the headstock. Tune to pitch and trim the excess string at both ends with some wire cutters.

Stringing a steel-string acoustic with slotted headstock

Requires a simple combination of the two previous operations described above. Naturally the steel strings won't 'knot' but they can be looped back on themselves to form a half-hitch.

Unconventional stringing

■ The traditional Gypsy Jazz tailpiece has looped strings.

■ The Ovation bridge is without pins and adopts a more 'classical' through-string approach.

■ The Baroque Flamenco and Torres guitars use wooden pegs, the most crucial element of which is a little Hill's violinist's Peg Paste applied to the peg to prevent slipping and to smooth the pitch adjustment.

Replacing an end pin jack socket

Perhaps the most common output arrangement on electro acoustics is a jack socket in place of the end pin. These wear out and become noisy, needing replacement every few years depending on the level of use.

1 Remove the protective ferrule/ strap button. Undo the retaining nut – the 'enclosed' spanner is good for this as it can't slip and damage the guitar. The 'Jack The Gripper' tool keeps the socket from revolving whilst you loosen the nut (anticlockwise).

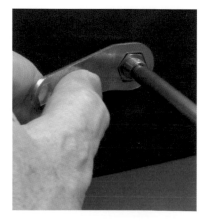

2 Push the freed socket into the guitar. Slacken the strings, sixth first, then first, then fifth, second, fourth and third – this evens out the loss of tension on the neck. Reach inside the soundhole and retrieve the jack socket.

3 Prise open the cable retainer to free the old wires. Unsolder the old connections carefully, making a note of the wiring colour coding – this particular jack socket is stereo wired with tip red, white ring, and black screen/ground to the 'sleeve'. Note the useful 'third hand'.

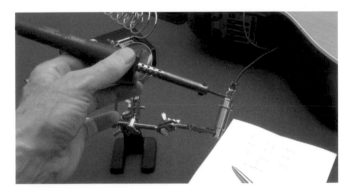

4 Solder the replacement socket using the same wiring colour codes.

5 Crimp the cable retainer to secure the wires.

6 A small amount of 'heat shrink' sleeving makes for a neat insulated finish. If this isn't available a little electricians' tape will do the job.

7 Carefully measure the depth of the exposed thread before the retaining nut on the old socket and set the new one to match – this will save a lot of fiddling! Install the new jack socket into the guitar via the soundhole.

8 Secure the new socket with a washer and retaining nut. Replace the cover/strap retainer.

9 It's also important to secure the internal wires to a brace in order to avoid acoustic rattles – handy self-adhesive clips are available from pickup manufacturers.

✏ Tech Tip

A piece of string attached to the new jack socket makes light work of getting this through the rear hole without a struggle!

Replacing defective machine heads

Machine heads are one of the few truly mechanical devices associated with acoustic guitars. As such they inevitably wear out, causing 'dead spots' in their compliance. This presents an opportunity to upgrade to better quality products such as those from Grover or Exagon. There are many options available depending on whether the guitar has a solid or slotted headstock and also if the old machines are arranged as 'singles' or sets of three. Choose something similar to the original in order to minimise any clean-up operations.

Solid headstock Dreadnought

The Yamaha solid headstock Dreadnought guitar (see page 130) has the very cheap machines expected at its budget price. Replacements will have a better gearing ratio, will lock to the headstock and have adjustable tension – all features that aren't on the originals. This will, however, necessitate relocating some retaining screws.

1 First remove the strings (always take the time to reduce the neck tension in a slow and balanced way to minimise the risk of upsetting the balance of the fixed neck). In this case the old fixing screws require a Phillips '0' point screwdriver for removal.

2 The ferrules will also need removal – don't be tempted to hammer these out, as you're likely to crack the lacquer or even worse the headstock; a gentle 'waggle' with a hole punch did the trick this time.

3 The old machines weigh 142g and the new ones 279g! – however, I have installed a preamp in this guitar so I'm hoping the overall balance will even out. An alternative would have been too install the lighter 'mini' version of the Grovers. On the plus side heavier machines *may* alter the position of the fundamental node on the neck, affecting the tone (possibly for the better). See page 106 for more on this.

4 The new machines drop neatly into place with a reassuringly snug fit. However, there are a couple of unsightly screw holes that need disguising.

5 I first trimmed the protruding 'burr' surrounding the old screw holes with a craft chisel.

6 I then filled the holes with a cocktail stick splinter and some superglue.

7 A fine abrade with a glass paper file flattens the fill.

8 This is then smoothed with some very fine abrasive paper.

9 Small dabs of Ronseal Deep mahogany varnish (satin) help to disguise the filled holes. A second coat feathered into the old finish has a reasonable effect.

10 One of the old ferrule holes is eccentric and I've had to enlarge it slightly with a rat tail rasp.

11 I confess that six coats of Ronseal were needed to fully hide the old screw holes! However, the time between coats is only 20 minutes. A light rub down with 000 grade wire wool between coats improves the final finish. The Dunlop polish system with carnauba also helped blend the old and new finishes.

12 The new machines are fixed by the front bolt bushings and washers. Tighten these, in this case with an 11mm socket spanner.

13 They're then aligned with the rear screw, which will need a small pilot hole. The relatively soft wood on the budget guitar means this can be achieved with a sharp-pointed craft tool – on a solid mahogany neck you may need a small drill. The screws themselves require a Phillips '0' point.

14 The new machines work substantially better and the guitar now stays in tune. As predicted, the tone is also better – probably attributable to adding some weight to the headstock.

Preserving the look

When replacing any parts on a *vintage* guitar to preserve the guitar's looks and value, get the nearest you can to an identical replacement and store all the vintage parts safely. They will help provide provenance for the instrument at any future sale.

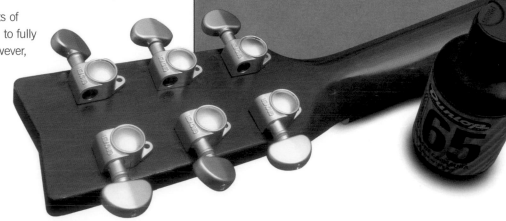

Classical slotted headstock

This is often a simpler replacement job as classic machines are more similar between brands. However:

- Removing the old machines reveals that the new screw holes don't quite align!

- I therefore filled the old holes with a cocktail stick and some superglue.

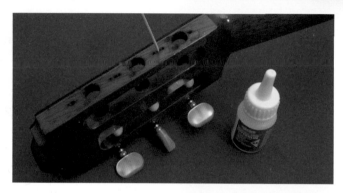

- A little candle wax on the ends of the new barrels sometimes helps for a smoother action.

- Aside from piloting the new holes replacement was straightforward, though be aware that the new screws supplied might be too long for the slotted headstock and could protrude – if so, simply reuse the old ones!

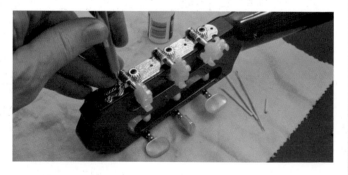

NB Exposed gears will benefit from light lubrication with Vaseline or a chapstick.

Slotted machines on a steel string guitar

Single tuners as seen on this Martin 0028 are often a better choice, as when one tuner fails you don't have to replace all three! They're a simple 'part for part' Grover replacement, and you can upgrade to gold if the guitar warrants it. Be sure to order the 'barrel' type tuner as they're almost identical to the solid headstock version – apart from the position of the string-threading hole! Notice also the cog size, which will affect the gearing ratio.

✎ Tech Tip

If you're replacing any machine heads and the existing headstock holes are a fraction too small don't be tempted to reach for the electric power tools! The safe solution is a razor sharp peg head reamer. A sharp reamer will trim the hole without chipping any lacquer – just be sure to support the headstock well as you ream!

Locking machines

Locking machines are also available for acoustics – these specific ones are by Planet Waves (see *Useful contacts* appendix) and were designed by Ned Steinberger. They offer the advantage of less 'wrap' and consequently less slippage. They're also 'self-trimming', so may make for swift stageside string changes. The string is simply locked from the rear and as the string is wound on to the post it is self-trimmed.

Correcting a loose saddle

The saddle on any guitar needs to be a snug fit in order to achieve a good mechanical couple with the bridge. A loose saddle, as on this Yamaha, will benefit from a very thin wooden shim to stop it rocking ineffectually. See 'The art and science of tone', page 99.

A fret polish

Any guitar will benefit from a smooth set of frets. Surprisingly the rosewood Yamaha NX had fairly rough frets as supplied, so I sorted them!

1 Remove the strings. As usual, avoid uneven stress on the neck by de-tensioning strings alternately, first, sixth, second, fifth etc.

2 Mask off the fingerboard with some low adhesion masking tape.

3 Carefully polish the frets with a Planet Waves abrasive paper if things aren't too bad, or a little 0000 gauge wire wool if more work is needed. Always wear gloves and eye protection when using wire wool.

4 A final polish with an old leather belt attached to a wooden baton and a little Duraglit metal polish will work wonders. Be sure to remove the nut and saddle in this case – it's easier and they won't get broken!

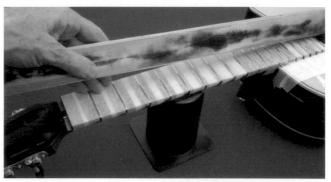

5 After removing the masking tape remove any surplus adhesive and condition the ebony with some Dunlop 02 oil or equivalent.

Truss rod adjustment

The truss rod is a relatively modern innovation patented by Gibson in 1921 and now almost universally fitted to all steel string guitars. Surprisingly Martin didn't fit adjustable truss rods on their guitars until 1985, though Vintage reissues will have them. Nylon string guitars with their lower string tensions tend to manage without, though the Yamaha NX series and the nylon string Ovations *do* fit rods.

All acoustic necks require a degree of 'relief' or bow to allow the strings some excursion without fret rattle. However, you may adjust the rod if the relief becomes excessive and makes the guitar difficult to play. If your guitar has no adjustable rod then you'll need to ask a luthier to see if it's cost-effective to remove the frets, flatten the fingerboard and replace the frets. This is only worthwhile on the very best vintage instruments.

First let's assess the relief on your instrument:

1 Check your tuning (which should be at standard A440 pitch or your preferred and consistent 'custom pitch'). Install a capo at the first fret, depress the sixth string at the last fret.

2 With a feeler gauge, check the gap between the bottom of the string and the top of the eighth fret. This well set-up Martin Dreadnought has a very shallow relief at .006in – fine for light fingerpicking and gentle chords. For heavy flatpicking you may want a little more relief in order to be able to 'dig in' and get the strings working the top.

If the neck on your guitar is too concave (indicated by too big a gap when measured with the feeler gauge) you may need to consider adjusting the truss rod for *less* relief.

Do not do truss rod adjustments on a rare and precious guitar if you feel unqualified, talk instead to an experienced guitar tech via your local music shop.

3 There are two common sites for truss rod adjustment: at the headstock under a small shield, as with a Taylor or Yamaha; and from within the soundhole, as on this modern Martin. In order to reach within the soundhole the Martins currently require a special long 5mm Allen wrench, available from Stewmac (see *Useful contacts* appendix). Other makes may require different sizes.

CLOCKWISE IF CONCAVE

4 If you wish to remove some relief, adjust the truss rod screw a quarter-turn *clockwise*.

OR

ANTICLOCKWISE IF CONVEX

5 If the neck has too little relief (the strings are too close to the fingerboard), turn the truss rod nut a quarter-turn *anticlockwise* to allow the string tension to pull more relief into the neck.

NB: For obvious reasons the truss rod was originally conceived to adjust situations with too much relief, and is much more likely to be successful in this application.

6 Recheck the relief gap with the feeler gauge and readjust as needed.

Headstock adjustment

Exactly the same principles apply for headstock adjustment, but you'll need to remove the shield first, often with a Phillips No.0.

Then (for the Taylor), using a ¼in truss rod wrench, turn clockwise to remove relief, anticlockwise to add relief.

NB: If you meet excessive resistance when adjusting the truss rod, or your instrument needs constant adjustment, or adjusting the truss rod has no effect on the neck, take your instrument to a guitar tech via your local musical instrument shop.

Classic guitar relief

Classic guitars are designed to be played purely acoustically and need more relief for clean *fff* articulated notes across the whole fretboard. This one has .014in at the eighth fret, so don't be surprised if yours similarly has .008in more relief than the Martin Dreadnought.

Nut maintenance and replacement

The simple nut is possibly the single most critical component of a good working acoustic guitar. Yours should ideally be made of bone or fossil ivory, the worst scenario being that it's one of the hollow moulded plastic nuts found on many inexpensive guitars – a replacement will sound better and be less prone to binding than coarse brittle plastic.

Securing a loose nut

A loose nut will tend to fall out at a string change or move out of position, and should be secured with a small amount of Loctite (just two small drops, as you may want to replace the nut at some stage).

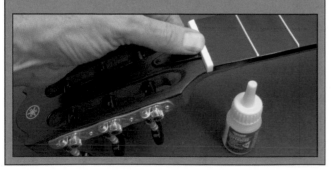

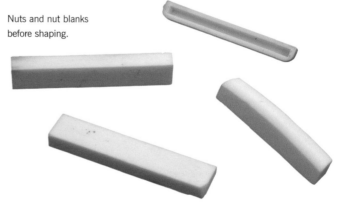

Nuts and nut blanks before shaping.

NB: Please use bone, fossil ivory or synthetic Micarta, not endangered ivory!

Adjusting and lubricating a nut

Much of the time all you need to do with a nut is set it up for your ideal height and ensure the strings don't bind.

If the string slots aren't too deep already then you can simply calculate your optimum depth and carefully file each slot.

1 A good guide to the individual string heights at the nut will be the height at the 2nd fret with the nut excluded from the equation. To calculate this, take a measurement at the second fret with a capo at the first fret – use a car feeler gauge. In this case the strings were approximately .006in above the frets, slightly less on the first and second strings.

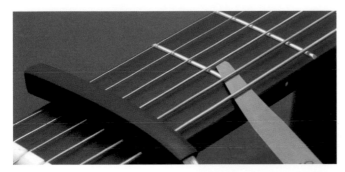

2 Now measure the *fret* height with the feeler gauge. I used a fret rocker as a straight edge (the present figure is .031in).

3 These two added together give you a *minimum* nut height, in this case .037in. You should add a little to this for a working starting point (it's easier to lower a nut slot than to raise it). This combined height made up as a feeler gauge composite provides a useful 'stop guard' for your files – I will try .040in as a starting guide and work down. (**NB:** This nut is way too high as supplied.)

4 Put your feeler gauges in place and file the nut slots to the estimated depth one at a time. I'm using Stewmac gauged nut files at widths of .012–.050 for string gauges .012–.053, the file generally slightly smaller than the string gauge but 'rolled' for fit.

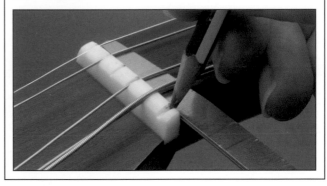
It's important to 'roll' the file to achieve a rounded bottom to the slot, but with the effective sounding edge still defined at the fret side of the nut – this is naturally critical to accurate intonation. The angle will ideally follow the string break angle to the machine heads.

Bear in mind that the fourth, fifth and sixth strings require slightly more height at the nut as their heavier gauge means they have a longer excursion when played.

5 A polish with a little gauged abrasive chord makes for a good smooth finish, avoiding the string snagging in the slot. A little pencil graphite will also help lubricate the new slot.

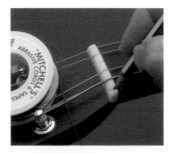

Stewmac.com do a handy 'Nut Slotting Gauge' for calculating the precise string height if you do a lot of this kind of work. This enables very accurate measurements of string heights to be taken.

Sometimes, if the slots require drastic deepening, you may have to take a little bone off the top of the nut. This avoids the strings sounding 'trapped'.

Replacing the nut

1 Remove the strings – take the usual precautions to avoid shock to the neck (one string at a time etc).

Carefully score any overlapping polyurethane or lacquer to avoid accidental chipping.

If present, remove any truss rod cover with a Phillips '1' point screwdriver or whatever is required.

If you're not a skilled luthier I recommend masking the fingerboard and headstock with several layers of protective masking tape.

2 Remove the old nut. Tap the nut *gently* using a small hammer. With luck the nut should eventually become loose and can be removed as one piece reasonably easily. I'm using a piece of scrap wood to spread the impact of the hammer evenly – the nut came off with two very gentle taps!

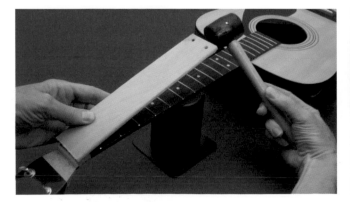

3 As a last resort you could prise the nut out with a pair of smooth-ended pliers. The smooth ends will avoid damaging the old nut – which, assuming you were happy with your original string spacing, provides a perfect template for the new spacing.

4 If necessary clean the nut slot of any surplus adhesive, lacquer, etc. A narrow and sharp file can be used as an effective tool on both the end of the fingerboard and the bottom of the nut slot. A file slightly narrower than 1/8in is required – these needle files were £3 for a set of six at a thrift store. I'm using the narrowest triangular file. Make sure the surface remains very flat!

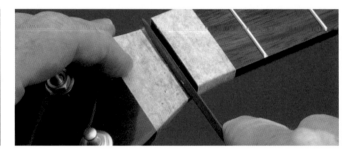

Smooth the nut slot. It's important to avoid chipping the neck finish, so gently file the sharp edge of any lacquer and also file the nut bottom with inward strokes from both ends of the nut slot, thus avoiding accidentally pulling any lacquer from the neck.

5 Approximate the new nut blank. Begin with an oversize blank, which can then be shaped down to a custom fit.

I like the shape of the old nut so have temporarily stuck the old and new together with a tiny dab of superglue. This makes it easier to pencil the outline and indicate the waste. Luthier John Diggins doesn't need to do this, but I do!

6 Cut off the excess length with an X-Acto saw, leaving a little bit of leeway at present. Note the rubber guards in the vice, which prevent damage to the nut.

7 Grind to size. It's a lot easier to do this on a belt sander with a fine grit, though in the past I've done this by hand with a regular file. Note the pliers to keep my guitar-playing hands off the sander – I also wear safety eye goggles.

8 Measure your nut slot width and mark the required nut slots on your new blank, based on the precise measurements of your nut slot and your old nut. Ideally you should carefully copy the string spacing from the old nut. Pay particular attention to the spacing of the sixth and first strings from the outside edge. Having strings too close to the edge will make finger vibrato difficult.

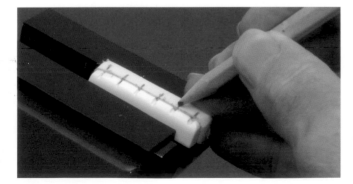

9 I'm simply copying the dimensions and shape of the old nut. Bear in mind you'll certainly need to allow a little more height towards the bass strings, as they need a bit more room to vibrate without 'choking' on the first fret. It's easy to lower a nut – much more fiddly to raise one.

10 When the nut is close to correct you can position the first two outer strings on the new nut by making pilot notches with a fine craft saw (X-Acto or similar, with a blade of .010 gauge or less).

If for some reason you don't have the old nut then a specialist tool called a 'compensated nut spacing template' (see *Useful contacts* appendix) is the easiest way to get even spacing between the outsides of adjoining strings – a more important factor than equal spacing at their centres. Use this or the old nut to determine the position of the remaining string slots.

Surprising as it might seem, expert luthiers often determine the individual string spacing by eye. Though this sounds a little unscientific, the precise calculations in thousandths of an inch are made very complex by the fact that each string is a different gauge. (This is where the 'compensated nut spacing template' makes an ideal reference.) You can adopt this pro method to a degree by positioning the strings in very shallow 'pilot' slots and then making any minor adjustments by eye before completing your filing of the final slots.

11 Here I'm using a regular file to fine shape the nut.

12 Check constantly for a snug fit in the nut slot. At this juncture the nut should still be left slightly overlong for flexibility at the later stages of shaping. A $\frac{1}{16}$in overlap will be enough to allow for some 'fine tuning'.

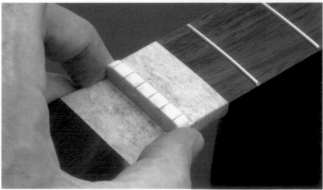

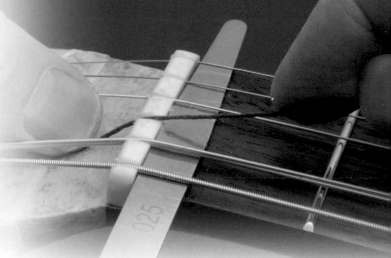

13 Having done a little more shaping, I carefully file the new slots to depth. In practice this is best 'fine tuned' on the guitar, so I've temporarily fitted the nut.

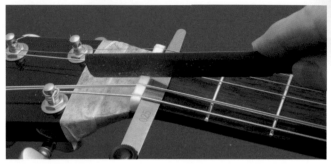

Specialist precision nut files (see *Useful contacts* appendix.) will allow smoothing of the nut slot bottom without damaging the sides of the slot. These files have smooth edges and a round bottom and are available in the precise size for your chosen string gauges. In practice a luthier would use a slightly smaller file than the requisite slot and use a rolling technique on the forward motion to widen the slot with more control and less chance of the file snagging. A carefully chosen feeler gauge can be a useful guide whilst filing, preventing any chance of filing too deep (you can apply the formula given on page XXX for calculating the nut depth).

File at a back angle, to shape the floor (or bottom) of the slot correctly. This enables the string to slide through freely. Emulate the break angle at the headstock. If the slot isn't correctly shaped it will prevent smooth tuning and will hamper the instrument's ability to return to tune.

When a string binds in the nut slot it makes a pinging sound as it breaks free of the slot. The nut will eventually need lubricating with graphite (see page 65).

The back angle of the slot will give good contact for the string, important for tone, whilst a first contact point at the front (fret end) of the nut will ensure correct intonation. Ideally the bottom of the nut slot should be rounded as per the relevant string gauge. I use gauged abrasive chord.

14 Secure the new nut in place with a couple of drops of glue. Don't overdo the glue, as the nut may need removing again for correction.

15 Having filed the string slots I'm taking a little off the top of the nut to avoid the strings tending to be 'nut bound'.

16 This final shot is still 'work in progress', as for the best tone I would ideally like the bass strings to be in the nut slots to just half their depth. I'm doing some saddle work on the same guitar (see page 70) and will make my final adjustments when the saddle is complete.

Internal inspections

The inside of an acoustic guitar is best viewed by removing the strings and using one of these approaches:

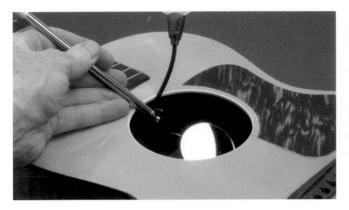

1 Inspection mirrors – the telescopic handle type is useful for examining smaller areas, such as bridge pin seatings. A separate light source such as a small torch is usually also needed.

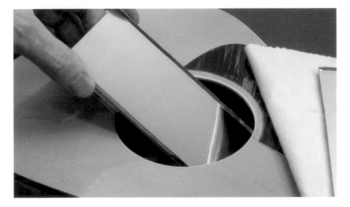

2 A better view can be had with a larger fold-up mirror set – I made this one from some sheet mirror glass hinged with gaffer tape. Be sure to take the sharp edges off with light abrasive paper. Once inside the guitar the mirrors are unfolded for a wider view.

3 A modern approach is to use a 'Snakescope', a variant of the medical endoscope. These self-illuminating remote-controlled video cameras plug into your computer via a USB and give you a recordable image. Be aware that the image quality varies, and if your use is only occasional it may be better to hire a more expensive model.

4 The internal photographs in this book were done using an Olympus IPLEX FX Videoscope. Obviously there are snags with this kind of imaging, particularly the lens distortion produced by the short focal lengths required in confined spaces. Lighting is also tricky – I used a separate very powerful but cool-running mini light, also from Olympus. Anything is better than working blind!

This image shows the Videoscope in use on the Gibson L5. The camera and additional ILP2 light source both enter through the F holes. The Olympus can also record moving images, which can be extremely helpful sometimes.

Bridge and saddle work

For hundreds of years most acoustic guitars have managed with very simple compensation for the intonation discrepancies caused by different string diameters. This usually amounts to a saddle that simply sits at an angle, with the thicker bass strings given more scale length than the thinner treble strings. Many classic guitars manage without even this, as the string gauges are fairly similar.

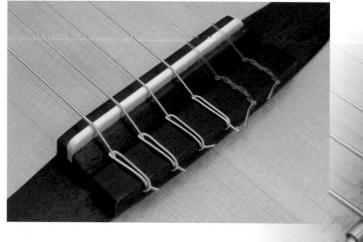

However, acoustic amplification also highlights any small pitch discrepancies and puts them under the microscope, as Leo Fender discovered with his Broadcaster and subsequent electric guitars. It's this acoustic amplification that has prompted luthiers to offer compensated saddles on their newer more expensive guitars.

If you have a cheaper or older guitar you can effect some accurate compensation by fitting a new saddle with custom filed adjustment. One of the easiest methods to gauge the position of the necessary custom shaping is to use a luthier's 'Intonator' (see *Useful contacts*); this temporary saddle enables you to find the optimum fulcrum point for each individual string and then copy those findings on to a permanent saddle.

You may need a new saddle, as a compensated saddle is often as wide as 3mm to accommodate the necessary adjustments. Maybe this is the opportunity to upgrade to a substantial bone saddle? I'm going to see what can be achieved using an existing fairly standard 3mm slot.

1 Check the radius of the guitar fingerboard. Note how the old plastic saddle conforms exactly to that radius.

2 The 'Intonator' has sleeved ferrules to enable individual height adjustment – you should use these and set them to approximately the same radius as your guitar. I found placing the old saddle in position and testing the first and sixth Intonator rods for a rough height guide very useful. I will then set the remaining rods to suit the fingerboard radius.

3 I temporarily filled the old saddle slot with a sliver of wood to give me a flat bridge surface to work on – I found a large kitchen match an almost exact fit! A slight shim was needed, however, to get the height right.

4 I then covered this with very thin masking tape to make a good pencil surface for marking up intonation points.

5 I then installed the outer two strings and tensioned them enough to keep things in place. I have put the largest sleeve on the sixth string – the first string didn't need any sleeve to achieve a good height.

6 I next installed the remaining strings at a workable low tension.

7 Using a radius gauge for reference you can add appropriate height rings.

8 Turn the thumbscrews to achieve all the saddles behind the old saddle line – this ensures that any kinks in the strings (which naturally upset the intonation) end up behind the effective string length.

9 You can now intonate the acoustic as you would a standard electric guitar – tuning the open string initially and then adjusting the 12th fret note sharp or flat as required – clockwise lengthens the 'octave note', making it 'flatter'.

…and anticlockwise the reverse. An electronic strobe tuner will make this a lot easier!

14 I'll get the saddle to an approximate shape with the belt sander.

15 Place the roughly shaped saddle in the slot and then transfer the string length measurements to the top using a vernier and a ruler.

10 When you're happy with the tuning you can mark up each side of the saddles with a sharp pencil. Take care to be consistent with the angle of your markings. When removing the Intonator keep the ferrules on the pins, as these are a record of the string heights – which will be copied to the new saddle.

11 The ideal saddle fulcrum is going to be in the centre of these two marks for each saddle, which I marked up in blue. This gave me an unexpected set of marks but all feasible using the existing saddle slot.

12 Carefully measure these centre points with a set square and a ruler or vernier and make a careful note.

16 Shape and file the top of the new saddle to accommodate any variants from the straight line. Take care to maintain the fingerboard radius with the overall shape of the saddle (this is an interesting three-dimensional sculpture!).

13 Roughly shape the new saddle – I'm using the old saddle as a template and leaving 2mm spare on the bottom to give me some leeway as I do the shaping. I've lightly glued the two saddles together for now to make it easier to mark up, and then scored an outline with a craft needle.

17 Naturally the height of the new saddle is critical, so observe the height established using the Intonator by filing the bottom of the new saddle as required.

18 This is my roughed out compensated saddle. I'll restring and 'tweak' as necessary for the best possible intonation.

19 The saddle needs a final polish with some very fine 3M flexible polish paper 281Q (grade 3MIC); this is micron graded aluminium oxide on a non-woven synthetic backing. Alternatively you can use some abrasive talc. You rub the talc block on some abrasive paper to create an abrasive dust and then polish the bone with this for a silky textured result. (Incidentally, the talc also gives a great polish to classical finger nails!)

In conclusion

Overall this saddle work is a fiddly job, and as bridge spacings naturally vary I did have to trim one of the brass string saddles to fit them in! However, it does give results. The bone saddle and nut have given the guitar a boost in the 200–400Hz area and the intonation is the best it has ever been. I will persevere!

Bridge pins

Bridge pins are in direct contact with the bridge, and via the strings the bridge plate. This suggests their mass may have some influence on sound, so as they're inexpensive why not treat your instrument to something better than five cents' worth of plastic? Planet Waves and others offer bridge pins in brass and ebony that look good and may contribute *something* to the sound of my old Seagull.

1 The safe way to unseat a jammed bridge pin is to employ the lever notch on most string winders.

2 The new pins fitted perfectly on the Seagull, with just one slightly overtight pin.

3 If they're too tight as on this other guitar a bridge pin reamer, used carefully, will open them up slightly.

PlateMate

Another inexpensive refinement is the PlateMate. This simple brass gizmo provides a secure and robust seating for the strings and adds a little mass to the bridge plate. It's designed to solve wear problems on vintage guitars but may be a worthwhile investment on any pin bridge acoustic. Installation is simple, with the only major consideration being getting the right size, as pin spacings have varied over the last 100 years. You can check the spacing on top of the bridge.

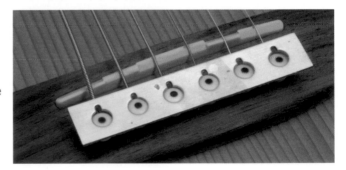

The keyhole notch naturally faces the soundhole when installed under the bridge. You could make one of these from a piece of brass but the Mitchel's version is self-adhesive, which means you only need make sure the bridge plate itself is free of loose wood splinters and any grease; a light abrasive paper will solve both issues. I found that placing a couple of bridge pins either end helped position the bridge plate. On the Seagull the plate subjectively enhanced the high frequencies, which may be a good thing – depending on what you play on the guitar!

Accessories and guitar care

On the face of it nothing could be simpler than an acoustic gig – just turn up, tune up and play. However, a few essential accessories may make for a smoother show. Start back at home by keeping the guitar itself at peak performance.

Raw wood

I confess I've played acoustic guitars for the last 50 years without much thought for the raw wood that sits under my fingers. Acoustic fingerboards of ebony and rosewood are completely exposed to the elements and abused by perspiration, water vapour and grime

Treat the lady right – slap on some body wax!

from our busy fingers. Cleaning the fingerboard with some lemon oil is a great start and conditioning the raw wood with ebony wax or rosewood wax makes a lot of sense. Dunlop also offer a two-pack cleaner and conditioner that will do a similar job.

Finish care

Depending on its vintage and price your guitar body is finished in nitro cellulose lacquer, French polish or polyurethane. You should *never* polish these surfaces with furniture polish as these often contain potentially harmful silicone. Also guitar waxes are emulsified to avoid any sticky residue, especially on exposure to stage lighting. Good guitar polishes are available from Gibson, Martin and Dunlop – they may seem expensive but they're designed for the job and one pack will last for years.

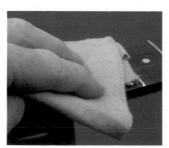

■ Different picks serve different roles. For recording I use specific plectrums for specific string gauges. Sometimes you need a big beefy plectrum to actually get a certain guitar to respond (a beautiful vintage J200 comes to mind).
■ On stage, brightly coloured picks are easier to find if dropped (we all do that). Gaffer a few spares to your mike stand!

■ 'Worn' picks

On the big Nationals where a steely sound is appropriate consider trying ProPik steel fingerpicks – they're loud but not *too* raucous. Many great players have also used finger-mounted thumbpicks and celluloid fingerpicks, though usually in pursuit of volume in a pre-electro acoustic world.

Picks, plectrums and nails

Whatever you choose to pick your guitar with will naturally have a profound effect on your tone. My great college tutor James Eastham insisted 'good tone is apt tone', and he's right – a brittle tone may not be beautiful in itself but maybe it's just the ticket for that killer intro. Equally a Bach Sarabande may call for a mellow warmth, which means looking after your nails.

In my youth plectrums or picks were made of turtle shell (though we thought it was tortoise). Though I was presented with one of these on a Japanese tour I have confined it to curio status – turtles have enough problems. Plectrums these days are made of a bewildering range of plastics and only you can know what works best for your tone, so experiment.

Here are a few things I've picked up along the way;

■ Thin picks sound thin and fat picks sound fat; and, curiously, thin picks may actually slow you down! Choose a pick for the sound you need.
■ A good grip is useful, especially with the perspiration induced by stage lighting – try the non-slip types with the 'Velcro' feel.
■ A 'two-stage' pick which is very flexible at the back and more rigid at the front makes for a versatile switch from 'rhythm' to 'lead'.

Nails – guitarist care

In a perfect world I prefer the sound of real fingernails on nylon or steel. This makes available an unrivalled range of tone and timbre from flesh to nail, varied by an infinite range and variety of angles and levels of attack. I recently directed Julian Bream's DVD *My Life In Music* and included a two camera angle analysis of the poetry available from this, the most 'organic' method. I find that even on steel strings there's no more expressive an option.

■ Nail care

Fingernails are made from the same translucent keratin as our hair – a protein of amino acid-based tissue – and are almost as fragile. The nail plate is formed from strong flexible layers of dead flattened cells. This appears pink due to the underlying blood-filled capillaries. Its transversal shape is determined by the underlying bone.

Good fingerpicking tone depends on smooth polished nails that generally follow the shape of the fingertip (there are alternative approaches to this but most players stick to this simple formula).

An overlong nail gives a thin 'naily' tone and too short a nail gives a similar brittle attack. So the best option is a short nail which allows some flexibility and some flesh contact with the string (which often warms up our tone).

■ Nail files and buffers

Pro fingerstyle guitarists of either sex, and especially Classic players, often have better manicure kits than their girlfriends.

Basic shapers include glass files, which are very effective, and diamond-coated metal files, which can be a bit fierce, but last a long time! Stone-based files are also useful, especially the shaped variety. Some players use Arkansas stones and smooth pebbles for finishing.

Once you've achieved your desired basic nail shape, regular buffers available from chemists and drugstores are brilliant for

finishing and fine-shaping. Start with the coarse buffer and work through in stages to the fine-grade finishing buffer. I personally give the nail edge a chamfer just like a decent plectrum, which seems to produce a softer less edgy tone.

I then finish the nail with a fine polish using a piece of scrap leather. This started out with a piece of my school satchel, which is now glued to an old paperknife to make a useful leather strop like those used by traditional barbers to hone their razors.

Capos

The humble capadastro is the perfect transposing tool; one click, and tenor keys suit sopranos. However, the capo has many more creative applications:

■ Taking a simple chord sequence up a fifth and playing it in the same shapes completely changes the character of the sound – which can be inspirational.

■ Try overdubbing two guitars playing the same chords, one with a capo and one without, *eg* E shapes in the open first position (EAB) combined with a capo at the seventh fret playing in A shapes (ADE) – this will result in interesting contrary motion in some of the changes, used to great effect by guitarists Peter and Paul of Peter, Paul and Mary in the 1960s.

Emergency measures

Sods law says you'll break a nail just before an important gig (for me it was the day of my grade VIII classical exam*). The answer is a repair kit as used by manicurists for glamour purposes. These are now also marketed to guitarists as 'Instant Nail' kits – guitarplayernails.com are one source.

Basically these kits provide everything you need for emergency 'false nail' construction. They comprise:

■ The plastic 'nail' material – which you trim to shape with scissors.
■ Some pipettes for accurately applying the supplied 'superglue'.
■ Some high-quality abrasives for shaping and smoothing the false nail.

These kits work, though I find the sound is a little coarser than a real fingernail – but any port in a storm! The show must go on etc.

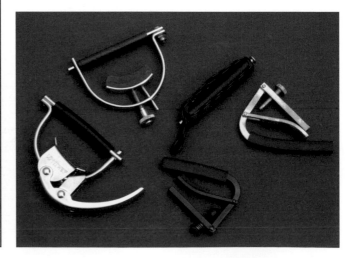

* I passed the exam with a Merit, walked out of the room – and the false nail fell off! In music timing is everything!

■ Capos can also be found with individual release catches. This presents a fascinating range of possibilities – open drone strings combined with stopped octaves etc The 'SpiderCapo' makes 'open tuning' possible without all

that time-consuming retuning. It also opens up an entirely new world of playing *both* sides of the capo. Each string has its own individual lever that smoothly slips in to stop the string as required. This device may change your playing forever!

■ Even the regular vanilla 'all stop' capo comes in a range of options. From simple elastic to adjustable clamps to the useful quick-release Shubb. Some of mine are becoming relics! The mechanical ones may benefit from an occasional very light lubrication in the metal to metal friction areas.

Locking straps

On many acoustic guitars the conventional straplock solution can be applied – just screw on the Schaller or equivalent straplock retainers in place of the standard ones and attach the catches securely to your strap. For the Schaller's this requires a 13mm socket wrench.

For some electro acoustic guitars where the end pin is also the output socket and can't be replaced, the Planet Waves approach makes a good alternative. Here the strap itself has a locking device that grips conventional and output jack strap pins via a thumbwheel.

The simplest and cheapest solution is a couple of Grolsch rubber beer bottle washers – the Grolsch itself may also provide useful lubrication and Dutch courage.

Bottlenecks

The first bottlenecks were just that – a broken-off bottleneck smoothed on a stone. Small pill bottles were a ready-trimmed alternative and metal types are popular – these heavy ones really produce a big blues tone. In the 21st century authentic-sounding bottlenecks come from the swampland delta of Birmingham, England, courtesy of Diamond Bottlenecks on the Stourbridge Bayou. Cheap and cheerful bottlenecks are also available, but the blues ain't always cheerful.

Mbrace

This is the perfect device for those 'Santana' moments, when you need to switch from acoustic for the intro to electric for the solo. The brace has a thread that fits a regular microphone stand (you'll need a very heavy old-fashioned one for stability). The guitar then attaches using the supplied mini-strap, with some rubber feet on the brace protecting the guitar's finish. I'm not about to advocate this for a prized Hauser I, but for an economy electro acoustic I'd take the chance for the novelty value!

The Mbrace attached to somebody else's guitar! It is quite stable, just a little scary!

Temperature and humidity issues

Fine acoustic guitars are very sensitive to temperature and humidity,
but with a few precautions your instrument can remain stable.

C.F. Martin and other makers construct their guitars at a controlled temperature of 72–77°F (22–26°C) and 45–55% humidity. Achieving this ideal consistently in a home living room isn't easy and when touring we're presented with the extremes of potentially very dry hotel rooms and searing stage lights.

The simple answer is to observe the tried and tested practice adopted by violinists and keep your expensive guitar in a case when it's not in use. The hard case is potentially a microclimate and can be kept at a good even temperature and humidity. The trick is to monitor your guitar's microclimate and avoid extremes. Combination hygrometer and thermometers are useful, relatively cheap and do an effective job.

Exposed wood is naturally hygroscopic; it absorbs water from the surrounding air, and air retains water in a direct relationship to temperature. Absorbing water can cause a guitar to swell and distort, and drying out can cause the lacquer or the guitar itself to crack. Thus the best practice is to keep your guitar at roughly the temperature and humidity in which it was constructed.

Generally guitars are inclined to dry out due to over-enthusiastic central heating and air conditioning systems. This can be counteracted in the guitar case by a simple humidifier. These generally contain water, which the guitar will naturally absorb.

The potential danger with humidifiers is to overdo matters and end up with a soggy guitar – hence the need for monitoring.

In a very damp tropical climate silica gel packs (often found with new guitars) can absorb moisture more effectively than your guitar and restore a balance.

The key is to try and avoid rapid changes of temperature and humidity, as this is when cracks, damage to glue joints and/or swelling are most prevalent. In my studio workshop in central England I find the difficult months of the year for temperature humidity are November–February. During these months I counteract the drying tendencies of central heating by using a simple humidifier obtained from a local store. Though intended for humidifying a child's nursery it can achieve 40–45% humidity in a garage-sized room despite my television lighting.

The guitar-friendly summer months here in England present temperatures and humidity similar to Nazareth, Pennsylvania. Beware, however, that relatively high ambient room humidity may not be ideal for your tape or book collection!

Dryness and guitar necks

Sometimes the neck of the guitar can also dry out, causing microscopic shrinkage. This manifests itself when the inert frets tend to protrude from the shrinking wood – see below.

Water-based humidifiers

■ Gibson Montana type

For this type you simply immerse the open unit in water for five minutes, wipe off the excess and place it in the guitar case. The unit contains an absorbent chemical.

■ Planet Waves type

This type is similar but uses a sponge to absorb and retain the water. The filled unit clips between the guitar strings and is fairly secure. Take care not to over dampen the sponge.

■ Dampit type

This is also a sponge type and sits within the guitar. It comes with its own Brannan hydrometer and thermometer.

Using a Planet Waves Humidipak

One solution recommended by Bob Taylor of Taylor guitars is the Planet Waves Humidipak. This utilises replaceable humidity packs that respond to the humidity in the guitar interior and automatically compensate to achieve optimum humidity – provided you remember to change the pack when it's spent.

The disposable humidifier packs sit in a double pouch in the guitar's soundhole with a separate pack designated for humidifying the neck area.

A neck repair

The Achilles heel of *any* acoustic guitar is the headstock/neck area, and in the Selmer design the neck may be a particularly weak spot due to its player-friendly slimness. John Diggins, the great repairer and luthier, reckons he sees one guitar a month sans neck!

1 The neck is first stripped of all hardware including the machine heads, and I've wrapped the body of the guitar in protective bubble wrap.

2 Titebond brand original aliphatic wood glue is then applied well into the break. This glue has a 30-minute setting time but benefits from being left for 24 hours when used at such a critical stress point. The glue is aided into the extremes of the break by a combination of gravity and a lollipop-stick spatula.

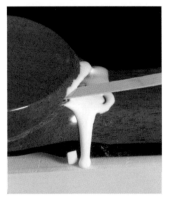

3 A G clamp is then applied with a rubber protector on the break side and a 2in x 1in baton on the fretboard side. Any excess glue must be wiped off with a damp rag before it attacks the neck lacquer.

The accompanying picture shows the typical 'sprung' nature of the break. The neck itself tends to break cleanly, but the headstock front veneer keeps the guitar together – though often a crease appears in the veneer at the break point.

I'm personally going to conduct this typical repair – overseen by John, who stresses that a very valuable guitar is best left to an expert unless you have a thorough competence in woodwork and a suitable workshop. As I'm not a luthier I'm not going to strip the neck finish to effect an 'invisible' repair – I don't have the skill or facilities. What we'll do here is a good effective working repair.

4 Do not overtighten the G clamps as they could distort the join and leave a mark.

5 Removing the clamps after 24 hours' drying enables us to check the strength of the bond, which is usually better than the original wood.

6 All excess dried glue is removed with a warm damp cloth and a gently persuasive fingernail! Some belligerent remnants responded to a soft plastic pen top.

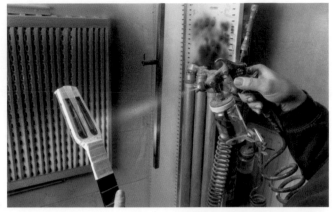

7 I then smoothed the joins with a little 320 3M Fre-Cut abrasive.

8 I touched-up the flaked-off lacquer with a little clear nitro cellulose tinted with a hint of mahogany – the brush is a craft workers' '00' point.

9 I then masked off the 'good' lacquer with a little tape.

10 John then applied a few coats of clear nitro cellulose over my paint repairs.

11 The main rear join was next given another fine sanding.

12 John then further disguised the faint crack with some slightly tinted nitro cellulose and a clear overcoat.

13 On removing the masking tape a faint line shows on the face of the guitar marking the limit of the new clear lacquer – this is removed with a little T-Cut (the car renovation abrasive/polish).

14 Reassemble and reinstall the machine heads. This shows John's final pro finish before returning the guitar to Peter Cook's shop.

Light restoration work

Vintage acoustics are often distorted and distressed due to the ravages of time and temperature/humidity variations. There are a few possible restoration measures that can be taken.

*This guitar has many characteristics of the KGN12 'Oriole' except that there is no evidence of the Oriole decal.

This Kalamazoo 'Robert Johnson' KG14* is of a type made in the 1930s to 1941, when the frugality of the Depression encouraged Gibson to manufacture an affordable guitar from, in this case, local maple, with a spruce top and a nut made of black ebony. The guitar sound has great character and is interesting from a constructional point of view in that it theoretically lacks both a truss rod and X-bracing.

The ladder bracing of the top (similar to the common back bracing) is common to all the other great blues guitars made by Stella, and although substantial has succumbed to the stress of the strings over the last 75 or so years. This has caused the top to 'over belly', making the action very high. The unmatched machine heads are also in a terrible state, which makes tuning a nightmare. So it needs a little TLC to make it a viable working instrument again.

Tuners

I'm fairly sure that the original tuners are the Klusons on the bottom three strings, as these have straight-slot screws in the gears and the plastic buttons show typical plastic/ Bakelite shrinkage.

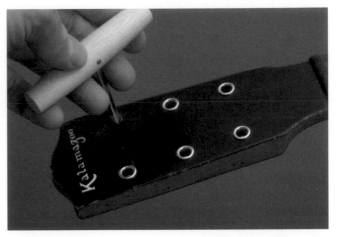

Luthier John Diggins thought single Waverley open-back type Grovers would make good replacements, single machines being a better choice than the economy three-in-a-row type. I'm considering this alongside the merits of keeping the guitar as authentic as possible. The Grovers look terrific, but would entail some reworking of retaining screw holes and ideally a peg reaming of the headstock to accommodate modern bushings (not present on the original).

Searching the Internet for more 1930s 'period correct' open-back Klusons, Jay Hostetler at Stewmac suggested a new line in antiqued 'Golden Age' three-in-a-row tuners. He also suggested these authentic push-fit 'mandolin' bushings – the originals had gone missing in action. Other than enlarging one of the holes slightly with a pin reamer for a push-fit this was a simple job.

The tuners look brilliant – I even prefer the white buttons, as they complement the white Kalamazoo logo. A 'non invasive' installation was effected as all the barrel and screw holes line up – brilliant! And the tuners are even pre-aged so that they look like they belong. Note the included straight-slot screws, 1930s pre-machine assembly correct.

Similarly these Wilkinson Kluson lookalikes have a great '50s vibe but will still leave a couple of redundant holes revealed.

The moral of this story is that whilst it's tempting to make practical alterations to important historical guitars, these days it is possible to find exact replacements that leave the guitar entirely unaltered. Just explore what's available.

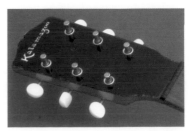

Solving over belly

Most steel-string flat-top guitars eventually succumb to 'over belly' – given the tension of your average set of light-gauge strings at circa 61kg this should come as no surprise.

Breedlove guitars have for some years fitted a brace between the end block and the bridge to counteract this effect and a retro-fit version made by JLD can help restore the equilibrium on some vintage guitars.

The Kalamazoo has a typical problem for an aged flat-top:

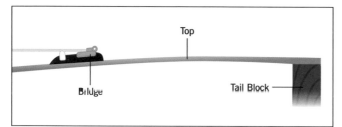

a pronounced bow behind the bridge and a dip in front of it. The saddle has been filed down to almost nothing in order to keep the action playable as the top has come up. Because the bridge pin holes are almost even with the top of the saddle, the strings don't exert much downward force on the top. Consequently this guitar is hard to play and the tone has suffered. The 'Bridge Doctor' or 'Bridge System' is a brace that can restore the over belly without drastically altering the guitar.

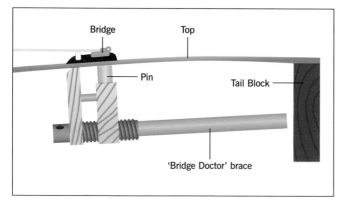

The picture above shows the brace in position prior to tensioning. The bridge pins have been replaced with a set of pins similar to the ones shown at right. The brace has been inserted through the soundhole and is held in place by one of the new bridge pins, which has been threaded into the top of the Bridge Doctor. A small locknut keeps the additional pins in place. Strings now pass through holes in the sides of the pins instead of being inserted into the bridge pin holes.

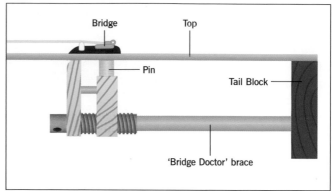

In this picture the brace has been adjusted to counteract the pull of the strings and the warping of the top. The top is now permanently flat and a playable action has been restored. The strings exert proper downward pressure on the saddle, enabling them to transmit more vibration to the instrument. Luthier Celine Camerlynck tells me the Bridge Doctor may, however, act as a spring, absorbing some vibration! But the guitar is not modified in any irreversible way. It is easier to play, and may have more volume.

Practical installation of the 'Bridge Doctor'

1 Having removed the strings (one at a time to spread the de-tensioning process evenly as expounded elsewhere in this manual), determine the size of the bridge and hence the optional position of the 'attachment post'. I will use the smallest leverage on this 'classical'-like oblong bridge.

2 Sort the replacement pins to suit your string gauges (they have different size string holes).

3 Install five of the pins using the locking nuts provided. Do not overtighten the pins – a paperclip makes a good 'tension sensitive' lever (don't bend the pin!). Leave the 'D' pin empty for installation of the attachment post.

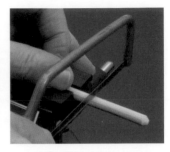

8 Saw the rod ⅜in shorter than the mark to allow for the tension screw.

9 Reinstall the tension rod pointed end first and then the tension screw, using a ³⁄₁₆in Allen wrench.

4 Remove the tension screw from the system block with a ³⁄₁₆in Allen wrench.

5 Install the block through the soundhole.

10 Tension the rod with the ³⁄₁₆in Allen wrench – go gently, allowing the top to reposition slowly without splitting!

11 Restring and check for realignment 'at tension'. Remember that few flat-tops are totally flat – this is intentional.

The Bridge Doctor remedy is NOT an ideal arrangement, though with the new bone saddle required to accommodate the slightly flatter top alignment the guitar did work and sound better than before. I did have to build a new saddle however! (See 'Bridge and saddle work', page 70).

One other factor is that I also tried lessening the tension on the ageing top by using 'Silk and Steel' strings. These not only come up to A440 at a lower tension but give a consequent softer warmer sound. I found this worked well on this specific guitar.

Also, as I prefer the sound without the brass bridge pins I have in fact replaced the old plastic pins, except naturally the fourth string, which is the fixing for the Bridge System.

NB: A type of Bridge Doctor called the 'JLD Bridge System' is also available. This is almost identical in principle but necessitates drilling a hole through the bridge. Naturally this is not ideal on a rare vintage guitar but does have the advantage of leaving the guitar with a conventional through-bridge stringing arrangement.

6 Attach the system block using the pin through the bridge at the 'D' hole.

7 Insert the tension rod into the system block, pointed head towards the soundhole, and make a pencil mark where it protrudes from the system block.

A neck reset, bridge replace, neck reinforce, refret, new saddle & nut

In a perfect world the best *long-term* solution for a guitar with 'over belly' is likely to be a full neck reset. This means removing the neck and resetting it with a different pitch to the body. As we will see, this can get complicated!

Our Kalamazoo initially responded fairly well to the Guitar Doctor approach (see pages 84–85). However, the (presumed) non-truss rod neck is now tending to have too much relief and the over belly is returning. Brilliant French Luthier Celine Camerlynck, of Luthiers Corner in London's Denmark Street, feels a full reset, with a re-fret and new nut, bridge and saddle, is required. This is time-consuming and expensive work, and the law of diminishing returns applies, since this work will cost as much as the guitar's market value! However, there is so much history and character in this instrument that I feel it deserves a new lease of life. I'm sure the authentic 'Early Music' enthusiasts of 2050 will be performing Robert Johnson's music on Gibson L1s and Kalamazoo KG14s.

Bridge work

1 Celine first compared the Kalamazoo bridge with a contemporary 1930s Gibson L00 and concluded that a previous repair had removed a considerable amount of the Kalamazoo's bridge. This was now beyond effective repair and needed replacement from a new slab of Indian rosewood.

2 Having released the attaching bolts, the old bridge is removed by melting the glue through applying up to 300° heat using an LMI heat blanket.

3 Once loose the bridge is gently levered, with a small card protecting the guitar surface. The pallet knife levers are from Leyland decorators' supplies.

4 The bridge comes off cleanly, though all the old dry glue must now be removed.

5 The adhesion area is first marked up and the old glue is removed with a Stanley blade.

6 Celine feels that the bolts are no longer needed in the bridge, and fills the holes with custom cut timber, shaped by being temporarily superglued to a dowel. The plugs are glued in place and then trimmed. To maintain the 'vintage correct' appearance she intends to inlay two mother of pearl dots over the absent screw holes in the new bridge.

7 Pilot holes for the new bridge pins are drilled using the old bridge as a template.

8 The new bridge is roughly sized and then shaped with a carving gouge and a Herdim luthiers' rasp.

9 Finer work requires some light abrasive paper wrapped on a pencil and a sanding stick. Lemon oil is used as a polish with 240–1200 grit paper.

10 After considerable shaping – following a vintage profile and the contour of the guitar top – the new bridge is ready to be glued and clamped. To aid adhesion, Celine removed excess oil from the rosewood with some meths and scored the underside of the bridge. Final shaping is done in situ.

11 These custom cauls ensure even pressure from the five clamps. Any extruded glue is quickly removed with a custom-cut plastic straw. The inside of the guitar is lined with paper to collect excess glue drips, and the bridge plate is protected with some thin strips of cork.

> ### ✎ Tech Tip
>
> **It's good practice to 'dry-run' all repair clampings before any glue is applied – any snags can then be addressed and corrected.**
>
> *Celine Camerlynck – Luthier*

Neck work

1 The need for a neck reset is demonstrated by applying a straight edge to the fingerboard and comparing the height at the bridge. If the neck pitch were adequate for a good tone, the straight edge would clear the bridge. As it is there's a considerable shortfall.

2 To remove the neck for resetting, first the 15th fret is lubricated with lemon oil to avoid splintering, heated with a soldering iron, and then gently removed with some Stewmac flat profile fret pincers.

3 Heat is then applied with the neck blanket...

4 ...and some gentle leverage applied.

5 Two 2mm holes in the 15th fret slot are drilled into the dovetail joint...

Bridge Height = projection or elevation of the fingerboard at the bridge end.

6 ...and the joint edges are scored to prevent any lacquer cracking.

7 A 'wallpaper stripper'-type steam generator is attached to an LMI or Stewmac steaming tube, which is inserted into the 15th fret holes. This forces steam into the joint cavity.

8 After 10 minutes an extractor jig is used to gently lever the neck from the dovetail. (The less heat the better).

9 The neck came off fairly cleanly after about 40 minutes. Some slight splintering is carefully repaired.

10 Surprisingly the neck *does* have a hidden truss rod!

Fingerboard removal

The concealed truss rod is not adjustable on assembly, so Celine suggests removing the fingerboard, straightening the neck and reinforcing it with two new carbon fibre rods, thus setting the new shape.

1 Heat is now applied to the fingerboard using the 'blanket' approach.

2 After several hours of heat and gentle coaxing the fingerboard starts to come off.

3 Though a slow process, the neck and fingerboard are both intact.

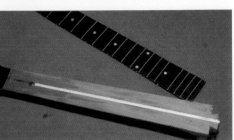

Neck reinforcement

1 The carbon fibre reinforcing rods are Stewmac types. These are custom cut to size – be aware that the dust generated by this is an extreme health hazard. Two rods will be fitted, one either side of the current truss rod packer.

2 A pilot hole is drilled in the neck for the router.

3 The router depth is carefully set so as to correspond to the rod depth. The router is carefully guided to cut the rod channels.

4 The two parallel channels are now ready for the rods, and Celine checks the neck is sanded perfectly flat.

5 The rods are glued in place with a two-pack epoxy resin. Wooden spacers are used to ensure that the clamps apply pressure directly to the rods themselves.

Reinstating fingerboard

1 Celine first ensured that the neck was perfectly flat using a custom-made sanding block, 120 grit for shaping and 180 for finishing; the papers are Jepuflex Antistat by MIRKA of Finland. It's important that the neck is flat in the diagonal plane as well as the parallel.

2 Celine uses French chalk to help identify any 'high' spots. When sanding, the 'high spots' are the first to lose the chalk.

3 The rear of the fingerboard also needs to be both flattened and subtly hollowed in the centre area, to allow room for the adhesive. For this Celine uses a custom steel scraper based on a violin tool. This produces thin shavings, not dust.

4 The neck lacquer is protected with broad Sellotape that Celine has carefully made less sticky by applying some textile fluff. Then the Titebond glued neck and fingerboard are bound with an old cycle inner tube, which ensures even pressure on the currently uneven fingerboard surface. As before, the rear fingerboard surface was degreased with meths and scored with a Stanley blade to aid adhesion. Alignment is achieved with two pins at the 1st and 12th frets.

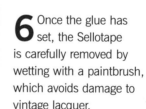

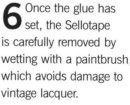

5 The end of the fingerboard required additional clamping, with a radiused block over the dovetail.

6 Once the glue has set, the Sellotape is carefully removed by wetting with a paintbrush, which avoids damage to vintage lacquer.

Removing frets

Celine removes the old frets with some lemon oil (avoiding splinters). A soldering iron applies some gentle heat.

Adjusting the neck pitch

NB: The faded neck number seems to be 88925(8).

1 The old body dovetail is first cleaned up with a custom 120-grit sanding block.

2 The neck dovetail is similarly tidied but needs some chisel work.

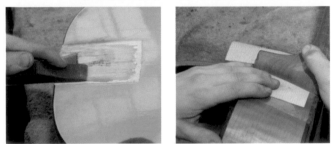

3 It's important that all old glue and lacquer are removed from the old top surface to help the new joint adhere. Celine fine-tunes the joint edge with very fine abrasive paper.

4 The interior joint is currently and intentionally very loose – the aesthetics of the exterior joint are matched to the required neck pitch, established with a straight edge to the new bridge. Celine also checks sideways with the pin holes as reference. The neck must be centred.

5 To create the eventual tight and stable fit, oversize 'wings' are now added to the interior of the joint, and having been glued and set are gradually reduced to a useful and snug fit. A thin wedge of maple is shown attached under the fingerboard to compensate for a gap created by the new neck angle.

6 Once again French chalk is used to check the areas that 'rub' and need slight adjustment.

7 One last check before gluing and clamping.

8 A special interior clamping block is required, with a channel to accommodate the ladder brace.

9 Two braces hold the reset neck in place for 24 hours. The top block has the correct radius to ensure an even pressure on the neck.

Refret

1 The fingerboard is marked with French chalk and any deviations in the radius corrected with a 120 and later 180-grit and 320-grit paper.

2 Using a straight edge, constant checks are made on the fingerboard shape and the clearance at the bridge. The clearance issue is difficult, as this style of guitar has a flat bridge and a 10in radius fingerboard, so the clearance is correct at centre but necessarily down at the edges. Celine is aiming for a 3mm saddle height above the bridge height.

3 Celine is careful not to over-thin the fingerboard, which would expose the inlayed side position dots.

Fretting

1 This requires a fret saw with depth guard and fret grips with interchangeable radiused jaws. As with most acoustic luthiers, Celine avoids hammering in frets, preferring the grip approach.

2 The fret slots are recut, with attention to the radius of the bottom of the fret slot.

3 A triangular needle file is used to microscopically 'open up' the slot.

4 The fretwire is 'period correct' 1.6mm from David Dyke (see *Useful contacts* appendix). A gentle radius is coaxed into the fret wire with a Stewmac fret bender.

5 The frets are roughly cut oversize with some fret pincers. A little Titebond adhesive is dabbed at the edges of the slots and the fret is squeezed into the fret slot.

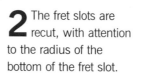

6 The frets may need a gentle seating tap at the edges.

9 Once dry, the frets are gently dressed with a series of sanding blocks, the grit gradually getting finer. The angle of the sanding blocks is critical. The edges are rolled off with the 3-corner file. See page 96 for more on fret dressing.

7 For the higher fret positions Celine uses a 'Fret Buck' to take the strain of the guitar body and absorb vibration as the frets are clamped in.

New nut 1

1 The original period-correct nut was ebony and Celine is maintaining that tradition.

2 The nut slot needs a little adjustment and the removal of old glue. Celine used a fine chisel and needle file.

3 The new nut itself is sanded to size on a belt sander and by hand.

8 The excess is trimmed from the fret edges and the glue left to dry.

Position and cut a saddle slot

1 To correctly position the new saddle slot, Celine first determined the scale length from the original frets. From the nut to the 12th fret is 314mm and total string length therefore 628mm. This is marked on the new bridge with a pencil. 'Compensation' is 3.5mm on the bass side and 2mm on treble.

6 A jig is used to cleanly guide the router in the new bridge.

7 A bone saddle blank is tested in the new slot.

2 To achieve a saddle angle to roughly compensate the different string gauges, Celine checked the intonation with two dummy saddles and the two extreme strings at pitch. The exact position is then marked.

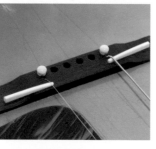

8 A 10in radius is marked on the blank and roughly shaped on a belt sander.

9 The saddle is further shaped with a sanding block.

3 This also necessitated roughing the first and sixth string nut slots with gauged nut files, and the bridge pin slots using a tiny pad saw.

10 The profile of the top of the saddle is critical – it must be rounded and polished for good tone and intonation. 1200 paper and T-cut are used for a smooth finish. The set heights are $\frac{3}{32}$in at the 12th fret bass, and $\frac{1}{16}$in treble.

4 Having checked the intonation at the 12th fret, Celine drilled two small pilot holes as guides for the slot router (interior view).

5 The router guides need a flat surface to cut an even depth slot, so the pickguard thickness is compensated with a business card.

New nut 2

1 The nut string spacing is determined using a sheet of paper behind the strings as a visual guide. Celine thinks in terms of 'two sets of three' – first to third, and fourth to sixth, but with a D in the middle between A and G, and G in the middle of D and B – and largely sets the spacing by eye (as each string is a different gauge the precise mathematical spacing can be extremely complex).

2 The nut slot depth is determined by establishing the height of the string fretted at the third fret – this is approximately 0.5mm and is the same at the next fret.

The finished nut, profiled and polished and glued in place.

Shaping the frets

1 The frets are stoned to an even height...

2 ...and then shaped or 'crowned' with some 320 fine abrasive paper wound over a hollow fret file. Note the Stewmac fret guard to protect the fingerboard. The frets are finished with 600/1200, then 000-gauge wire wool for a mirror finish.

3 The ends of the frets are polished with a decorators' abrasive pad.

4 The fingerboard is cleaned of any glue with a Stanley blade.

To complete the repair, Celine French polishes the areas of the neck that have lost any lacquer, and touches up any joins with dark stain or shellac as appropriate. This is very challenging, as in the 1930s parts of the dark mahogany neck were stained 'white' before being lacquered.

Another nice touch is the two mother of pearl inlays on the bridge which would have covered the bolts on the original guitar. These had been lost and Celine made new ones. The bridge is also French-polished.

Coda

This restoration took a total of nine long days (though there were elements of waiting for glue to set and lacquers to dry). The repairs are all nigh on invisible and the guitar is now fully working in a way that it hasn't been for the last 15 years. All the frets now ring true up to the highest positions, and the guitar plays well and is noticeably louder (due to the proper break angles at the nut and saddle). However, it retains its distinctive ladder brace tone and vintage character. As Celine often says, 'Nothing is beyond repair – it's just a matter of cost and time!' Guitar history is worth preserving and guitars like this are irreplaceable.

A little fret dressing

This interesting guitar built by Victor Payne in 1989 is modelled on an 1888 Antonio de Torres, probably made in Torres' 'late period' specifically for his young daughter. The guitar has a short 60cm scale length and a very small body. It is currently the property of guitarist Wendy Plowright, who allows me use it in concert when performing the 19th-century repertoire to which it is ideally suited.

Fret dressing and polish

1 When de-strung the neck returns to being almost flat, as revealed with an accurate straight edge. As expected the guitar has no truss rod and depends on the strength of the neck and the ebony fingerboard to remain true.

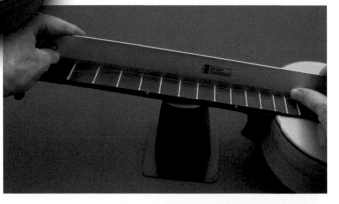

Since 1989 the fretboard has shrunk a little and one or two frets are sitting a little proud. When strung the guitar has an appropriate amount of relief – more on the bass side than the treble.

2 However, a fret rocker helps me locate the odd proud fret. Proud spots can be indicated with a permanent marker.

3 Before filing I like to mask the fretboard itself to avoid accidental damage.

4 A diamond dressing stone is used to take the top off the proud frets.

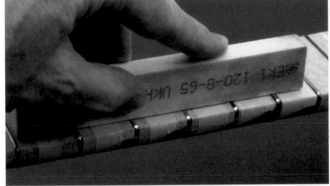

5 Some sharp protrusions of the fret edges due to wood shrinkage are also addressed using the same diamond file.

6 The 'flattened' frets are now restored to the correct contour with a Stewmac contoured fret file, initially 150 grit then the finer 300 grit.

7 The frets are then polished, initially with 400 Fre-Cut paper and a soft-backed sanding block then a 1200 grit wet-and-dry.

8 I further polish the frets with a short length of timber surfaced with an old leather belt and some metal polish. A similar finish can be had with a D'Addario polishing paper and their fret polishing template, but it takes longer.

9 I cleaned and conditioned the ebony board with the Dunlop 01/02 system.

10 The guitar was then restrung with three-quarter scale D'Addario EJ27N short scale strings, and the nut and saddle slightly compensated for the lower frets. See pages 64 and 70 for advice on nut and saddle adjustment.

The importance of correct tension and gauge strings applies to any guitar, but perhaps more so for these small, lightly braced historic reproductions.

When restringing a flamenco or historic instrument the wooden pegs benefit from a little Hills' violin peg paste; this prevents slippage and stops the pegs binding – miraculous! Note the pegs are numbered, each being individually crafted for a specific hole and once settled surprisingly more stable than most machine heads!

If you get the opportunity to work with a wooden peg guitar try it – it's a very illuminating experience. They have great character and naturally suit earlier music styles as well as flamenco.

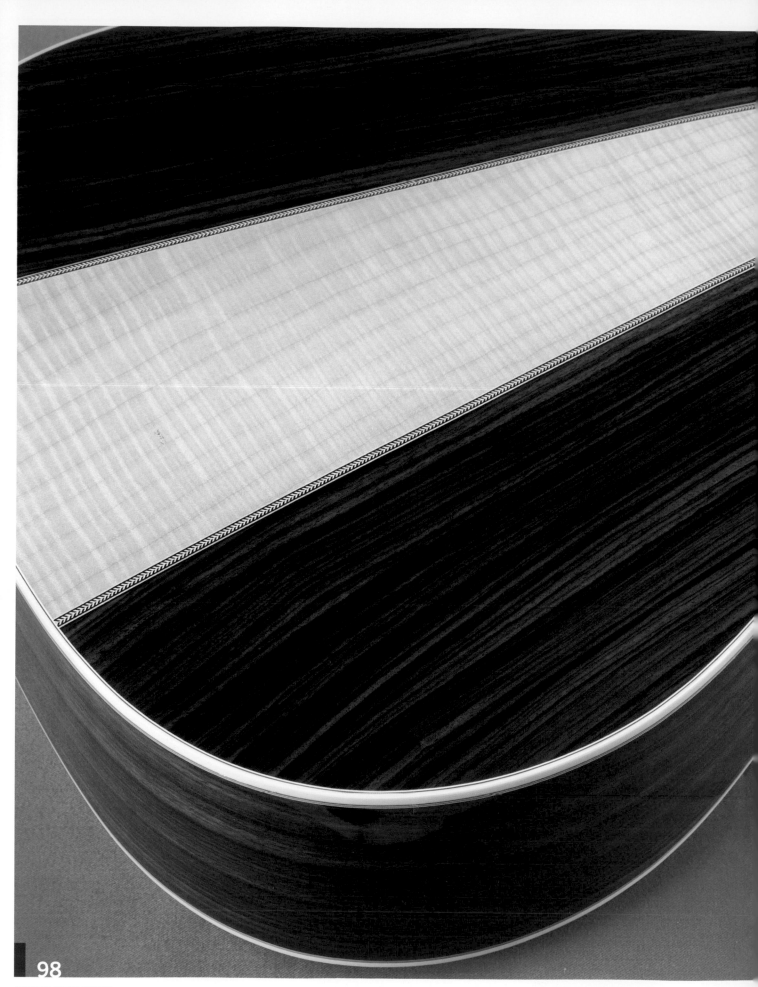

ACOUSTIC GUITAR MANUAL

The art and science of tone

The acoustic guitar of the 21st century represents in all its variants at least 1,000 years of evolution. Latterly a luthier's training passes on all the trials and errors of countless generations of artists and craftsmen, all of whom made some contribution to the fabulous instruments available today. However, perhaps the most exciting thing about the acoustic guitar is its continuing evolution. As musical styles change and performing situations evolve the guitar moves with those changes – perhaps the reason why the guitar is the most popular musical instrument ever. In choosing and maintaining our guitars it may help to know a little of the art and science behind that elusive but essential quality 'tone'.

LEFT A Martin '12-fret' Dreadnought.

RIGHT A 'Belleville' Grand Bouche.

The art & science of tone 1 – 'Unplugged'

Fretted strings – the guitar's 'engine room'

The guitar is one of the many musical developments of the prehistoric hunting bow. Its most often six gauged and fretted strings offer 72 semitones within the common 12 frets. With the added scope of the typical 19 frets, this gives us three octaves and a fifth on most acoustics. We then have a choice of timbres offered by the availability of most pitches at three positions. Add to this that fretting makes quadruple stopping and kaleidoscopic open and stopped string options relatively easy and you have an unprecedented potential for harmony and counterpoint, chords and melody.

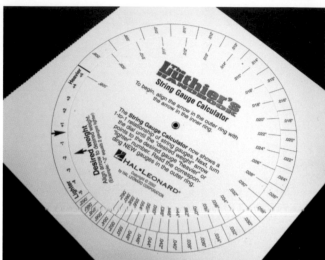

Experiment with string gauges

Our strings are the engine of tone and their materials – from gut to nylon, phosphor bronze, copper, silverplate, silk and steel – offer a myriad range of useful timbres. Gauges and tensions offer another layer of possibilities. The magic is to find the perfect complement to match your guitar's top and your individual style. It's amazing how some rather ordinary guitars can suddenly come to life when you find their optimum stringing, so experiment – but take care with very high tension strings on a lightly made top; Roger Siminoff has devised a very useful string gauge calculator available from Hal Leonard. This takes the guesswork out of matching up custom string sets.

The top and its bracing

Understanding the flat-top guitar

Ironically most 'flat tops' are not quite flat – even Classic guitars tend to a gentle pliage of the top, which contributes to the dissipation of the energy generated by the guitar's 'engine', the strings. The top acts like the head or skin of a drum. In fact many good guitars make excellent drums, with a range of resonances dispersed about the top (witness players like Rodrigo y Gabriela). The very best guitars are almost invariably the ones with the most responsive and finely tuned tops.

Some luthiers will 'tap tune' the top – literally listening for certain resonances inherent in the raw wood and cmphasising or damping these by microscopic planing of specific thicknesses at specific points. A thickness gauge designed primarily for carved-top guitars is sometimes employed. The Dreadnought top in the accompanying picture varies in thickness from 3.0–3.5mm (thicker near the soundhole). Other guitars, like the Taylor shown here, have a thin area specifically at the edge of the top, encouraging freedom of movement.

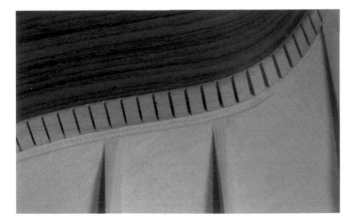

The size of the top is also important, with the bouts 'tuned' to respond in different ways to the fundamentals and harmonics of the vibrating strings. One reason we have so many different-size guitars is not unlike drummers having different size 'toms' in their kit: the upper and lower bouts of the top are sized to coincide with important nodes in the guitar's frequency range. Naturally, if we had a bout with a node that coincided with an important low frequency such as E (open sixth) then that guitar would have a rich low end and the high E's would also benefit due to sharing related harmonics. However, a guitar that only emphasised one frequency would be a difficult guitar to use in performance.

■ Fan bracing

Most Classic guitars use a variant of Torres 'fan' bracing. Contrary to legend Antonio de Torres didn't actually invent fan bracing, but like many great innovators he made the principle work in practice.

This lighter strutting lends depth and warmth to the classic Spanish sound, and again, few modern luthiers conform precisely to traditional fan bracing – the search for the elusive magic tone goes on.

In fact many of the great classic guitarists, including John Williams, are now using Greg Smallman and Matthias Dammann guitars, which use a radical 'lattice' brace.

Back and sides

On both classic and steel-strung flat-tops the back and sides are generally considered less important than the top in terms of tone production – though they provide a sturdy frame for the top and are usually constructed first.

The back and sides lend themselves more obviously to the successful employment of laminates. There is no doubt that different woods used for these components impart a different character to the sound of the top, but in the 21st century this is tending to be more a source of creative variety. Traditional rosewood and mahogany does impart a deeper resonance to most guitars than, say, brighter-sounding maple, but happily there is room for both in today's modern musical palette. The bracing of the back tends towards the simplicity of three or four transverse ladder braces, often tapered rather than scalloped as on this Martin example.

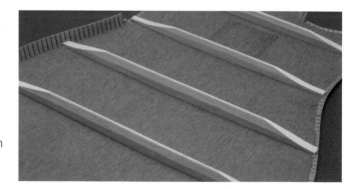

The top and back are usually attached by glued kerfed linings. Ramírez are currently experimenting with un-kerfed linings (see case study on page 183).

The traditional
dovetail.

Neck

It was Les Paul who first drew my attention to the importance
of the neck to guitar tone. Though now universally associated
with the electric guitar that bears his name, Lester's first loves
were his two prized acoustic Gibson L5s. He often spoke of
the importance of rigidity
and stability in the neck,
avoiding any tone dissipation.
A laminated neck is usually a
stronger neck and bodes well
for tone. A good stable neck-
to-body join is also vital and
traditionally this is achieved
with a glued dovetail or
sometimes a tenon joint.

Though great for tone and stability, the downside of this
arrangement is that shrinkage in the area of the joint can cause
a misalignment and distortion of the fingerboard as it crosses
the upper bout. Since the 18th century many luthiers have
experimented with 'floating necks' and bolted necks, which escape
the rigidity of the traditional joint and are easier to realign. The latest
and most successful version of this approach is that of Californian
Bob Taylor, whose bolt-on NT neck offers stability and adaptability
in a winning combination. Though perhaps consequently lighter in
bass resonance this amplifies well, with less propensity to acoustic
feedback. (See 'The art and science of tone 2: Plugged', pages
107 and 170 for more on this.) The further advantage of this
'new' approach is the opportunity to easily employ corrective
shims if the neck-to-body angle needs adjustment.

Bolt-on neck.   Corrective neck shims.

Sustainable luthiery

The NT neck approach is also allied to modern pressures
on timber supplies and a 'green' approach to sustainable
rainforests.

Bob Taylor says: 'I have to get *more* primitive, back to the
donkey and whip-saw days, to pull out a few logs in negotiation
with the indigenous population. Go back in time to go forward.

'It struck me that we had always used rectangular aspect
ratios (in cutting wood), which are grain specific, but a *square*
isn't grain specific so I changed to a 4in by 4in instead of a
2½in by 4in. The eco part of this way is I can buy the entire
tree instead of 40% of the tree. This works for us in that
we can splice the peg head on with the scarf joint and glue
the heel on from the piece that was adjacent – it's the same
amount of wood per neck but *more* necks per tree! This allows
us to make what I call an "acoustic electric guitar neck".
We don't put the heel on until the last minute, so it's flat
like a Fender neck or a Gibson Les Paul neck and it's freed
us up from that 14-fret problem of being tied to the whim
of humidity and so on! The NT neck fits an NT body
– two things working together.'

Fingerboard

On many top-end guitars ebony is the first choice of wood.
This isn't just the most hard-wearing but also its weight
and rigidity tends to move the fundamental resonance
node of the neck towards the headstock joint – often an
arbiter of good tone.

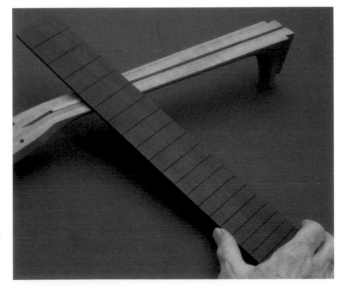

Headstock

A light headstock with lightweight wooden pegs produces an airy, light-sounding guitar – perfect for Baroque guitar and flamenco. A heavy headstock with sturdy metal machines tends towards a beefier more robust sound, great for churning out a compulsive rock rhythm. Hence a professional chooses a guitar appropriate for the job in hand. The practical trade-off is balance, with a heavy headstock pulling the guitar towards the ground – not usually a big problem on a guitar worn with a strap.

Ironically, however, some cheap guitars with flimsy machine heads can really come to life with the added weight of a decent set of pro tuners. This 'added mass at the headstock' principle is also exploited by Groove Tubes' patented headstock clamp, the 'Fat Finger', the heavier 'bass' version of which adds 3.8oz (108g) to the headstock, which may sometimes be beneficial. You could experiment by carefully applying a conventional hardware store G clamp and listening. If it works on your guitar then the more aesthetically attractive proprietary version may be worth the investment. **NB:** Protect the guitar lacquer from damage before applying any clamps!

Nut

A major contributor to good tone and accurate intonation – best made of hard dense bone and definitely NOT of flimsy hollow plastic (top right).

Carved-top guitars

Orville Gibson and Lloyd Loar were the main protagonists in creating the early 20th-century carved-top guitar, based on similar principles to the violin and more particularly the violoncello. This method has been taken to new heights by the modern Italian/New York school of James L. D'Aquisto, John D'Angelico and, most recently, Robert Benedetto. The best of these guitars have elaborately hand-carved and meticulously 'tap tuned' tops and are often braced with a longitudinal bass and treble bar (see Gibson L5 case study, page 174).

The distinctive short attack, high middle frequency heavy sound of the archtop is reinforced by its pressure bridge, which transfers energy to the top in a pumping action, just like a violin. This is in contrast to the rocking bridge of the flat-top. The short decay of the archtop is further exaggerated by the F holes, which are designed and sited to interfere with vibration radiating across the top from the bridge, thus emphasising the faster 'along the grain' vibrations. This also contributes to a violin's characteristically short plucked pizzicato. Again, you choose an archtop for its inherent characteristics, perfect for authentic jazz rhythm and Gypsy Jazz solos.

Acoustic ports and baffles

While engaged in 'the quest to be heard' there have been many attempts to port or baffle the acoustic guitar. These include the Tornovaz of Antonio Torres, the double-backed and ported guitars of Mario Maccaferri, and Lloyd Loar's (rare) ported L5. The latest venture into this arena is called the 'O' port, which retro fits very simply to many roundhole acoustics. Its parabolic lens effect is difficult to perceive from a player's perspective but may enhance forward projection of purely acoustic sound.

The art & science of tone 2 – 'Plugged'

The last half-century has seen enormous progress in the area of amplifying the acoustic guitar's true timbre. In a live performance before about 1965 you made do with a poor microphone on an inadequate stand, through a very poor PA – probably designed for the cinema or for use by a bingo caller. This was nearly always a disaster.

In the 1950s and early '60s there were large round piezo-electric contact microphones available, but these glued to your guitar, sounded terrible and were extremely prone to acoustic feedback. From the early 1950s Django Reinhardt and others experimented with retro-fit magnetic pickups, the best of which were made by the De Armond company. However, they were crude, cumbersome and struggled with the varying magnetic properties of acoustic strings made of brass and bronze alloys. At their very best they made your acoustic sound like a cheap electric guitar – not very useful.

Gibson tried a very bold move in 1951 with their CF100E, and in 1954 with their J160E. This included a single coil P90 magnetic pickup built into the last fret of a conventional Jumbo and an onboard volume and tone with a built-in output jack – very neat. The Beatles bought two! Unfortunately, through a VOX AC30 it also sounded like an inexpensive electric guitar, which mostly defeated the object.

Two great strides were made in the '60s. Firstly, in 1963 the violinist John Berry teamed up with electronics wiz Les Barcus and developed a range of tiny piezo contact transducers. The 'Barcus Berry', though still glued or velcroed to your guitar, soon had an associated preamp that by amplifying and equalising the feeble piezo signal made a decent stab at an acoustic sound.

The other great stride came from the Ovation guitar company which began installing ceramic piezo-electric transducers under the saddles of some of their revolutionary Lyrachord guitars. Now, with a lot of EQ, a little reverb and wad of compression these guitars did sound a little like acoustic guitars. However, the piezos were hearing the rocking excursions of the saddle NOT the resonant timbre of the top or the body cavity. So the sound was initially a little compromised – but it was loud enough, without acoustic feedback, to be stage usable, and that was considerable progress.

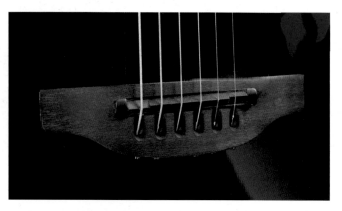

Other experiments with capacitor-type contact devices, like the C-Ducer, largely faded into obscurity though they have found applications in amplifying the piano and harp.

For the last 40 years the undersaddle piezo-electric device has tended to rule the acoustic guitar scene, and has been adopted by esteemed makers such as C.F. Martin. There have been refinements, such as split piezos for individual and groups of strings, but the biggest strides have been in the area of onboard and external preamps. These now commonly have three-band EQ and master volume, a useful built-in tuner and

often an anti-feedback device that seeks out feedback-prone frequencies and automatically attenuates them. A phase reversal switch is often added too, which can also help cancel feedback and/or restore phase relationships between onstage monitors, backline 'acoustic' amps and the main PA.

Many of the piezo systems benefit at high amplitudes from the use of a soundhole bung, or as Planet Waves call it a 'Screeching Halt'. These help reduce the Helmholtz resonator effect, as the 'tuned' cavity of an acoustic guitar encourages acoustic feedback at specific 'tuned' frequencies.

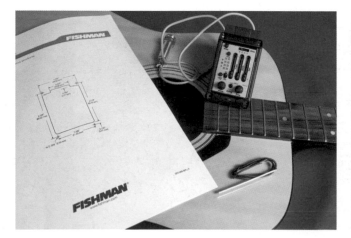

Alternatives – the electro-acoustic

Over the years many musicians have complained about the 'different' timbre of piezo devices and manufacturers have sought solutions that come closer to the acoustic sound of a quality guitar, only louder!

Add a conventional microphone?

It has to be said that for guitar amplification, nothing so far invented can beat the actual output of a quality capacitor microphone. No surprise here, as 21st-century capacitor mikes are the result of 100 years of development of a device designed to be transparent – the mythical transducer with gain, the sound engineers' dream. The snag, however, is resonance. When we put a guitar near a microphone the microphone 'hears' not just the guitar but everything else in the vicinity, including a whole lot of frequencies 'tuned' by the guitar's resonant cavity. These tuned frequencies are then amplified in the exponentially expanding loop of audio we know as acoustic feedback. Tune out these frequencies with EQ and you also tune out most of the frequencies that carry the tone we are seeking! So in the studio fetch your best two capacitor microphones. But on stage?

■ Put the microphone inside the guitar?

Several manufacturers offer internal guitar microphones – usually inserted via the end pin hole and self-suspended with an integral jack socket. These run off a small 1.5V battery and work quite well at low volumes. They're suitable for simple reinforcement of solo acoustic guitar. I've used the GHS miniflex to successfully match the volume of an acoustic string quartet to an acoustic classic guitar.

Fishman and others offer 'blend' systems. These mix an internal microphone with a piezo undersaddle (see page 122 for more on this). They work quite well and sound good, but again at fairly conservative volume levels – the microphone is prone to feedback beyond a simple 'sound reinforcement' or solo acoustic level. It does, however, open up a fascinating range of Tommy Emmanuel-style 'body percussion' possibilities.

■ Put the microphone outside the guitar?

In the 1970s and '80s I did a long spell as a 'live audio' supervisor for BBC network TV. All my fellow audio colleagues and I struggled as a team trying to crack the daily dilemma of successful broadcasting, a live PA feed for a studio audience and a musicians' monitor feed of acoustic guitars, violins cellos and even the odd bouzouki. We tried everything! The least nasty in terms of fulfilling the complete remit was a Sony ECM 50 electret condenser microphone clipped just *outside* the instrument's soundhole.

Designed for speech work as a lavalier microphone, the Sony was omni-directional and fairly robust. Applied to various guitars it wasn't a beautiful sound but it sounded more like an acoustic guitar than a set of bagpipes and we lived with it. It definitely worked better *outside* the guitar.

Several manufacturers now supply high-quality electret microphones fitted with suitable body clamps for mounting externally on an acoustic guitar. These can sound good but present the obvious practical limitations and are prone to feedback if used at full frequency.

A DPA 4099G clip microphone.

Try a moving coil approach?

The moving coil principle, which depends on a coil of very thin wire vibrating around a magnet generating a tiny EMF (electrical signal), has been successfully used in such stalwarts of the live music scene as the Shure SM58 microphone.

Several guitar manufacturers, including Yamaha and Taylor, have experimented with dynamic moving coil transducers fixed strategically within guitars. The Yamaha NX model (see page 134) currently has two transducers placed one at the treble and another at the bass end of the 'under bridge' area with independent volume controls available on the preamp. This works really well and with some custom modification is seen in concert with artists such as Antonio Forcione and Rodrigo y Gabriela and can be used successfully via a large modern concert PA at considerable volume. I have personal experience of this system and in conjunction with a good external preamp such as those by L.R. Baggs it can come very close to a convincing 'loud' acoustic sound.

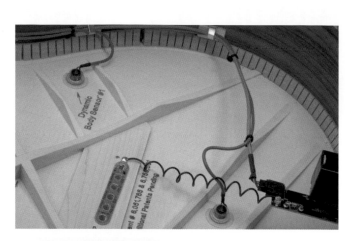

There are two moving coil transducers (note the balanced wiring in the picture), which are fixed to the table, one at the upper waist and one almost in the middle of the lower bout.

Additionally the system has a 'magnetic string sensor' built into the table just below the last fret.

The NX transducer.

■ The Taylor Expression system

This sophisticated system was developed by esteemed audio engineer Rupert Neve, and received a TEC award at the AES convention for Neve and co-developer David Hosler. It combines several transducers of different types via a comprehensive onboard amplifier, EQ and mixing circuit.

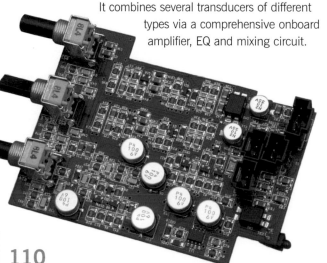

All these transducers are linked to the complex preamp and mixer housed discreetly in the guitar's upper bout.

Yamaha
Compass Series.

The volume and tone controls for this preamp appear very tastefully on the exterior of the upper bout. David Hosler says 'We hoped to improve feedback rejection as well as create a pickup system that doesn't require cutting big holes in beautiful wood – as "stealth" a system as possible.'

Additionally the Expression system has a fused string ground safety feature and a very tidy concealed battery unit, both located near the balanced line output jack.

David tells me that Taylor are currently working on a simplified one dynamic sensor version of the Expression system that addresses the complex phase issues arising when using multiple sensors. The single sensor is also re-voiced significantly by adjusting the magnetic structure and number of wraps. The new preamp system is based on discreet bipolar junction transistors, which offer a hugely improved signal to noise ratio as well as improved transparency and extra bandwidth. This is all good news!

I heard an interesting demonstration of this system using high-quality Bose L1 amplification; the Taylor 600 series guitar is heard first acoustically (and quietly), then gradually the Expression system linked to the Bose is introduced and the volume goes up but the timbre remains largely unchanged – Nirvana? Well, getting very close – especially if you're a solo guitarist or singer/guitarist in a small 'acoustic' group. The only outstanding issue now is how that 'ideal' sound blends with the mix when you introduce an electric guitar, bass and drums etc. See below for practical solutions.

Sample the studio microphone sound?

Another direction being investigated by Fishman and Yamaha is the area of 'modelling' – this implies sampling the characteristics of a guitar's timbre in a high-quality studio environment, using optimum microphone type and placement and storing these responses as 'sonic images' in the preamp software. Fishman, for its 'Aura' system, offer four onboard images (at any one time) of a range of high-end guitars from diverse makers; whilst Yamaha, with their SRT (studio response technology) system, simply offer three (at any one time) high-quality images of their own excellent guitars in diverse miking arrangements, with a 'blend' option that means you can have the guitar's own piezo blended with as much or as little of the onboard modelling as you wish. You can also adjust the 'closeness' of the miking (altering the mix of close and distant microphones) at the preamp and also add 'resonance'.

Both Fishman and Yamaha offer downloadable and updateable softwares so they have a certain measure of future-proofing and the potential to develop as technology inevitably marches on. **NB:** Also see page 145 for an electrostatic approach.

Go back to magnetics and hybrids?

Companies such as L.R. Baggs in the USA have returned to the magnetic 'in the soundhole' approach of the early De Armond systems but with the benefit of modern technology. These new magnetic pickups are different in that they are also sensitive to the vibration of the guitar top and, again in conjunction with a great preamp, can produce some useful acoustic-like sounds. They are especially suited to very loud stadium PA situations.

Magnetic options are available from several manufacturers including the great Seymour Duncan. The specific L.R. Baggs unit pictured here has a very useful built-in volume control and an integral connection to a self-switching strap button output jack. The pickup has a built-in active preamp powered by a concealed button type battery. The adjustable pole pieces are preset for bronze acoustic strings and are adjustable for alternative magnetic

responses and gauges by raising or lowering the individual poles with a 3/32in Allen hex wrench. Additional pole pieces are provided for the first and second strings should you wish to try nickel-based electric guitar strings on your acoustic.

The wiring of the unit shows great forethought, with the ring connection on the 'stereo' jack left available as an output carrier for another transducer, *eg* an existing built-in undersaddle piezo. The L.R. Baggs is a very professional unit with a useful −10db output at 800ohms and is a world away from the primitive high-impedance units of the 1950s.

Use good 'balanced' cables when possible?

Taylor, on advice from Rupert Neve, have taken the very sensible option of offering an electronically balanced 'three wire' output from their Expression system. 'Balanced' circuits offer the maximum resistance to induction and interference from the many stray electrical signals present in our modern world. To take advantage of this balanced line your Taylor or any other balanced guitar needs to be routed with a good quality balanced cable to a good quality balanced direct injection box and fed to a good PA. Just as important is taking time to get the input and output levels right. Too high a level into the DI box can overdrive the input circuit and cause distortion. Too low a level will bring up the inherent noise in the circuit. Never skimp on sound checks and always be nice to the PA guy – come show time he has your sound in his hands!

In the common unbalanced situation a good switchable cable such as the one from Planet Waves means you can disconnect your acoustic mid set without deafening the crowd – keep the audience on your side! (See page 113.)

Equal loudness curves and perspective

One of the dilemmas faced by engineers trying to amplify acoustic guitars relates to 'equal loudness curves'. Put simply our ears perceive frequencies differently as audio gets louder, so a simple linear amplification of a guitar's sound doesn't work. Players perspectives and perceptions are also a factor; David Hosler, a senior developer at Taylor, had these thoughts on the matter:

'In my opinion the challenge is as much about perception to sound in specific listening positions – from playing the guitar to listening – as anything. A player hears a completely different sound and has a completely different experience than a listener. The player feels and hears at the same time; he is also off axis from the main sound plate (the top) in a playing position and hears high end that is not present directly in front of the instrument. I will also note that people do not always recognise or identify the differences and that the mind tends to equal the experiences from playing position to listening position as oppose to define them separately.

'It's the same phenomenon as happens when listening to a guitar unplugged and then plugging it in and listening to it through an amp or PA. The mind tends to blend the two experiences and relate them as equal…unless (and this is a good experiment) a person plays (strums a chord) and someone slowly turns them up during the playing. Then the differences become really obvious.

'Trying to gather sound information from the surface of a guitar is basically amplifying a speaker or an amplifier. The real problem for accuracy is gathering sound waves that are usually in a plane state when you hear them at a distance, from a solid surface that hears or creates the wave in a more spherical wave type of identity. As you may know, spherical waves become plane waves after a distance dependent on the many contributing factors. In the end you have to keep the coils as low as possible in impedance and you still have to filter mids because of their energy. In the end it is still somewhat of an electrical interpretation of the real experience, also dependent on the signal chain it's subjected to.'

Practical solutions

Having looked at the electro acoustic dilemma for over 40 years both from the perspective of a player and as a professional audio engineer I have these practical suggestions.

General

I think we have to be realistic about what we do when we amplify the acoustic guitar, and accept that it does become a different instrument when amplified. This need not be a negative. The boomy 'low and mid-frequency heavy' nature of a flat EQ amplification doesn't always sit well with other instruments so we should accept that some mixing EQ and dynamic compression is necessary to benefit the overall 'front of house' mix of guitar and band.

Solo and small ensembles

The reinforcement of a purely classic sound to achieve the levels required to compete with louder acoustic instruments is still currently best achieved with a very high-quality capacitor microphone on a good stand attached to an excellent full audio bandwidth PA system. See acoustic amplifiers, page 115.

Small gigs

At still fairly conservative volume levels, the compromise arrangement of a small external or internal microphone, dynamic transducer or piezo/mike blend attached to the guitar will produce quite acceptable results for most situations where a 'different' modified kind of guitar sound is appropriate. This includes playing popular repertoire on a classic or steel-strung guitar in a non-concert situation such as a small club, bar or restaurant.

The large auditorium

■ Classical

For a classical concerto situation with an orchestra the good quality microphone/wide bandwidth PA is still likely to produce the most authentic sound.

■ Rock, Pop, Country etc

When an acoustic guitar is expected to sit in the mix alongside drums, bass, keyboard, fiddle, vocals, percussion, electric guitar and the kitchen sink I think we must accept that a very different approach is required other than just amplifying the flat acoustic bandwidth.

In this situation piezo-electric and dynamic transducers of the Taylor and Yamaha type and the L.R. Baggs magnetic types come into their own. These lend themselves to selective EQ and compression of the dynamic range of the instrument to 'find a place' for the amplified acoustic guitar in the overall sound design.

■ Mobility

Microphones and transducers attached to an acoustic guitar offer the performer the mobility often needed in a live situation and are a natural first choice for most popular music scenarios. But when the sound is really critical, as with Mark Knopfler's solo Ramírez at the end of a Dire Straits concert – out come the expensive microphones!

Conclusion

The acoustic guitarist has never had a better choice of amplification options than at present – the challenge is to choose the solution appropriate to the gig – whether that's a concerto with an orchestra or rhythm guitar with a country band, there are solutions, though they take time, patience and a good sound check, preferably with a great engineer and a first rate PA. If you have to do it all yourself, see the following chapter!

A useful 'Planet Waves' switchable jack.

Acoustic amplifiers and PA

We've seen enormous developments in acoustic guitar transducers in recent years, and this mirrors a parallel improvement in PA technology and expertise. For the smaller gig a whole new breed of dedicated acoustic guitar amplifiers has appeared. However, the best solution for a decent acoustic sound in a *very large* venue remains the main PA, with its associated team of expert sound engineers. A good PA is acoustically 'tuned' to the frequency response and reverberation of the venue and with luck the engineers know the venue and the changes in acoustics that occur as the hall fills up with people and the ambient noise levels rise.

LEFT Bose L1 control station.

RIGHT Yamaha 310 fitted with Fishman Aura.

Getting the best from a PA

Make a friend of the house engineer! He likes to provide a good front of house sound and you can work together to achieve that. Come early for the sound check and come prepared. Don't hassle the sound guys – they have multiple pressures from diverse artists and you're currently just a name on a list! Just let them know you're ready and be patient.

Make a friend for the day. Offer the sound crew an XLR balanced line DI output with a switchable ground lift; this tells them you care about good audio and know where it starts – at source. Many companies now offer good floor-mounted acoustic preamps that also offer balanced line XLR outputs. If you're a gigging acoustic guitarist they'll change your life!

When your time comes to sound check, play a consistent riff or chord sequence for the sound guys that typifies your set and style, and play it until asked to stop! This allows the PA guys to sort a good 'front of house' sound, which they can then feed to your monitors. Naturally they can't feed you a decent monitor feed until they have one to send! Then you can comment (via a handy vocal mike) on the sound they send you. Be positive but don't be afraid to ask for the earth – it's YOU that has to face the crowd!

Engineers have a rich palette at their disposal these days – parametric EQ, compression, reverb, chorus – but it takes time to set these parameters, so if you really need them at very specific settings provide them yourself before that XLR you offer the engineers. You can then say 'This is the sound I want – just make it louder!' Be polite and patient; these guys may have just spent half a day rigging the PA hardware, and they're often hungry, tired and overstretched. You may feel the same!

Smaller gigs

For many smaller gigs the electro acoustic guitarist needs to be self-contained, and thankfully there are many manufacturers offering dedicated 'acoustic' amplifiers, often usefully combined with some kind of small-scale vocal provision; even if you're purely an instrumentalist you'll need to address your audience.

So why do we need an 'acoustic' amplifier if we already perhaps possess a perfectly good electric guitar amp?

Acoustic amps

All amps do essentially the same job. However, the best conventional electric guitar amps are coveted for having a distinctive sound of their own – witness the number of 'modelling' devices that offer 'Tweed '50s' and 'Marshall stack' as options.

Electric guitarists rightly love the distortion and colouration offered by specifically 'tube'-powered amps. However, the acoustic guitarist wants the complete opposite – a transparent amplification of his coveted vintage Martin perhaps?

Acoustic amps therefore often employ 'Hi-Fi' components based on silicon chips and microprocessors, their sole aim being audio utopia – the perfect amp, a piece of wire with gain. The same applies to 'acoustic' loudspeaker design: a quest for transparency.

Two specific case studies

Let's take a look at a small portable 'combo' and a line array combination unit with an 'eye-level' mixer.

A Roland Chorus

Roland have a long history with transparent transistor or chip-based amps, going back to their association with keyboard amplifiers, which have similar requirements.

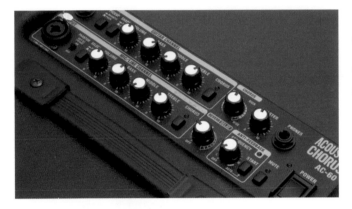

There have been many 'Roland Choruses' and there will no doubt be a new model out next week. However, the principles remain the same and share common ground with many other useful acoustic combos:

■ A small but necessarily fairly heavy 'ported' cabinet enclosure – most good audio still depends on efficient, heavy, magnet-based, substantially engineered loudspeakers of 1930s-type design.

■ Two discreet input sockets offering a range of input levels suited to magnetic, piezo, microphone and line level inputs. XLR and mono jack options.

■ Phantom power – for powering capacitor microphones.

■ Input levels and three-band EQ.

■ Reverb/delay and chorus options – both very useful.

■ An anti-feedback control – usually an automatic notch filter that can 'seek and attenuate' feedback prone frequencies.

■ A master volume control and headphone output.

The Roland also offers comprehensive rear panel outputs:

■ Stereo-balanced XLR line out. ■ Mono jack out.

■ A sub woofer out – for adding an additional 'bass' speaker.

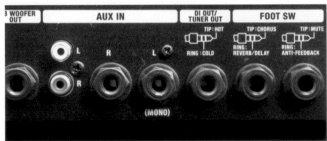

■ An aux 'in' for feeding backing tracks from MP3 CD etc – via jacks and RCA phono connectors.

■ A tuner out (also serves as another jack DI out) and some specific footswitch options.

This is a good example of a small acoustic amp offering everything you need for a small self-contained gig (100-seaters?) and has been heavily emulated by other manufacturers in smaller and larger packages to suit your needs. In practice I find this kind of rig works great for discreet (literally under my seat) situations where you should really be able to work acoustically but the acoustic of the venue and/or the ambient noise levels make this difficult – think wedding receptions, and smaller-scale concerts where you have to keep up dynamically with louder instruments like violins and woodwind. It would also suffice in a small pub or any domestic party. Hooked up to a front of house PA via the XLR line outs you have a very respectable 'backline' for bigger gigs.

A Bose line array system

The Bose company have developed a reputation in the wider field of quality audio through their medium-scale PA and compact Hi-Fi systems. More recently they've pitched a Hi-Fi approach to a triple purpose sound reinforcement system intended for all musicians. The triple purpose refers to one preamp, power amp, woofer and inline audio array supplying backline, monitor and main PA for each performer. This is quite radical but makes a lot of sense, especially in medium spaces (up to 400-seaters) at more conservative levels.

The problem often experienced with traditional PA arrangements is that it can be very hard to know what you're really hearing, with perhaps three versions of your sound washing over you onstage and all the consequent delay/phase/EQ variables that presents.

The basic Bose L1 version II consists of a sophisticated preamp (called a T1 Tonematch), a B1 bass module and a 7ft high cylindrical line array radiator multi-array of mid to high drivers.

For the acoustic/vocalist guitarist working independently this system offers portability (broken down it will easily fit in a small car boot) and very sophisticated audio with lots of sound processing power available when required, Reverb/Delay/Parametric EQ etc.

As is fitting for the 21st century, the system controller has programmable presets, meaning that any guitar changes and corresponding EQ and level changes can be called up as required. The same applies to any vocals, backing tracks, rhythm machines and loopers that you might conceivably wish to incorporate in the set.

In practice what I enjoyed about this approach is knowing that the sound I'm hearing is the sound the audience is hearing, which puts the musician back in the driving seat. Now, I effectively have a degree in sound engineering so that works for me. It will also work well for any seasoned player who has lots of experience with EQ etc – perhaps through operating his home studio.

However, this is not for the inexperienced performer still struggling with basic audio, though we can all learn and the results are very rewarding. Budget issues will exclude many beginners, so that all adds up. Bose (and others) offer these 'line array' self-contained systems as a radical alternative to three-way systems and I can hear a place for it in the small to medium-size venue, for acoustic guitarists supporting vocals and playing with other 'acoustic' instruments.

My only personal difficulty with this type of set-up comes when using backing tracks to accompany solo guitar – the tracks come up in the same 'audio space' as my guitar, and in 'mono', so I missed the spatial discrimination that sometimes helps me distinguish the 'live' from the 'Memorex'; and I was also reminded that mixing in mono is harder! (I hadn't tried this since 1979.) Naturally, the 'stereo' component is restored for the audience when multiple L1s work together.

However, if you work primarily as an acoustic guitarist in 200–400-seaters, you should certainly give this self-contained line array approach a try. The actual quality of the audio is superb and though rated at a nominal 350W RMS with one bass unit, it sounds much louder than that figure might suggest. This is the ideal type of system for achieving a true 'acoustic' sound at moderate amplification levels.

The Bose L1 system.

Installing a Fishman Aura Pro piezo-electric transducer

Here we'll be fitting a sophisticated transducer and preamp to a Yamaha F310 Dreadnought budget guitar to make a good live workhorse.

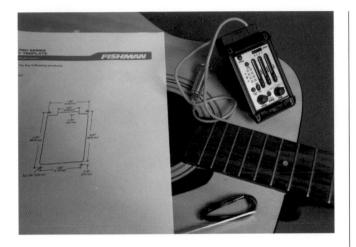

The piezo-electric 'crystal' system has been used for over 50 years to convert the acoustic vibrations of the guitar into an amplifiable electronic signal. Initially these systems were very crude and almost unusable. However, computer analysis has now enabled sophisticated tailoring of the tiny signal from a piezo to something very usable in a professional live music situation.

There are many hardware systems available but the most common types all tend to involve a piezo strip installed under the bridge saddle, a preamp sited somewhere accessible to the player and an output jack often concealed as a strap button on the endpin of the guitar.

Currently industry leaders Fishman are offering self-install 'imaging' systems that offer tailored studio-recorded microphone 'images' as onboard software, blendable via a preamp pot with the guitar's actual onboard piezo pickup output.

The following case study shows the procedure for installing a simple 'one' piezo device (with Aura capability). **NB:** The case study on page 122 looks at an alternative arrangement incorporating a blended microphone and piezo pickup.

Fishman recommends the Aura Pro system for a guitar with the following dimensions:

Minimum saddle slot length: 2.775in (70.48mm)
Maximum E to E string spacing at saddle: 2.5in (63.5mm)

This would encompass most full-size standard-scale guitars.

Fishman *prefer* their systems to be fitted professionally and I would only recommend the DIY approach if you're very confident with basic carpentry on frail musical instruments. I did this installation under the watchful eye of luthier John Diggins.

1 Carefully de-string the guitar, minimising the neck stress by doing it one string at a time in the order sixth, first, fifth, second, fourth, third. This reduces the tension on the neck evenly.

2 Before you cut the cavity on the side of the guitar choose a workable location. Ideally this should allow the preamp to swing freely for battery replacement and have a flattish profile in order that the preamp can sit neatly. The minimum clearance inside the guitar is 4.3cm for this specific model. The flattest and most comfortable location is often at the upper bout, just above the instrument's waist and well below the shoulder. The surrounding bezel will bend enough to conform to the curves of most instruments.

Fishman recommend a thin veneer applied inside the mounting area to provide extra support for the preamp.

As this guitar has relatively strong laminated sides I'm choosing to omit this stage – though I would recommend it on a more 'sensitive' solid-sided guitar.

3 Apply a little masking tape to the fixing area and measure the template placement in order to be parallel with the top. Apply the supplied template.

4 Establish the extremes of the cavity with four holes at the corners of the template – take your time with a hand drill to avoid internal splintering! Join the holes up with a sharp pad saw. This one from Hobbycraft is ideal.

5 Smooth the edges with a simple and gentle file. Coarse nail files are ideal and less likely to tear the laminate. File on the 'in'-stroke only – this also avoids the laminate tearing on the visible exterior. This home-made file is custom-sized for the job (made by John Diggins from a scrap of timber and some self-adhesive grit).

6 I also used a small round needle file to shape the corners and top indentation.

7 Use a .082in (2mm) drill to make the preamp retaining screw holes. Don't secure the preamp yet as it needs connecting to the pickup!

8 Remove the existing end pin – these pincers proved ideal.

9 Widen the end pin hole to 15⁄32in (11.9mm) to accommodate the new end pin jack. John suggested using a 60° countersink for this as it's less likely to tear or drift in the existing hole.

10 A piece of string tied to a jackplug makes easy work of getting the jack socket in place. This is then secured with a washer and nut and then an external cover, which doubles as a strap pin.

11 Remove the existing saddle. Drill a 3⁄32in (2.4mm) hole in the saddle slot for the pickup wire, no less than .100in (2.5mm) from the nearest string.

12 Install the pickup, feeding the output wires through the guitar body.

13 The saddle will require adjustment to accommodate the extra height added by the pickup strip – in this case 1.38mm thick, so the same amount removed from the saddle should put us back on track!

14 Mark the saddle with a sharp scoring tool and file the excess material with a flat file. In practice I find it's easiest to do this with the file in a vice, checking constantly for an even base to the saddle – crucial to good tone.

15 Open the input compartment on the preamp. This requires a small screwdriver to click open the hatch.

16 Connect the pickup wires to the preamp terminal block (the signal wire goes to the terminal marked 'I' and the shield wire goes to the 'G'. Tighten the screws on the block with a jewellers' size Phillips to secure the wires.

17 Loop the pickup wire to the right and press it into the slot on the edge of the chassis. Snap the trap door shut. Place the preamp in the cavity.

18 To install the screws and mounting brackets, swing the preamp open. Insert the mounting screws in their holes. Reach inside the soundhole and fasten the screws to the mounting brackets with a Phillips '1' point driver. Snap the four covers in place over the screw heads. Secure the loose wires inside the instrument with the supplied adhesive-backed clips. Cleaning the mounting surface with an alcohol wipe or a cotton swab moistened with rubbing alcohol will aid a secure fixing.

19 This Aura system, and I imagine many that will follow, requires the installation of updateable interpretive software to optimise the amplified pickup and 'Aura' blend. The software is first installed on your computer from a CD or website then uploaded to the preamp via a USB cable that connects to the side of the preamp.

20 The onboard preamp offers volume, EQ – bass, middle and treble – phase control, an automatic anti-feedback control, and a 'blend' between the pickup and the four switchable onboard 'images', which can be a similar guitar to your own but apparently 'heard' with a range of studio microphones – Schoeps, Neumann etc.

The straight pickup option sounds fine and with a little EQ and reverb comes quite close to an acoustic sound. **NB:** See page 122–123 for further useful illustrations.

121

Installing a pickup and internal microphone

Many players prefer the sound produced by the combination of a Piezo pickup with the output of a small internal microphone. The installation of a Premium Blend Fishman device follows the same principles as our previous install with the exception of the larger preamp cavity and the sighting of the microphone:

1 Remove the strings as before. Mark up and cut out the preamp cavity. Smoothe the new cavity as before by gently filing. Check for a good fit.

3 This guitar has no end pin so a bradawl mark, pilot hole and then a conventional 12mm drill is required. The masking tape protects the finish and also makes for easier marking up of the hole site.

2 Drill the securing holes and leave the unit unfixed for the present.

4 A good way to keep the jack from turning whilst tightening the securing nut is to thread a small drill through the provided end hole.

5 Drill the pickup hole. Install the pickup.

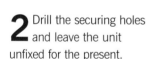

The Fishman Premium blend piezo and microphone.

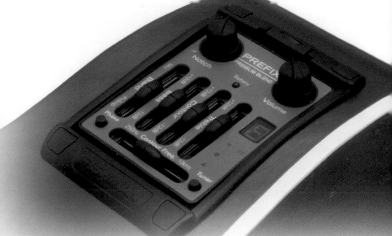

6 The pickup is 1mm thick so it's worth filing 1mm off the bottom of the saddle to restore the original string height.

7 Connect the pickup wires observing the polarity – braid to 'G' or ground and the 'hot' pin to the left. Tighten with a jewellers' size Phillips. Loop the wire through the exit hole and clamp the retaining lid.

8 Position the microphone and secure with the self-adhesive pad supplied. I'm trying a fixing to the neck block!

9 Screw the preamp in position using the supplied rear clamps and hide the screws with the supplied caps.

10 Fix the cables to the 'inside sides' of the guitar with some self-adhesive clips. Restring the guitar.

NB: Every guitar has a different acoustic character and some experiment will be needed with the mike position, the 'pickup microphone' balance and the EQ.

The preamp offers the usual volume and EQ facilities – in this case plus or minus 12dB at 60Hz, and 10KHz and a parametric 'contour' at 250Hz–10Khz with a Q of 0.05, plus a blend control for the mike/pickup mix and a variable notch control for attenuating any feedback-prone frequencies (30–300Hz) by 15dB.

With this particular unit it is also possible to split the two outputs using a stereo to 'two mono' splitter lead and feed the mike and pickup to separate channels on your amplifier or mixer – an ideal scenario.

The recommended starting point for the mike position is pointing back.

Results

This unit works very effectively, with a useful range of sounds – especially at the lower volumes you'd expect from a 'parlour' guitar and with a 50/50 mike/piezo balance. In higher volume situations it would be possible to rely on the piezo pickup alone and still generate a usable tone. The built-in tuner has a useful large display and is extremely accurate.

I particularly enjoy the way the mike opens up lots of interesting percussion effects from the body of the guitar – excellent!

ACOUSTIC GUITAR MANUAL

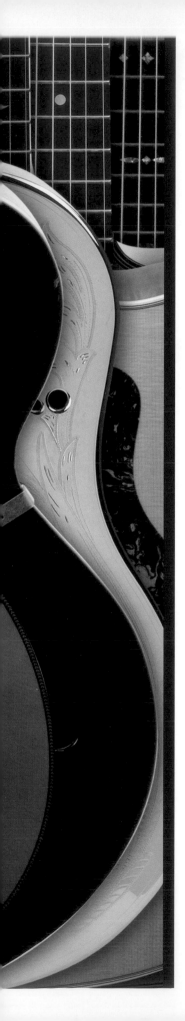

Specific case studies

It has been very difficult to choose the guitars for these case studies – but fascinating! The range of the acoustic guitar, from Spanish and flamenco to Dreadnought and National, and six to twelve strings, is tremendous. I've also included a ¾-size beginner guitar, alongside the glory of a Taylor, several Martins, including an Eric Clapton Grand Auditorium, and an individually made Fylde Ariel. The aim is to give an overview of what's available, how they differ both externally and internally, and the broadly applicable maintenance issues that they raise. Enjoy!

LEFT The Case Study guitars.

RIGHT A National Style 3.

Chinese-made Yamaha CG 122MS 'classic' Spanish guitar

Serial No QPZ180551

An inexpensive 'beginner's' nylon-strung Spanish-type guitar with a reasonable tone that will improve as it's played in.

Ideal for

Getting started – many students start on a nylon-strung guitar as it's easy on your fingers and single-string melodic lines can work well, as can warm root position chords. I've never seen a Yamaha guitar that didn't provide a reasonable tone and good intonation – just what you need.

Signature tone woods

This economy guitar features a solid Englemann spruce top, nato back and sides, and a matte natural finish. Nato is a collective name for wood from *Mora* trees. The best-known species are *Mora excelsa* (mora) and *Mora gonggrijpii* (morabukea.)The timber is sometimes called Eastern mahogany.

Condition on arrival

The guitar arrived reasonably well set up and just needs a little fret polish and a nut tweak to be set to go. The flight case is the economy cardboard variety.

General description

The guitar has the classic 'post-Torres' shape and size; specifically 37cm lower bout, 28cm upper bout, with a 24cm waist (all very similar to the current Ramírez specification). The small 8.5cm soundhole is decorated with an elaborate set of faux inlays.

■ The one-piece 49cm back is of nato and has a very slight pliage or curvature.

■ The 9.75cm deep sides enlarge to 10cm at the lower bout. The sides are also factory-made from nato. The guitar is faux bound in black.

■ The rosewood bridge has a plastic saddle with some lone compensation for the G string intonation. The strings are secured traditionally in a knot known as the timber hitch, bowyer's hitch, lumberman's or countryman's knot depending on your geography!

■ The guitar weighs a very light 3.25lb (1.476kg), slightly lighter than the Ramírez featured later in this book.

■ The seven-piece neck is obviously made with a very frugal use of materials, with even the headstock made of a three-piece laminate. The laminated neck has a traditional U profile with a fairly flat and comfortable back and the usual 12 frets to the body. The scale length is approx 65cm with 18 full frets and a 19th part fret giving top 'B' on the first and sixth strings.

■ Despite the separate headstock joint the headstock angle is only approx 13°. However, Les Paul himself told me not to fret too much over this break angle!

■ The three-a-side machine heads are very lightweight stamped steel.

■ The black-stained rosewood fingerboard traditionally has no inlays, but a couple of discreet side dots at V and VII will be appreciated by students. The frets are light 1.9mm gauge shaped quite low and in need of a finishing polish.

■ The slotted headstock carries the distinctive Yamaha logo. The 51.8mm nut is plastic and slightly narrower than the classic size, which will aid some beginners.

Yamaha musical instruments

The roots of the Yamaha Corporation can be traced back to Torakusu Yamaha, the third son of a samurai. Apparently, in 1887 a local school needed some repair work on their reed organ. Torakusu, who had originally trained as a watchmaker, became so fascinated by the workings of the instrument that he decided to build one himself. Having completed this, the Yamaha founder then carried the instrument on his back to Tokyo (a round trip of 250 miles) and sought the opinions of an eminent music professor. Following that meeting the Yamaha legend was born.

Through constant innovation and technological leadership, Yamaha has grown to be the world's largest and most successful maker of quality musical instruments. I visited the Yamaha factory myself in Hamamatsu, Japan, and was stunned by the attention to detail and the dedication to music education. I've never encountered a bad Yamaha instrument – the samurai spirit lives on!

Specific routine maintenance

Setting the action: The action on a classic guitar is traditionally set quite high to facilitate a heavy dynamic without fret rattle. This new guitar has been set a little over high, allowing the player to decide his or her preference on delivery.

With a capo at the first fret to take the nut out of the equation, and the string stopped at the last fret, check the neck relief with your feeler gauges. The neck should have some relief for acoustic volume, perhaps .011–.012 at the seventh fret sixth string but this is a matter of personal taste. Naturally the guitar has no truss rod.

See the nut and saddle work guides on pages 64 and 70 for any saddle height and nut adjustment.

The strings on this guitar are .028–.044 medium tension monofilament one to three and wound-on nylon four to six.

When changing strings it's worth checking the machine head fixing screws, which tend to work loose. On the Yamaha this requires a Phillips '0' point. The bushing cogs require a Phillips '1' point. Do not overtighten either of these – just enough to stop the machine head drifting in normal use. A tiny amount of Vaseline or ChapStick on the open gears will prevent the threads stripping with use.

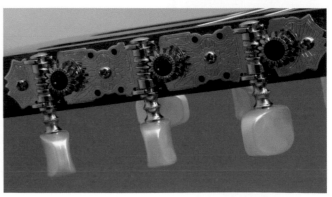

A little graphite from a pencil tip will keep the strings moving at the nut when tuning.

A little lemon oil will usually clean the fingerboard, but beware – this may upset any colour stain on cheaper guitars.

Periodically examine the saddle – good tone depends on a correct fit and avoiding any gaps between bridge and saddle. Also the intonation will be upset by any tendency to 'lean' from the vertical. The current set-up on this guitar is fine. A good secure string knot is essential if the guitar is to hold its pitch.

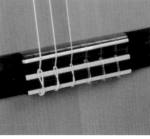

Under the hood

■ The top has a variant of traditional Torres non-scalloped fan strutting with a simple neck block and tenon neck-joint. All the back and side joins are neatly kerfed.

Signed off

This economy guitar offers a good 'in' to the classical arena for adult beginners. I have a similar Yamaha student guitar that has given good service for 20 years without need of a refret or replacement tuners. The current guitar plays in tune and sounds OK – it just needs 'playing in' to achieve its full tonal potential. The intonation is OK, especially in the lower positions likely to be encountered in Royal College Grades I to V.

■ The back of the guitar has *three* parallel slim-tapered and 'end-scalloped' braces. All the interior woodwork is wisely left unfinished.

■ It's worth checking occasionally for any loose braces; with time and humidity changes these can come unglued, resulting in warping of the top – an expensive fault to repair. Loose braces often produce a rattle that's easily detected. However, it's not always this obvious. Another symptom is a loss of bass response – the guitar sounds inexplicably 'thin'. A gentle check once in a while can save an expensive repair.

■ This traditional-type guitar naturally has no transducer electrics.

Indonesian-made Yamaha F310 Dreadnought

Serial No ONN254118

A remarkable entry-level '14 frets to the body' Dreadnought combining a laminated spruce top with meranti back and sides. The guitar arrived in a plain cardboard box with lots of useful goodies.

Ideal for

Getting started on a steel-string. For almost 40 years these economy Yamahas have provided a remarkable 'in' to the standard Dreadnought-size guitar for the beginning guitarist, and a very useful robust songwriting aid for the professional tour bus.

Signature tone woods

A laminated spruce top and meranti. Meranti grows in various South-East Asian countries and is sometimes known as seraya, lauan or Asian mahogany, depending upon country of origin. Meranti is the commonest name in the United Kingdom and the type most often used is the red variety. This instrument sounds fine for any teaching or songwriting situation, just 'smaller'-sounding than the real thing.

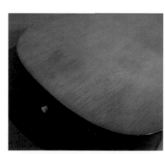

Condition on arrival

This is a good example of Yamaha's commitment to affordable but musical entry-level instruments. I personally paid £29 for mine (about $42.50 at the time of writing), new, including a tuner, plectrums, strap, spare strings and DVD tutor! The average shop price is £100 in 2010, and that's still a bargain.

See the previous case study for some background on Yamaha company history.

■ The guitar weighs a light 4lb (1.8kg), lighter than the average modern Dreadnought, and is tapered from a relatively shallow 9.25cm deep at the neck and 11cm at the end pin, with an almost flat back.

■ The unbound neck is manufactured from nato, a collective name for the wood from mora trees. This wood is dense and not particularly easy to dry or to work. However, it is available in large dimensions and demonstrates well above average strength, durability and resistance to wear. The neck is made in three pieces: a heel, a main body and a clever splice to the headstock with no obstructing volute. It has a very slim U profile with a tapered heel and 14 frets to the body.

General description

Most luthiers seem to agree that the top is the most critical element of an acoustic guitar's tone woods. Some even say the sides are just there to keep the back and top apart and can be made of anything! The great luthier family of Ramírez have famously used laminates and even papier mâché here (purely for demonstration). The Yamaha's sides and 51cm back are meranti. This has an average dry weight of 550kg/m³ but it can be heavier (up to 705). This wood takes stains and finishes well and there's a lot of stain here, but it looks OK.

■ The guitar has the classic *modern* Dreadnought 'square-shouldered' shape and size; specifically 41.5cm lower bout (larger than the Judy Collins Martin), 29.5cm upper bout, and 27cm waist. The black plastic scratchplate is attached directly to the top.

■ The round 10.5cm soundhole is lightly decorated with some plain black rings.

■ The rosewood bridge is nicely shaped but has a simple uncompensated plastic saddle with the expected slant towards a 'shorter scale' treble. The saddle is a poor fit, which will affect the sound – relatively easily fixed.

■ The unbound rosewood fingerboard has simple dot markers. The 20 frets give access to a top C and are narrow 1.9mm gauge and a little unfinished. The fingerboard virtual radius is 15in (38.1in).

■ The headstock is inlaid with the familiar leaf logo and a plain 'YAMAHA' insignia. The headstock angle is a generous 14°.

■ The 43mm plastic nut arrived set a little high and is a little narrow for fingerpicking but fine for a plectrum-style beginner.

■ The screw-fixed machine heads are economy units that might be usefully replaced with Grovers or similar. See page 58.

■ The strings are secured with simple white plastic bridge pins. The bridge has a marked rear 'belly' to help distribute vibration to the top, unlike the traditional rectangular 'Spanish' bridge.

Specific routine maintenance

Setting the action: With a capo at the first fret to take the nut out of the equation and the string stopped at the last fret, check the neck relief with your feeler gauges. The neck should have some relief, perhaps .010–.015 at the seventh fret sixth string for light fingerpicking, slightly more for hard bluegrass flat picking. If the neck relief does need adjustment the 310 requires a 5mm truss rod wrench (the Stewmac types are easier to handle than the supplied hardware-store Allen. See *Useful contacts* appendix).

See the nut and saddle work guides on pages 64 and 70 for any saddle height and nut adjustment.

The strings are Yamaha .012–.052 acoustic bronze and it would be unwise to try anything heavier on this economy guitar.

When changing strings it's worth checking the machine head fixing screws, which tend to work loose. On the Yamaha this requires a Phillips '0' point. All the screws were loose due to post-manufacture shrinkage. Do not overtighten them – just enough to stop the machine head moving in normal use.

The simple machines are not tensionable.

A little graphite from a pencil tip will keep the strings moving at the nut when tuning. Graphite dust mixed with ChapStick or Vaseline is another solution.

If you're removing *all* the strings then a little lemon oil will usefully clean the rosewood fingerboard.

Always examine the string retaining pins for wear – good tone depends on a correct fit and the correct break angle at the bridge. Excessive wear at the bridge string contact point needs professional attention. The current set-up on this guitar is fine if a little high. A jammed pin needs careful extraction with some masking tape and cushioned pliers, as the pins and bridge are easily marked or broken (as are those in the picture). The extraction lever found on most peg winders will do the job for all but the most firmly fixed.

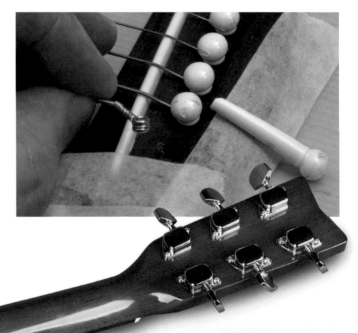

Whilst you have the tools out it's worth checking for a secure end pin – this is a traditional friction fit.

Under the hood

■ The truss rod access is via the sound hole and requires a 5mm hex wrench for any relief adjustment. See page 62 for more on neck relief and adjustment.

■ The top has a variation on the Martin X-braced arrangement with fairly crude unscalloped braces and taping and some ill-fitting joints. Under the bridge there is a supporting bridge plate.

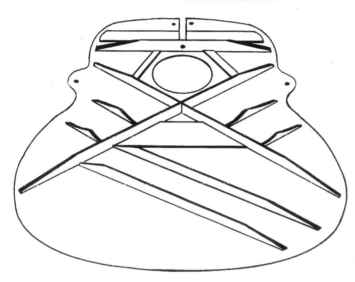

■ The back of the guitar has four parallel 9mm thick, end-tapered ladder braces, all of which are visible through the soundhole.

■ The guitar has very simple and heavy 'block' kerfing and a substantial 'square' neck block.

■ Note the importance of correctly fitting string-retaining pins.

Kerfing and ill-fitting tone bars.

■ All the interior woodwork is traditionally left as bare wood.

■ It's worth checking occasionally for any loose braces; with time and humidity changes these can come unglued, resulting in warping of the top – an expensive fault to repair. Loose braces often

Interior bridge plate and string pins.

produce a rattle that's easily detected. However, it's not always this obvious. Another symptom is a loss of bass response – the guitar sounds inexplicably 'thin'. A gentle check once in a while can save an expensive repair.

■ This economy instrument naturally had no transducer electrics as supplied, though on page 119 we show the installation of a Fishman Aura system on this guitar.

Signed off

This is a great economy guitar that I feel may even be usable professionally, especially when amplified. The intonation is accurate throughout. Fitting a good set of tuners (see page 58) will double the price of the guitar but make it even better. I used this guitar for teaching for a year and feel it's one that I could comfortably recommend to any pupil.

Japanese-made Yamaha NCX 2000FM electro-acoustic

Serial No QP1204A

A modern electro acoustic cutaway classic hand-crafted in Hamamatsu, Japan, this guitar represents the core production of Yamaha professional guitars not franchised to Indonesia or China. This particular guitar innovates around the traditional mid-20th century Classic guitar pattern with a cutaway and integral onboard electrics. It's currently the guitar associated with jazz virtuoso Antonio Forcione and duo Rodrigo y Gabriela.

Ideal for

Almost any professional application where you need an amplified nylon string tone. Great for top octave improvisations, aided by the Florentine cutaway.

Signature tone woods

The two-piece top is from Hokkaido spruce that has been artificially seasoned to create a 'played-in' sound from a new guitar – the Yamaha ARE or 'Acoustic Resonance Enhancement'. The back and sides are solid flamed maple and the neck African mahogany.

Condition on arrival

This interesting guitar arrived beautifully set up and ready to play – a refreshing change. The tone is soft and mellow rather than brash and strident, well suited to a range of music from bossa nova to Bach. The guitar has a substantial textile-covered solid but lightweight case.

General description

The guitar is a variant on the classic 'Spanish' shape and size, specifically 37cm lower bout, 28cm upper bout (same as our Ramírez), with a lightly larger 24cm waist and, of course, a 6.5cm Florentine cutaway. The small 8.5cm soundhole is decorated with an elaborate set of inlays and supplied with a rubber 'bung' for amplified applications.

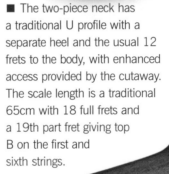

■ The beautiful two-piece 49cm back is matched from flame maple with a simple double-line centre inlay and a slight tension arch.

■ The 10cm deep solid maple sides diminish to 9.5cm at the lower bout and the neck joint. The guitar has black edge binding front and back.

■ The guitar has an unusual shaped ebony bridge, with a saddle made from a simple piece of uncompensated bone. This was a little loose, and a tiny side shim would help the tone. The strings are secured traditionally with a timber hitch.

The Hamamatsu tradition

Established in 1887, the Yamaha Corporation in Japan (then Nippon Gakki Co Ltd) has since grown to become the world's largest manufacturer of a full line of musical instruments. Their Hamamatsu factory in Southern Honshu – Japan's main island – epitomises the Japanese industrial ethic, with management and workers engaged in a cooperative effort to achieving excellence.

■ The two-piece neck has a traditional U profile with a separate heel and the usual 12 frets to the body, with enhanced access provided by the cutaway. The scale length is a traditional 65cm with 18 full frets and a 19th part fret giving top B on the first and sixth strings.

■ The guitar and electrics weigh a light 4.25lb (1.93kg).

■ There is no separate headstock joint and headstock angle is 13°.

■ The traditional flat ebony fingerboard has side dot position markers at V and VII and the frets are medium 2.1mm gauge shaped to a high crown and nicely polished.

■ The slotted headstock has a Maccaferri shape and carries the distinctive Yamaha crossed tuning fork logo on a rosewood veneer. The 52mm nut (just a millimetre less than the Ramírez) is a well-cut piece of plastic set at a playable height.

■ The three-a-side machine heads are beautifully made and gold-finished with marbled plastic buttons.

Specific routine maintenance

Setting the action: The action on a classic guitar is traditionally set quite high to facilitate a heavy dynamic without fret rattle. This new guitar has been set to a good working height for a moderate acoustic 'attack'.

With a capo at the first fret to take the nut out of the equation and the string stopped at the last fret, check the neck relief with your feeler gauges. The neck should have some relief for acoustic volume, perhaps .011–.012 at the seventh fret sixth string, but this is a matter of personal taste. Unusually the guitar *does* have a truss rod, which does not, however, upset the balance of the guitar due to the electric preamp acting as a counterweight!

The rod requires a 5mm Allen accessed at the headstock, under a shield removed with a Phillips No.1.

See the nut and saddle work guides on pages 64 and 70 for any saddle height and nut adjustment.

The strings on this guitar are .028–.044 medium tension monofilament one to three and wound-on nylon four to six.

When changing strings it's worth checking the machine head fixing screws, which tend to work loose. On the Yamaha this requires a Phillips No.1. The bushing cogs also require a Phillips No.1. Do not overtighten these – just enough to stop the machine head moving in normal use. All the screws on this guitar were very loose. The button retainers also tend to work loose and require a Phillips No.1.

A little graphite from a pencil tip will keep the strings moving at the nut when tuning. Curiously, the nut isn't actually glued in! A small drop of Loctite superglue is needed.

A little Dunlop 02 Deep conditioner will benefit the ebony fingerboard. This is part of the 'System 65' maintenance kit, which also includes guitar polish and a fret polish abrasive.

Periodically examine the saddle – good tone depends on a correct fit and avoiding any gaps between bridge and saddle. Also the intonation will be upset by any tendency to 'lean' from the vertical. The current set-up on this guitar is excellent. A good secure string knot is essential if the guitar is to hold its pitch.

Periodically tighten the end pin/jack socket with a Phillips No.0 and strap retainers with a Phillips No.2.

Under the hood

■ The top has a very lightweight variant of traditional Torres non-scalloped fan bracing. Note also the two 'treble' and 'bass' sensors under the bridge. These are connected to the preamp.

A variation on traditional fan bracing, with additional tone bars.

■ The back of the guitar has *three* parallel 8.8mm wide end-scalloped braces and an ellipse centre splice, all of which are visible through the soundhole (*four* rear braces are often found on bigger-bodied Dreadnought-type guitars). There is 14mm traditional kerfed support to the back and lighter 12.8mm to the top.

■ Unusually the inside of the soundhole has a thin reinforcing veneer. This may be allied to the removable rubber acoustic bung.

■ All the interior woodwork is wisely left unfinished.

■ It's worth checking occasionally for any loose braces; with time and humidity changes these can come unglued, resulting in warping of the top – an expensive fault to repair. Loose braces often produce a rattle that's easily detected. However, it's not always this obvious. Another symptom is a loss of bass response – the guitar sounds inexplicably 'thin'. A gentle check once in a while can save an expensive repair.

Electrics

This guitar has two moving coil transducer pickups under the bridge. These are mixed at the upper bout as a pair labelled 'High' and 'Low'. There is also EQ High, Low and Mid +/– 12dB, a main gain and tuner OFF/ON switch.

Pickup placement is apparently determined to within one-tenth of a millimetre. Having found the 'sweet spot', Yamaha then redesigned the internal bracing of the guitars to allow for ideal placement while maintaining the tonal character of the guitars. To reduce unwanted feedback caused by vibration, the NX Series contact pickup utilises an additional multilayer damper to ensure the tone is captured in its purest form.

The battery compartment reveals a PP3, which will need replacing every 40 hours max.

The preamp electrics are easily accessible for servicing simply by unscrewing two No.1 Pozidrives. The transducers and battery connections are simple push-fit and 2.5 and 3.5mm jacks.

Signed off

This is a fine guitar, suited to amplification but also very pleasant to play as a purely acoustic instrument. The extra high octave access is very welcome given the demands of much modern repertoire. I tried restringing the guitar with D'Addario J45s plus a wound Savarez third; this improved the sound significantly.

The intonation is accurate throughout. This guitar represents a really refreshing diversion from the conventional classical approach but with no sacrifice of sound.

A beautiful rosewood back and sides version of this model is favoured by Gabriela of Rodrigo y..., and this has a different character – not as bright as the maple, but with more depth and a little quieter overall.

USA-made 'Judy Collins' Martin HD 355SJC Dreadnought

A classic '12 frets to the body' Dreadnought, signed by Judy Collins and C.F. Martin IV. This particular guitar is number 27 of a limited edition of just 50 made in Nazareth, Pennsylvania.

Serial No 882956

Singer songwriter Judy Collins' association with Martin goes back to the early 1960s – in 1962 she even gave a concert in the loading bay of their new factory with Tom Paxton! She remembers 'I was wearing this little blue dress and my slip was showing!'

Judy with this guitar in 2010.

With a lightly braced table specifically designed for light picking, this guitar is actually branded inside with the familiar Martin 'Nazareth PA' and also 'Use light or medium strings only'.

Ideal for

The pro songwriters' muse – you could work on the new album inspired by this guitar's tone, confident that in the studio it's going to sound great! This is not the ideal instrument for a stadium thrash, though Judy used hers with great grace at Glastonbury and Fairfield Hall in 2010.

Condition on arrival

Apart from the 'modern' X-bracing, this is a great development of the original 12-fret 1916 Dreadnaught design made by Martin for their distributor Ditson. This design is considered by many to be the most powerful and resonant Dreadnought. The rework is by Martin legend Dick Boak in consultation with Judy herself. The guitar comes in a custom five-ply hardshell case and is also available in a more heavily braced 12-string version.

Signature tone woods

An unusual combination of premium solid tone woods gives this instrument its unique sound. A centre wedge of flame figured Pacific bigleaf maple in the traditional Style 35 three-piece back stands out against adjacent wings and sides of East Indian rosewood. Visually striking, the maple wedge also adds crisp definition to the rich tone and enhances the higher frequencies. The beauty of the back and sides is matched by the Sitka spruce top, supported by ⁵⁄₁₆in X-bracing scalloped for a full, open timbre.

General description

This guitar has the classic *early* Dreadnaught 'round-shouldered' shape and size, specifically 40cm lower bout, 29.5cm upper bout, with a 27.5cm waist. The black plastic scratchplate is attached directly to the 3.3mm solid Sitka spruce top.

■ The round 10cm soundhole is decorated with 'Style 45' – maple and black fibre inlays and a green abalone inner circle.

■ The beautiful 53.5cm back is crafted from solid East India rosewood with a Pacific bigleaf maple wedge and back purfling Style 00-21 GE.

■ The sides are also solid East India rosewood and 'herringbone' bound.

■ The bridge is ebony with a very complex custom-filed compensated bone saddle with the expected slant towards a 'shorter scale' treble. The strings are secured with white plastic abalone-decorated bridge pins.

■ The guitar weighs a light 4.5lb (2.04kg), somewhat lighter than the average modern Dreadnought, and is tapered 10cm deep at the neck and 12.5cm at the end pin, with a very slight arch to the complex back.

■ The headstock joint results in an unusual volute that doesn't actually cause any playing obstruction. The headstock angle is a very healthy 13°.

■ The screwed and bolted machine heads are Martin-branded Schaller chrome minis, with ebony knobs.

■ The fully bound solid mahogany neck has a slim U profile with a tapered heel and feels very short due to the now unusual 12 frets to the body. The scale length is approx 64.5cm.

■ The fully bound African ebony fingerboard has tasteful snowflake and diamond abalone markers. The frets are narrow 1.96mm gauge and beautifully dressed and polished. There are 19 frets – top B like a 'classic Spanish' guitar. The fingerboard radius is a flattish 15in (38.1in).

■ The headstock carries the Judy Collins 'Wildflower' (a columbine), Judy's signature and a version of the classic Martin logo in 'silver' foil, all inlaid into the black African ebony overlay. The 45.94mm nut is a beautifully cut piece of yellowing bone.

Specific routine maintenance

Setting the action: With a capo at the first fret to take the nut out of the equation and the string stopped at the last fret, check the neck relief with your feeler gauges. The neck should have some relief, perhaps .010–.015 at the seventh fret sixth string for light fingerpicking, slightly more for hard bluegrass flatpicking. If the neck relief does need adjustment the Collins requires a 5mm truss rod wrench (the Stewmac types are easier to handle than a hardware-store Allen – see *Useful contacts* appendix).

See the nut and saddle work guides on pages 64 and 70 for any saddle height and nut adjustment.

The strings on this guitar are Martin .012–.054 aco bronze SP and it would be unwise to try anything heavie on the lightly braced table.

When changing strings it's worth checking the machine head fixing screws, which tend to work loose. On the Collins this requires a Phillips No.1 at the back and a 10mm socket for the front locking nuts. Do not overtighten these – just enough to stop the machine head moving in normal use. Due to wood shrinkage all the screws and nuts on this guitar were slightly loose.

The Schallers are tensionable and should be loosened for string changes and retightened for a comfortable working setting. This requires a 4mm straight-slot driver.

A little graphite from a pencil tip will keep the strings moving at the nut when tuning. Graphite dust mixed with ChapStick or Vaseline is another solution.

A little lemon oil will clean the ebony fingerboard.

Always examine the string retaining pins for wear – good tone depends on a correct fit and the correct break angle at the bridge. Excessive wear at the bridge string contact point needs professional attention. The current set-up on this guitar is excellent, as expected.

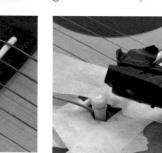

A jammed pin needs careful extraction with a peg winder lever, or as a last resort some masking tape and cushioned pliers – the pins and bridge are easily marked or broken.

Whilst you have the tools out it's worth tightening the end pin – this is a traditional friction fit. The pin is grained ivoroid and the endpiece inlay is black/white Boltaron, a recycled ABS/acrylic PVS extruded alloy sheet material used by Martin since the 1960s.

The Martin dynasty

'My great, great, great, grandfather Christian Freidrich Martin (1796–1873) lived in Neukirchen in Saxony and was a cabinet maker. Despite training in Vienna with the great luthier Stauffer, the local Guilds prevented him making guitars. So he took his tools and his family and moved to Soho, New York, and eventually Nazareth, Pennsylvania. Still to this day the craftsmen are from the local community and the work ethic is strong. We are making an "American guitar" with a German heritage. Even though our early guitars were all gut-strung they were not really identifiable as a "Spanish' guitar".'
Current CEO C.F. Martin IV (born 1955)

Under the hood

■ The truss rod access is via the soundhole and requires a 5mm hex wrench for any relief adjustment. See page 62 for more on neck relief and adjustment.

■ The earliest Dreadnaughts were fan-strutted. However, this return to the past has 5/16in heavily scalloped X-bracing with an extra upper bout parallel strut and two top soundhole braces, also extra 'belly' struts behind the bridge. There is also a mahogany neck block and a dovetail neck joint.

■ The back of the guitar has two triangular centre splices and four parallel lightweight (6.3mm wide) end-scalloped braces, all of which are visible through the soundhole (these are nearly 3mm slimmer than the Yamaha 310 Dreadnought braces). The kerfed supports are 18mm wide but slim and tapered.

■ All the interior woodwork is wisely left unfinished.

■ It's worth checking occasionally for any loose braces; with time and humidity changes these can come unglued, resulting in warping of the top – an expensive fault to repair. Loose braces often produce a rattle that's easily detected. However, it's not always this obvious. Another symptom is a loss of bass response – the guitar sounds inexplicably 'thin'. A gentle check once in a while can save an expensive repair.

■ This vintage-type guitar naturally has no transducer electrics.

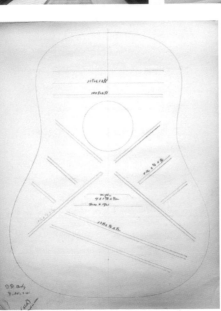

The 12-string version bracing.

Signed off

This is a true testament to the Martin heritage – beautifully finished A1 materials that result in a wonderfully responsive guitar. It is now owned by folk singer Sandy Clayton – 'Who knows where the time goes'.

 NB: The 12-string version has contoured rather than scalloped bracing, contributing to the necessary extra strength – Martin were originally reluctant to make 12-string guitars for this reason.

USA-made 'Custom Shop' Gibson J200 Super Jumbo

Serial No 00922032

This classic oversized Super Jumbo designated 'Montana Gold' represents a Gibson tradition stretching back to 1937, when in a pre-electric rivalry for acoustic volume, guitars were getting bigger and bigger.

The Martin Dreadnaught-size guitar had been firmly established by 1931, the first Gibson 'Jumbo' had arrived in 1934, and in 1936 came the even bigger 'Advanced Jumbo'.

When singing cowboy Gene Autry was filmed playing a Martin, the bigger and flashier SJ200 'Super Jumbo' was quickly developed by Gibson's Guy Hart for rival Hollywood cowboy singer Ray Whitley. Very soon Gene Autry had commissioned an even flashier SJ200 with his name emblazoned in mother of pearl across the fingerboard. The model has since been popular with many Country-influenced artists including Emmylou Harris, Elvis Presley and Bob Dylan. The Beatles' George Harrison used one for his acoustic version of *While My Guitar Gently Weeps*.

Ideal for

A brilliant studio guitar for adding expensive-sounding overdubs and lending warm support to any voice. The retro-installed Bluestick transducer extends the scope to any 'Unplugged' session.

Signature tone woods

The $200 SJ200 started life with rosewood back and sides, but after production was halted by the war the guitar was reissued as the J200 in 1947 with the rosewood replaced by maple. A simpler version of the guitar has also been available since 1939, known as the J100.

This particular 'special', designed by Gibson Acoustic's master luthier Ren Ferguson, has a combination of a relatively thick 3.5mm AAA grade Sitka spruce top with back and sides from AAA grade Eastern curly maple. It restores the elaborate tuners and bridge of the original Ray Whitley model but dispenses with the double binding and cowboy scenes on the fret markers. All the binding is 'yellow antiqued'.

Condition on arrival

This is a good example of the Super Jumbo and has a retro-fitted Schertler Bluestick capacitor microphone with active EQ powered by two CR2450 Lithium Manganese batteries. The guitar comes in a substantial Canadian-made TKL 'Custom Shop' hardshell case.

General description

This guitar has the square-shouldered Jumbo shape and is huge, specifically 43cm lower bout, 31.5cm upper bout, with a narrow 26cm 'corset' waist – the Dolly Parton of the guitar world. The 'tortoise' pickguard is hand-engraved with clusters of wheat with a 'Montana Gold' banner. The colouring and inlay are all done by hand and the pickguard is attached directly to the top.

■ The round 10cm soundhole is decorated with a hand-crafted abalone double-ring rosette with an abalone-filled middle. The main ring consists of seven-ply binding, and the second ring is three-ply binding, fairly restrained for this type of guitar.

■ The beautiful 53cm back is two-piece bookmatched crafted from eastern curly maple, the centre join decorated with an intricate black inlay.

■ The sides are of the same curly maple, all the joints bound and inlaid.

■ The unusual moustache bridge is ebony with six mother of pearl inlays and an uncompensated saddle with the simple slant towards a 'shorter scale' treble. The strings are secured with white plastic pins.

■ The guitar weighs 5.5lb (2.5kg), a pound heavier than the average modern Dreadnought, and is sharply tapered 9.5cm deep at the neck, reaching 11.5cm by the waist and 12cm at the end pin, with a very slight 'arch' to the back.

■ The fully bound dovetail jointed neck seems to be constructed from a two-piece longitudinal maple laminate and has a fairly slim 2cm U profile with a tapered heel and no headstock volute. It has the modern 14 frets to the body. The scale length is 64.5cm.

■ The fingerboard is constructed from the highest grade ebony, making it extremely balanced and stable. The block inlays are of genuine mother of pearl and are crafted into the fingerboard, eliminating gaps and without fillers. The fingerboard has a rolled edge instead of the usual right-angle where its surface meets the neck. The flattish radius is a bend friendly 12in (30.5cm).

■ The 20 frets are quite narrow 2.1mm gauge and beautifully dressed and polished.

■ The headstock has the Custom 'Montana Gold' banner peghead logo with wheat accents, made of gold mother of pearl, which sits below Gibson's modern logo. The 44.3mm nut is a beautifully cut piece of yellowing bone. The headstock angle is a solid 15°.

■ The guitar has gold Grover Imperial tuners. These are part of the company's vintage line, making their first appearance in the early 1970s. They are exact reproductions of the original 1930s type, including their unique three-step buttons, a design trademarked by Grover. With a gear ratio of 16:1, the Imperials have a durable housing that provides maximum protection for the gear and string post. All moving parts are cut for exact meshing, eliminating the possibility of slippage. A special lubricant inside the gear box provides smooth and accurate tuning stability.

A little lemon oil will clean the ebony fingerboard and prevent damaging drying out of the exposed wood. Always examine the string retaining pins for wear – good tone depends on a correct fit and correct break angle at the bridge. Excessive wear at the bridge string contact point needs professional attention. The current set-up on this guitar is excellent, which also means the pins come out easily.

A jammed pin needs careful extraction using the lever found on many string winders, as the pins and bridge are easily marked or broken.

Whilst you have the tools out it's worth tightening the distinctive Bluestick end pin/output jack. The cosmetic cover is a simple fingertight thread whilst the actual jack requires a socket wrench.

Specific routine maintenance

Setting the action: With a capo at the first fret to take the nut out of the equation and the string stopped at the last fret, check the neck relief with your feeler gauges. The neck should have some relief, perhaps .010–.015 at the seventh fret sixth string for light fingerpicking, slightly more for hard bluegrass flatpicking. This is currently set comfortably low at .008in. If the neck relief does need adjustment, first remove the truss rod shield with a No.1 Phillips. The J200 then requires a ⁵⁄₁₆in truss rod wrench (the Stewmac types are easiest to handle – see *Useful contacts*).

See the nut and saddle work guides on pages 64 and 70 for any saddle height and nut adjustment.

The strings on this guitar are D'Addario custom light .011–.052 phosphor bronze, though I suspect the guitar could cope happily with much heavier gauges for a bigger acoustic sound.

When changing strings it's worth checking the machine head fixing screws, which tend to work loose. On the J200 this requires a No.1 Phillips. Do not overtighten these – just enough to stop the machine head moving in normal use. Due to wood shrinkage all the screws and nuts on this guitar were slightly loose.

The Grovers are tensionable and should be loosened for string changes and retightened for a comfortable working setting. This requires a Phillips No.0 driver.

A little graphite from a pencil tip will keep the strings moving at the nut when tuning.

Under the hood

■ The top bracing is a variant on the classic X-bracing, with hand-scalloped radiused top bracing offering added strength and a lighter top. The X-brace has an unusual triangular section.

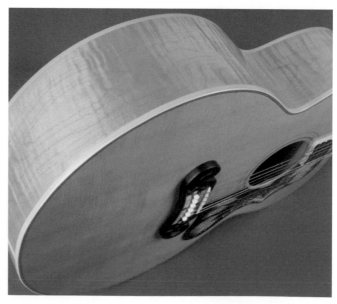

■ All acoustics produced by Gibson in Bozeman, Montana, have a radiused or 'tuned' top, this is slightly raised, and a special instrument is used to shape the top braces to the top radius. This process adds tension and strengthens the top, creating a less stressful joint where the top meets the sides and reducing the stresses of string pull. It also results in a 'speaker cone' effect that maximises sound projection, adding a significant boost to mid-range levels for a more balanced acoustic tone.

■ The back of the guitar has four parallel end-scalloped braces – two 'normal' 7.4mm ones at the top bout and two huge 17.5mm ones across the lower bout – a curved centre splice and a mahogany end block, all of which are visible through the soundhole.

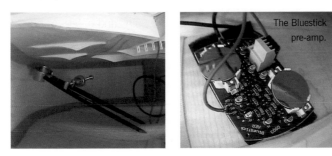

The Bluestick pre-amp.

■ The substantial bracing pattern is the same as used in Gibson's first Super Jumbo in 1937, constructed both to support and strengthen the very large surface and to allow the top more freedom of movement to vibrate and project sound. The kerfed edge supports are also fairly lightweight.

■ All the interior woodwork is wisely left unfinished. The exterior is finished in nitrocellulose lacquer, which is porous when cured, allowing the wood to 'breathe' naturally and mature. The microscopically thin finish involves seven main coats of lacquer. After drying overnight, these initial seven layers are then level sanded and given two additional coats. After being left to dry for five additional days the finish is wet sanded and buffed to its final glass-like sheen. This time-consuming process has been employed since 1894. A nitro finish means there's less interference with the natural vibration of the instrument, allowing for a purer tone. It's also a softer finish, making it easily repairable. You can touch-up a scratch or ding on a nitro finish, but you can't do the same on a poly finish.

Electrics

The guitar has been retro fitted with a Bluestick active transducer, a miniaturised equivalent of a studio-grade condenser microphone element under the guitar's saddle. Bluestick claim that this is the first acoustic guitar transducer to actually reproduce the sound of a

guitar instead of merely *recreating* it via imprecise piezo-ceramic mechanics. A couple of shims are required under the saddle to accommodate the centre connection of the capacitor.

The unusual centre mounting location.

In theory this unit should give an extended frequency response, more 'detail', and up to 30dB more dynamic range than piezos.

One-thousandth the weight of a piezo, the miniaturised electrostatic condenser microphone has a moving mass of just 0.0014mg. Being so light it can respond to the incredibly subtle harmonic vibrations that determine the sound of a guitar.

Offering up to 10dB more volume before feedback, the Bluestick microphone element is housed in an hermetically sealed sound chamber just two-tenths of a millimetre thick. This acoustic resonator evenly collects sound from each string and delivers it to the transducer via a logarithmically-scaled high pressure zone at the centre.

The microphone is linked to a micro-'Class A' preamp module claiming over 1,000 hours' playing time between lithium battery changes and an ingenious sound wheel that allows quick volume changes from just inside the soundhole. The retro-fit necessitated just one small hole to be drilled under the guitar's saddle. The unit also has a two-band adjustable EQ accessed at the soundhole thumbwheels.

The unit does work quite well, with the perhaps expected HF bias of a condenser system. This can be adjusted at the amp or PA to give a very convincing amplified acoustic tone.

Signed off

This is a wonderful Gibson with beautifully finished A1 materials, resulting in a very responsive guitar.

The intonation is reasonable, especially for first position chords. More accurate higher position tuning *could* be achieved by custom filing the saddle. A great guitar, however, which makes you want to play! The perfect guitar, in fact, for those 'Black Leather Elvis' moments, maybe *That's Alright Mama* from the '68 TV special?

British-made Maccaferri Selmer-style 'Model Orchestre' Gypsy Jazz

Serial No 252

A classic Quintette du Hot Club de France rhythm guitar as used by the Ferre Brothers and many others. Made in England in October 2009 by Belleville Guitars' luthier John Vickers, it is a very authentic development of the early Maccaferri-designed Grand Bouche guitar used by the rhythm section of the Hot Club Quintet in the 1930s. The greatest exponent of Gypsy Jazz, Django Reinhardt, also played this type of guitar but finally switched to the Petit Bouche version.

Ideal for

Gypsy Jazz enthusiasts, particularly rhythm guitarists, though this specific guitar has 14 frets to the body like the Petit Bouche so may also suit soloists. Luthier John Vickers tells me that Django didn't have a Petit Bouche until 1940, so most of the Hot Club Quintet material was in fact recorded on the Grand Bouche!

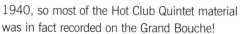

Signature tone woods

A European solid spruce bookmatched soundboard. Period-correct laminated rosewood back and sides, all of which (apart from the top) is authentically varnished internally, plus an ebony bridge with period-correct glued-on 'moustache'.

Condition on arrival

This particular guitar had suffered a neck fracture in transit (see page 80). The repair has set well and the neck is now very stable. The guitar comes in a very solid white hardshell case. All the appointments are very authentic.

General description

This guitar has the classic *early* Selmer Maccaferri shape and size, specifically 40cm lower bout, 29.5cm upper bout (very similar to a flat-top Dreadnought) with a narrow 26.25cm waist. There is no scratchplate and the solid European spruce top is 3.5mm at the soundhole with a noticeable pliage. The body bindings are ebony with white-black-white purfling.

■ The traditional Selmer horizontal cutaway gives good access to the higher frets.

■ The characteristic large 'D' soundhole is 15cm x 6.75cm (max), with a traditional multiple rosette surround.

■ The beautiful 47cm back (6cm shorter than a Dreadnought) is authentically crafted from laminated rosewood.

■ The sides are also three-ply laminated rosewood/poplar/mahogany.

■ The three-piece bridge is an ebony 'moustache' with a removable centre section supplied in two heights. The strings are secured with traditional 'banjo' loops though provision is made for ball-end types on the authentic brass and rosewood-decorated tailpiece.

■ The guitar weighs a moderate 4.75lb (2.15kg), about the same as the average modern Dreadnought, and is tapered a shallow 9cm deep at the neck and only 10cm at the end pin with a very slight pliage to the back.

■ The back of the neck has a slim flat profile very like an expensive classic guitar, there are an unusual (for a Grand Bouche) 14 frets to the body. The scale length is a very long 67.5cm (a typical 12-fret Dreadnought is 64.5cm).

■ The unbound solid mahogany neck has an ebony fingerboard and a traditional dovetail body joint. The fingerboard has simple abalone dot markers at V / VII / X / XII. The frets are substantial 2.6mm gauge and beautifully dressed and polished. There are 22 full frets and a part extension gives 26 on the first string, giving top F# above the extra octave, and top C on the second string. The fingerboard radius is a flattish 15in (38.1cm).

■ There is no (intended!) headstock joint and the headstock angle is 11.5°. The headstock carries the Belleville 'Vintage Strings' logo and the Ferre Brothers' endorsement, all in gold against an ebony veneer. The 45mm nut has an authentic zero fret.

■ The very unusual and complex machine heads follow the original 1930s design exactly, and like the brass tailpiece draw on Selmer's skills in working brass for their wind instruments. The machines have two separate back plates and individual removable covers for each worm gear with 12 individual ferrules! They're secured with sixteen 2.5mm straight-slot screws and eight 5mm screws, all in brass – a novel feat of early 20th-century engineering. Luthier John Vickers recommends that the concave worm gear, with three threads in contact at a time, needs lots of grease inside the enclosure – and this is currently the case!

The Belleville brand

The Selmer guitar originally designed by Mario Maccaferri has become synonymous with the 1930s work of the Hot Club Quintet of France. The brief to Mario – a renowned classical guitarist – was to design a LOUD guitar for the new Jazz that had arrived in Paris during the First World War. He responded with a radical design that blended archtop violin principles, flat-top appearance and an unusual cutaway. These guitars were made in very small numbers – a few hundred – so there is a burgeoning demand for soundalikes, fulfilled by enthusiasts like John Vickers.

Django's last 'Petit Bouche'.

Specific routine maintenance

Setting the action: there is no need for a capo due to the 'zero' fret! – just stop the string at the last fret and check the neck relief with your feeler gauges. The neck should have some relief, perhaps .010–.015 at the seventh fret sixth string for light picking and a good deal more for hard Manouche 'Pompe'. This guitar *does* have an adjustable truss rod, unlike the originals. The adjustment is made from inside the soundhole.

Bridge height adjustment is in the first instance a case of swapping the centre section of the bridge; the current one is set at 17.8mm and the second is set at 20.2mm – probably 'rhythm' and 'solo' settings? Note that the two end sections are glued directly to the guitar top. Beyond swapping the middle section I would suggest getting a luthier to carefully trim the top of the hollowed low mass bridge. A further complication is the piezo pickup connection (see below), which would need removing and refixing in the higher bridge.

The strings on this guitar are 'Argentine'-type authentic 1930s Gypsy Jazz strings now made by Picato gauges, .011–.045in with a wound third. Specific Gypsy Jazz strings are also available from D'Addario, though these are not supplied with loop ends.

When changing strings it's worth checking the machine head fixing screws, which tend to work loose. On the Belleville this requires a 2.5mm jewellers' driver and a 4mm straight-slot. Do not overtighten these soft brass screws – just enough to stop the machine head moving in normal use.

A little graphite from a pencil tip will keep the strings moving at the nut when tuning.

A light polish of the frets with a Dunlop light abrasive once in a while will make for very smooth string bends – note the ebony protected with some masking tape. A little Dunlop system 01 and 02 will also clean and condition the fingerboard.

Whilst you have the tools out it's worth tightening the end pin – this is also the output for the internal piezo. A cosmetic ferrule disguises a 12mm nut that also retains the tailpiece, which is further secured by two 4mm straight-slots. When in position a green felt protector keeps the tailpiece off the body. When replacing the retaining nut a jewellers' screwdriver through the thread pin keeps the output jack from revolving.

Under the hood

The earliest Maccaferri guitars had his version of the Turnovaz internal resonator system but this was discontinued following Mario's departure from Selmers.

■ The top of this Belleville has five substantial transverse braces, four of which are 9mm wide and under the body of the top, with a heavier 14mm one close to the neck – our videoscope photo shows three of these. Incidentally, Django's Petit Bouche had four braces, not five, though John Vickers has tried this and ended up with too much bass. This may provide a clue to Django's rich tone – far more resonant than most Gypsy Jazz guitars offer.

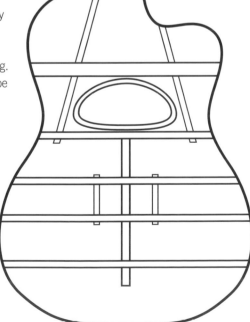

■ The guitar has very sturdy 14.5mm side supports with inverted kerfing. This videoscope image shows the end of the truss rod.

■ The back of the guitar has three very substantial 10.8mm transverse braces. The interior woodwork of the back and sides is heavily lacquered with two-part lacquer – this and the fact that the grain isn't filled contributes to the guitar's weight and tone.

■ It's worth checking occasionally for any loose braces; with time and humidity changes these can come unglued, resulting in warping of the top – an expensive fault to repair. Loose braces often produce a rattle that's easily detected. However, it's not always this obvious. Another symptom is a loss of bass response – the guitar sounds inexplicably 'thin'. A gentle check once in a while can save an expensive repair.

Electrics

Though a vintage-type guitar it nevertheless has simple transducer electrics consisting of a piezo device taped inside the hollow centre bridge section. This is routed directly to the output jack without any intervening preamp, thus an external preamp such as the L.R. Baggs unit on page 108 would be needed to give access to EQ and anti-feedback measures.

such as the L.R. Baggs unit on page 108

Signed off

This is a fascinating guitar that produces a very distinct, almost brass-like timbre, and the electronics with a preamp do a good job of amplifying the distinct Belleville voice.

A Petit Bouche version is also now available.

All are set up personally by John Vickers before shipping in the custom and stylish Belleville Hiscox case. They're supplied with a 12-month manufacturers' warranty.

Chinese-made 'Roy Orbison' Epiphone 'Bard' FT-112 12-string

Released 23 April 2009, on what would have been Roy Orbison's 73rd birthday, this particular guitar is based on the 1962 Epiphone 'Bard' 12-string on which Orbison wrote and recorded many of his early hits, including *Pretty Woman*, written in 1963 with his friend and fellow Texan Bill Dees.

Serial Nos 0908171 271 & 288

Ideal for
An affordable 'vintage vibe' 12-string for home studios and a useful composing aid.

Signature tone woods
This tribute model features a solid spruce top and two-piece bookmatched solid mahogany back. The sides are five-ply laminated mahogany.

Condition on arrival

Sadly the first of these Bards (serial number 271) arrived with a broken headstock, courtesy of an accident in transit; hence this is the guitar seen in the wide shot photography. The close-ups are of a second guitar that Gibson kindly supplied (serial number 288). This is a good example of a Dreadnought 12-string in the Gibson B45 mould.

The guitar comes in a custom five-ply hardshell case with Roy's signature, a signed photograph of Roy with the original 'Bard', and a certificate signed by Roy's widow Barbara and Roy Orbison junior. The package also includes a Roy Orbison 'Sunglasses' badge and a copy of the sheet music for *Pretty Woman*.

■ The neck, constructed from three pieces of mahogany, has a very slim U profile with a tapered heel. The scale length is a shortish 63cm.

■ The headstock joint is very slim and the headstock angle is a very shallow 11°.

■ The unbound rosewood fingerboard has simple plastic dots at III / V / VII / IX / XII and XV. The frets are medium 2.49mm gauge and in need of a polish. There are 20 frets, giving top C. The fingerboard radius is a fairly curvy 10in (25.4cm).

General description

The guitar has a classic Dreadnought 'square-shouldered' shape and size, specifically 40cm lower bout, 29cm upper bout, with a 27.5cm waist (identical to the 12-fret Martin Dreadnought). The brown-flecked plastic scratchplate is attached directly to the 3.3mm solid Sitka spruce top and has the classic Epiphone 'e' in silver. The back and sides have a cream PVC binding and four coats of urethane 'clear coat'.

■ The round 10cm soundhole is decorated with four simple black rings and the 51cm back is crafted from two-piece bookmatched mahogany.

■ The sides are five-ply laminated mahogany.

■ The bridge is rosewood with a fairly complex custom-filed compensated plastic saddle with the expected slant towards a 'shorter scale' treble. The strings are secured with white plastic bridge pins.

■ The guitar weighs 5lb (2.27kg), not heavy for a 12-string, and is tapered from 9.5cm at the neck and 12cm at the 'end pin', with a very slight arch to the back.

■ The headstock has a black veneer, a plastic inlay and carries a version of the classic Epiphone logo. The 48.1mm nut is plastic and needs a bit of work.

■ The machine heads are Kluson-type copies. Note the Orbison signature and the notated *Pretty Woman* riff.

Epiphone and Gibson

The Epiphone company has an older heritage than Gibson, dating back to 1873. During the 1930s and '40s Gibson and Epiphone were arch-rivals – the guitar world's Pepsi and Coke! However, in 1957 Gibson acquired the older Greek family company and remains the proud custodian of this additional great marque. In recent years Gibson have reissued many of the great Epiphone models, including Paul McCartney's 'Texan' and John Lennon's 'Casino'.

Specific routine maintenance

Setting the action: With a capo at the first fret to take the nut out of the equation and the string stopped at the last fret, check the neck relief with your feeler gauges. The neck should have some relief, perhaps .010–.015 at the seventh fret sixth string for light strumming and slightly more for hard *Pretty Woman* riffs. If the neck relief does need adjustment the 12-string requires a 4mm truss rod wrench (the Stewmac types are easier to handle than a hardware-store Allen – see *Useful contacts* appendix.

Follow the set-up guide on pages 64 and 70 for any saddle-height and nut adjustment. Bear in mind that the 12-string nut requires very careful filing – the high octaves usually found on the third to sixth courses being up to 0.5mm thinner than the low octaves. The two strings need to sit at the same 'floor height' in the slot but have very different width requirements to avoid sticking. Some of these slots are currently overtight, contributing to tuning instability.

The current strings on this guitar are phosphor bronze .010–.047, and it would be unwise to try anything heavier on this narrow-necked 12-string, especially at concert pitch. However, acoustic 12-string guitars are best tuned down to D or even C for a good bass response, and for that to work then appropriate strings would have to be sought – perhaps .012 for the first according to John Diggins. (See *The Luthier's Handbook* by Roger H. Siminoff for his string gauge calculator and more on this very specific challenge.)

When changing strings it's worth checking the machine head fixing screws, which tend to work loose. On the Epiphone this requires a No.1 Phillips at the back. Do not overtighten these screws– just enough to stop the machine head moving in normal use. Perhaps due to post-assembly wood shrinkage all the screws and nuts on this guitar were extremely loose.

A little graphite from a pencil tip will keep the strings moving at the nut when tuning. Graphite dust mixed with ChapStick or Vaseline is another solution.

A little lemon oil will clean the rosewood fingerboard following a necessary fret polish.

Always examine the string retaining pins for wear – good tone depends on a correct fit and the correct break angle at the bridge. Excessive wear at the bridge string contact point needs professional attention. The current set-up on this guitar is fine. A jammed pin needs careful extraction, with some masking tape protecting the bridge and cushioned pliers for the pins as they're both easily marked or broken.

Whilst you have the tools out it's worth tightening the end pin – this requires a No.1 Phillips.

Under the hood

■ The truss rod access is at the headstock and requires a 4mm Allen wrench for any relief adjustment (see page 62 for more on neck relief and adjustment).

■ The 12-string has heavily hand-scalloped X-bracing.

■ There is also an extra upper bout parallel brace and two top soundhole braces, and there are extra 'belly' braces behind the bridge. The guitar has a traditional dovetail neck-joint secured with Franklin Titebond 50 adhesive.

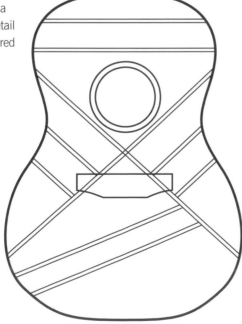

■ The back of the guitar has a centre splice and four substantial 8.5mm heavily tapered ladder braces, all of which are visible with the videoscope. These have substantially less mass than the six-string Yamaha 310 Dreadnought braces. The kerfed side supports are slim and tapered.

■ All the interior woodwork is wisely left unfinished.

■ It's worth checking occasionally for any loose braces; with time and humidity changes these can come unglued, resulting in warping of the top – an expensive fault to repair. Loose braces often produce a rattle that's easily detected. However, it's not always this obvious – my own 1960s B45 suffered some loose braces and the symptom was a loss of bass response. The guitar sounded inexplicably 'thin'. A gentle check once in a while can save an expensive repair.

■ This vintage-type guitar naturally has no transducer electrics.

Signed off

A very traditional 12-string originally manufactured for the folk boom of the mid-1960s. With a little nut work it will be a reasonable guitar. But take care over that very thin headstock/ neck area – my own B45 broke at exactly the same point as the first version we received of this one. For me 12-strings are better tuned down to C, putting less tension on the table and the neck and also giving a fatter sound.

Indonesian-made Yamaha ³/₄-size 'CS 40' Classic Guitar

Serial No ONJ014400

Made circa 2009, this nylon-strung classic is a small but working guitar for small hands. It's the perfect instrument for a seven to eleven-year-old working with a teacher in a small group situation, as found in many schools. The nylon strings are kind to small fingers and the tone is good enough for a school concert. An ideal guitar for the early 'classical' grade student.

The CS 40 is very similar to the Yamaha full-size Classic CG 122MS featured on page 126. However, the guitar provides a scaled-down instrument for junior beginners and anybody else with small hands. I have never seen a nylon-strung guitar cheaper than this that is actually a musical instrument as opposed to a toy.

A note to parents

A pupil with the right-size guitar, accurately fretted, tuneable and with a decent tone, *will* progress. Those without such guitars usually give up! I say this as a qualified teacher who has seen this happen too many times.

My own first guitar was poorly set up and had the wrong strings – I gave up aged nine! I fortunately started again aged 12 when by chance a schoolteacher spotted the problem guitar and helped me sort it out.

Please DO NOT buy children's guitars from thrift stores and Internet chains unless you're an expert and can spot a true bargain.

General description

This spruce-top guitar has the classic Torres shape but is proportionally smaller, specifically 34cm lower bout, 26cm upper bout, with a 22cm waist (about 2cm smaller all round).

■ The one-piece 45cm back (4cm shorter) is from two-piece laminate meranti.

■ The 8.2cm sides enlarge to 9cm at the lower bout. The sides are also meranti two-piece laminate. The guitar is faux bound in black.

■ The rosewood bridge has a plastic saddle with some lone compensation for the G string intonation.

■ The guitar weighs a very light child-friendly 2.75lb (1.25kg).

■ The three-piece nato neck has a traditional U profile with a fairly flat and comfortable back and the usual 12 frets to the body. The scale length is approx 58cm (7cm shorter than a standard Classic guitar) with 18 full frets and a 19th part-fret giving top B on the first and sixth strings.

■ The rosewood fingerboard traditionally has no inlays but a discreet side dot at VII will be appreciated by students. The frets are 2mm gauge shaped quite low and in need of a fret polish.

■ The 48mm nut is plastic – considerably narrower than the classic size and a good aid for young beginners. The three-a-side machine heads are very lightweight stamped steel.

Setting up

The CS 40 presents some small set-up issues that are likely to be of interest and are a feature of virtually every 'beginner's' guitar:

■ **Playability**

As with virtually every economy guitar the nut is too high and inaccurately cut – this is easily fixed (see page 64).

The saddle could also be lower to help a beginner fret the strings in the first position (see page 70).

■ **Tunability**

The nut and machine heads will last longer with light lubrication (see pages 58 and 65) and may benefit from an upgrade.

■ **String care and stable tuning**

Economy guitars always come with economy strings, so it's always worth having good and correct gauge strings fitted. D'Addario now do specific three-quarter scale strings. These aid intonation and tone when it's needed most – at the patience-trying 'first steps' stage.

Once the new strings are fitted wipe them down *after every playing* with a lint-free cotton cloth. They will then last for six months as opposed to six weeks. Neglected strings sound bad and are impossible to tune, a disincentive to any young player.

Signed off

A fine beginner's instrument. All you need now is a small dollop of talent and a huge dollop of perseverance – *five minutes a day and you will learn to play!*

NB: This guitar size is perfect for the average five to eleven-year-old. For younger children of five to seven years there are currently some excellent one-eighth size guitars coming out of the Czech Republic, manufactured by Strunal. Due to their small scale these will also need some setting up and custom gauge strings from Dr Junger (www.dr-junger-saten.de) in order to function 'in tune'.

British-made Fylde 'Ariel' parlour-size steel-string guitar

Serial No 80488

A classic '12 frets to the body' slotted headstock guitar made by craftsman luthier Roger Bucknall in Fylde, Lancashire. This particular instrument is a good example of his smaller steel string guitar, similar to those made in the USA in the early part of the 20th century. It is approximately 10% smaller than the regular Dreadnought and the body proportions are more like a late period Torres Spanish guitar.

With a lightly braced table specifically designed for light fingerpicking the guitar has no scratchplate. The guitar is a favourite of The Who's Pete Townshend.

Ideal for

This is the perfect guitar for the discerning steel string fingerpicker looking for a good professional acoustic for recording applications. It would be a shame to carve it up for acoustic electric work, as you could get similar results 'plugged' by other (and possibly cheaper) means.

Signature tone woods

West African sapele is used for the back and sides, a wood reminiscent of mahogany with a distinctive figure. The top timber is Western red cedar and the neck construction is one-piece Honduras mahogany with an ebony bridge.

Condition on arrival

With 'modern' X-bracing, this is a good example of a 12 frets to the body traditional non-cutaway guitar. It comes in a Hiscox Liteflite hardshell case. On arrival it was soon obvious that the saddle was set too low and Roger immediately dispatched a couple of shims to correct this.

General description

This guitar has a distinctive small and 'bottom heavy' shape, specifically 36cm lower bout, 24cm upper bout, with a 21cm waist.

■ The round 10cm soundhole is decorated with three concentric inlays.

■ The beautiful two-piece 47cm back is crafted from sapele.

■ The tapered sides are also sapele, 9.5cm at the heel and 11cm at the end pin.

■ The bridge is ebony, with a very simple uncompensated bone saddle with the expected slant towards a 'shorter scale' treble. The strings are secured with black plastic white dot decorated bridge pins.

■ The guitar weighs a light 3.5lb (1.59kg), a pound lighter than the average modern Dreadnought.

■ The neck is constructed in one-piece Honduras mahogany with an integral slotted headstock and 12 frets to the body.

■ There is no headstock joint but there is a strengthening 'volute' to the headstock taper, which doesn't actually cause any playing obstruction. The headstock angle is a useful 14°.

■ The unbound ebony fingerboard has no decoration but some simple dot markers on the side at III / V / VII / IX / XII / XV and XVII. The frets are narrow 2mm gauge and beautifully dressed and polished. There are 19 frets – top B like a classic Spanish guitar. The fingerboard virtual radius is a flattish 16in (40.6cm).

■ The slotted headstock, which is lighter and contributes to the balance of the guitar, carries the attractive medieval Fylde logo, gold on an ebony veneer. The wide 46.1mm nut is a nicely cut piece of yellowing bone, 5mm narrower than a classic Spanish guitar but significantly wider than many Dreadnoughts (though the Judy Collins is 45.9mm) Most significantly the Fylde has a zero fret – maker luthier Roger Bucknall told me: 'From my point of view, the zero fret is not a short-cut in manufacturing, in fact it takes longer than a standard nut to do properly. It is an attempt to give all the notes on the fingerboard a similar tonal quality. Having the six open notes defined in a different way to all the other possible notes doesn't make any sense to me.

'Some of the strings are very stiff compared to others, and this affects the intonation and harmonic content for each string in a different way. By having the open strings lie against a fret in the same way as every fretted note rather than in a tight-fitting nut slot, the string stiffness is less of a factor. Intonation and "harmonicity" are improved. Harmonicity is the relationship of one harmonic or partial to another, and only when all of the harmonics and partials are in a clear simple mathematical relationship does the note sound pure.'

Interestingly the Gypsy Jazz guitar described on page 146 also features a zero fret.

■ The slotted headstock has gold-plated three-a-side Gotohs with marbled plastic buttons.

Spanish-made Ramírez cypress Flamenco guitar model F656A

Signed by Amalia Ramírez and manufactured at No 8 Calle de La Paz, Madrid, in 2009, this particular guitar is a standard edition traditional Flamenco guitar with modern machine heads rather than wooden pegs. All Ramírez professional guitars are built in Ramírez's small artisan workshop under the direct supervision and participation of Amalia Ramírez, who also inspects each instrument once finished.

Ideal for
The serious flamenco student.

Signature tone woods
The combination of cypress and cedar gives this instrument its unique bright percussive flamenco sound.

Condition on arrival

This is a new example of the current Flamenco-type guitar as manufactured by the distinguished luthier family of Ramírez. It comes in a custom hardshell Hiscox case with the Ramírez logo. The guitar is also available in an Indian rosewood 'Negri' version and the top is optionally spruce or cedar.

General description

This guitar has the classic shape and size, specifically 37cm lower bout, 28cm upper bout, with a 24cm waist (slightly wider than our Ramírez Classic). Two transparent plastic golpeadores are attached directly to the spruce top, protecting the guitar from the vigorous and rhythmic rasgeudo. The small 8.25cm soundhole is decorated with an elaborate set of inlays.

■ The guitar weighs a light 3lb (1.36kg) – extremely light, enabling balance in the traditional flamenco playing position.

■ The three-piece neck has a traditional U profile with a separate heel unusually sculptured both outside and inside and with the usual 12 frets to the body. The scale length is approx 65.6cm with 18 full frets and a 19th part-fret giving top B on the first string.

■ The beautiful two-piece 49cm back is bookmatched from cypress with an elegant black splice veneer and heel decoration with a very slight tension arch.

■ The 9.5cm parallel sides are also cypress with inlayed edge binding front and back.

■ The bridge is rosewood with an unusual rear extension. The saddle is a simple piece of bone, not entirely seated at the treble side. The strings are secured traditionally in a knot.

■ There is a separate headstock joint resulting in a headstock angle of a substantial 17°.

■ The 53mm nut is a well-cut piece of bone.

■ The traditional flat ebony fingerboard has no inlays or position markers and the frets are medium 2.16mm gauge shaped to a high crown and in need of a finishing polish.

■ The slotted headstock carries the distinctive Ramírez shape and a rosewood cap.

■ The three-a-side Sintessi Pro machine heads are beautifully made by Exagon and gold-finished, with Ramírez crested buttons and nylon bushings. The gearing ratio is 18:1.

The Ramírez dynasty

José Ramírez of Galarreta and Planell was born in Madrid in 1858. At the age of 12 he began working as an apprentice in the workshop of Francisco González. In 1890 he established himself at Concepción Jerónima Nº 2, where his descendants continued to build guitars until 1995. It was José's brother Manuel who gave Andrés Segovia his first serious guitar. The dynasty continued with José Ramírez II, III and IV.

The team at Casa Ramírez currently comprises 14 people, led by Amalia Ramírez, sister of José IV, who began her apprenticeship under the direction of their father in 1976. The workshop employs three professional Level 1 guitar makers (Carmelo Llorena, Fernando Morcuende and Ricardo Sáenz); one professional Level 2 guitar maker (Samuel Pérez) and three apprentices (Gabriel Saar, Fernando García Mauriño and Enrique Ramírez). Our Case Study guitars were supplied by the Classical Guitar Centre Ltd UK and Josef's Pianos, Rothwell.

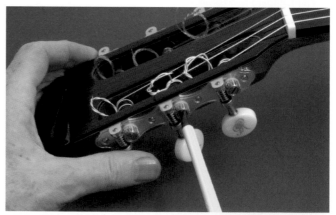

Specific routine maintenance

Setting the action: The action on a Flamenco guitar is traditionally set low as a little fret rattle is idiomatic to the 'falsettos'. This new guitar has sensibly been set a little high, allowing the player to decide his preference.

With a capo at the first fret to take the nut out of the equation and the string stopped at the last fret, check the neck relief with your feeler gauges. The neck should have some relief for acoustic volume, perhaps .008–.010 at the seventh fret sixth string, but this is a matter of taste. Naturally the guitar has no truss rod.

See the nut and saddle work guides on pages 64 and 70 for any saddle height and nut adjustment, but allowing a little more fret rattle than a classical player would tolerate.

The strings on this guitar are .029–.045 medium tension monofilament one to three and wound-on nylon four to six.

When changing strings it's worth checking the machine head fixing screws, which tend to work loose. On the Ramírez this requires a 4mm straight-slot. The bushing cogs require a very slim-bladed 5mm straight-slot. Do not overtighten – just enough

to stop the machine head moving in normal use.

A little graphite from a pencil tip will keep the strings moving at the nut when tuning.

A little lemon oil will clean the fingerboard.

Interior shot of the elaborate heel.

Periodically examine the saddle – good tone depends on a correct fit and avoiding any gaps between bridge and saddle. Also the intonation will be upset by any tendency to 'lean' from the vertical. The current set-up on this guitar is excellent apart from a gap beneath the treble-side saddle. A good secure string knot is essential if the guitar is to hold its pitch.

Under the hood

The top of the guitar has a variant on traditional Torres fan-strutting with a sculpted block and a Spanish heel neck joint.

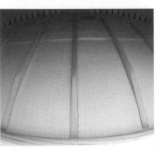

■ The back of the guitar has *three* parallel 6mm hardwood tapered ladder braces and an ellipse centre splice, all of which are just visible through the soundhole.

■ All the interior woodwork is wisely left unfinished.

■ It's worth checking occasionally for any loose braces; with time and humidity changes these can come unglued, resulting in warping of the top – an expensive fault to repair. Loose braces often produce a rattle that's easily detected. However, it's not always this obvious. Another symptom is a loss of bass response – the guitar sounds inexplicably 'thin'. A gentle check once in a while can save an expensive repair.

■ This traditional-type guitar naturally has no transducer electrics.

Signed off

This is a testament to the Ramírez heritage – beautifully finished A1 materials that result in a wonderfully responsive guitar. The intonation is accurate throughout. A good guitar that makes you want to play every Phrygian phrase you can muster!

NB: The Negri rosewood version has contoured rather than scalloped bracing, contributing to the necessary extra strength. Ramírez also offer urea or shellac finish, and traditional wooden pegs are also available, replacing the modern machine heads.

USA-made 'Eric Clapton' Martin 000-28EC 'Orchestral Model'

Serial No 15379
neck stamp 1345038

Made in Nazareth, Pennsylvania, and signed by Eric Clapton and C.F. Martin IV, this classic 14 frets to the body 'Orchestral Model' guitar is one of the six 'Eric Clapton' Martin models that have been made.

This one is based on Eric's own vintage 1939 0042 and is similar to the Limited Edition 000-42EC introduced in 1995. Just 461 of these special guitars were offered, and the edition sold out within days of its introduction. A further run of 500 ECBs in Brazilian rosewood were also immediately snapped up.

A turning point for the Martin Company, these signature editions were a direct result of the Eric Clapton MTV *Unplugged* show recorded on 16 January 1992 at Bray Film Studios in Windsor, England. Eric's 00042 has since gone on to inspire more signature editions than any other Martin. Ironically the original gut-strung style '42' of circa 1870 cost $42! Originally conceived as a plectrum 'Orchestral Model' this 1930s development of the style '42' has found popularity with many fingerstyle guitarists and is branded inside with the familiar Martin 'Nazareth PA'.

Ideal for
Avid collectors, but deserves to be played. It would acquit itself well in the studio for almost any steel string work, plectrum or fingerstyle. Andy Fairweather Low's personal version of this guitar is one of most responsive guitars I have ever played – it is played every night on extensive tours and this is clear in the sound.

Signature tone woods
Naturally this is a 'solid wood' guitar; East Indian rosewood, quarter-sawn Sitka spruce and ebony.

Condition on arrival

This is a good example of an update on Martin's original 14-fret OM design developed in the 1930s. The guitar comes in a Deluxe Vintage Series Geib-style hardshell case, featuring the vintage shape, deep textured black exterior, five-ply laminated wood shell, vintage green crushed velvet interior, antique white stitching, brass plated hardware, and a keyed lock.

General description

This guitar has a classic square-shouldered OM shape and size, specifically 38.5cm lower bout, 29cm upper bout, with a distinctive narrow 24cm waist. The tortoise-effect plastic teardrop scratchplate is attached directly to the one-piece solid Sitka spruce top. The top is 3.5mm thick at the soundhole.

■ The round 9.75cm soundhole is decorated with a rosette of finely patterned herringbone wood marquetry.

■ The two-piece bookmatched back is short (in comparison to a Dreadnought) at 49cm and is crafted from solid East India rosewood with a herringbone joint inlay.

■ The sides are also solid rosewood and bound with grained ivoroid.

■ The ebony bridge has a custom-filed compensated bone saddle with the expected slant towards a 'shorter scale' treble. The strings are secured with black dotted fossil ivory pins.

■ The guitar weighs a very light 4.25lb (1.93kg) and is tapered from a slim 8.5cm deep at the neck to 10cm at the end pin, with a gentle arch to the back.

■ The unspecified hardwood one-piece neck has a vintage V profile similar to the shape Eric likes on his Strats. The scale length is a short 63.5cm.

■ The headstock joint results in the distinctive Martin volute which doesn't actually cause any playing obstruction. The headstock angle is a useful 14°.

■ The ebony fingerboard features the pre-war Style 28 snowflake pattern in abalone pearl. Eric Clapton's signature is CNC inlaid in mother of pearl between the 19th and 20th frets; these are medium 2mm gauge and beautifully dressed and polished. There are 20 frets giving top C. The fingerboard virtual radius is a flattish 16in (40.6cm).

■ The squared headstock bears Martin's tasteful but elegant 'old style' decal logo.

■ The synthetic bone 45.2mm nut is beautifully cut – all of the slots follow the string break angle. This will aid tuning stability.

■ Vintage-style individual nickel-plated open-geared tuning machines are equipped with unique vintage Waverley-type 'butterbean' knobs.

Specific routine maintenance

Setting the action: With a capo at the first fret to take the nut out of the equation and the string stopped at the last fret, check the neck relief with your feeler gauges. The neck should have some relief, perhaps .010 at the seventh fret sixth string for light fingerpicking, slightly more for hard flatpicking. If the neck relief does need adjustment the Clapton requires a long-arm 5mm truss rod wrench – the Stewmac types are essential, as a hardware-store Allen will rarely reach the Martin 'key'. See *Useful contacts* appendix and illustration below.

Follow the nut and saddle set-up guides on pages 64 and 70 for any saddle height and nut adjustment.

The strings are Martin .011–.054 acoustic bronze SP and it would be unwise to try anything heavier on this lightly braced table.

When changing strings it's worth checking the machine head fixing screws, which tend to work loose. On the Clapton this requires a No.1 Phillips at the back and a ⅜in socket for the front locking nuts. Do not overtighten – just enough to stop the machine head moving in normal use. Due to wood shrinkage some of the screws and nuts on this guitar were slightly loose.

The Martin signature editions

Up until 1992 'if you played a Martin you paid for it – whoever you were!' I remember Chris Martin pointing this out to me personally in a studio in 1982 when he presented me with a free soundhole cut-out! However, the Clapton endorsement has opened a new door for Martin, introducing a whole new generation to the joys of traditional American guitars. There are now a range of signature guitars all steeped in tradition and with largely cosmetic nods to the endorsee.

A little graphite from a pencil tip will keep the strings moving at the nut when tuning. Graphite dust mixed with ChapStick or Vaseline is another solution.

A little lemon oil will clean the ebony fingerboard.

Always examine the string retaining pins for wear – good tone depends on a correct fit and the correct break angle at the bridge. Excessive wear at the bridge string contact point needs professional attention. The current set-up on this guitar is excellent. A jammed pin needs careful extraction using the lever slot found on most peg winders.

Whilst you have the tools out it's worth tightening the end pin – this is a traditional friction fit. The pin is grained ivoroid and the endpiece inlay is black/white Boltaron.

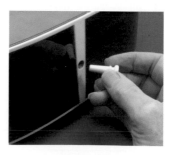

Under the hood

■ The truss rod access is via the soundhole and requires a Stewmac long-reach 5mm hex wrench for any relief adjustment. See page 62 for more on neck relief and adjustment.

■ The back of the guitar has one centre splice and four parallel lightweight 6.8mm wide end scalloped ladder braces, all of which are visible through the soundhole (these are over 2mm slimmer than the Yamaha 310 Dreadnought braces). The kerfed supports are 14mm wide but slim and tapered.

■ All the interior woodwork is wisely left unfinished.

■ It's worth checking occasionally for any loose braces; with time and humidity changes these can come unglued, resulting in warping of the top – an expensive fault to repair. Loose braces often produce a rattle that's easily detected. However, it's not always this obvious. Another symptom is a loss of bass response – the guitar sounds inexplicably 'thin'. A gentle check once in a while can save an expensive repair.

■ This vintage-type guitar naturally has no transducer electrics, though left-handed and transducer versions are available

■ The top bracing pattern is the standard Martin 000 14 frets to the body type.

■ This return to the past has 5/16in heavily scalloped X-bracing with an extra upper bout parallel brace and two top soundhole braces. There are also extra 'belly' braces behind the bridge. The neck has a traditional dovetail neck joint and block.

Signed off

This is a nice guitar – beautifully finished A1 materials and wonderfully responsive.

The intonation is accurate throughout. Another great guitar that makes you want to play! *'Before yer accuse me – take a good look at yerself!...'*

USA-made Taylor 614 CE
Grand Auditorium electro-acoustic

Serial No 20080717136

Signed by Bob Taylor, this particular guitar is a good example of his instruments, designed for amplification in a modern stage environment. It does, however, also have a good acoustic response, perhaps more reserved at the lower frequencies to intentionally minimise the acoustic feedback zone prevalent below 150Hz.

Ideal for

Professional 'plugged' acoustic work – everything from the pub band acoustic set to 'Live at The Hollywood Bowl'. It will work well both strummed and fingerpicked and has a 'balanced line out' capability for the PA guys to have a fighting chance of getting you a good acoustic-like tone.

Signature tone woods

Big leaf maple and Sitka spruce with an ebony fingerboard.

Condition on arrival

The guitar arrived beautifully set up and ready to go. It comes in a substantial hardshell plush-lined case.

General description

This guitar has a unique variant on the Grand Auditorium shape with a Venetian cutaway for those high spots in the music. Specifically the guitar has a 40cm lower bout, 29cm upper bout, with a 24cm waist. This is similar to the (non-cutaway) Martin 00028 'Clapton' but 2cm wider in the lower bout. The semi-transparent plastic scratchplate is attached directly to the 3mm solid Sitka spruce top.

■ The round 10cm soundhole is decorated with a very attractive abalone inner circle.

■ The two-piece 51cm back is crafted from bookmatched solid big leaf maple.

■ The three-piece hard rock maple NT neck has a slim U profile with a custom-tapered heel and gloss finish. The scale length is 64.8cm. See the accompanying boxout for more on NT necks.

■ The finger joint headstock results in an unobstructed playing area and the headstock angle is a useful 15°, giving plenty of tone-enhancing purchase at the nut.

■ The tapered sides are also solid big leaf maple, 9.5cm at the neck and 11.5cm at the end pin (considerably deeper than the Martin Clapton), giving a very slight 'arch' to the back.

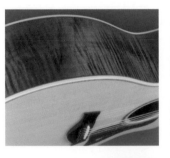

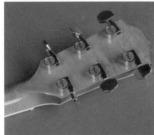

■ The bridge is ebony with a relatively simple second-string compensated Tusq saddle with the expected slant towards a 'shorter scale' treble. (Tusq is a patented artificial ivory made by the Canadian company Graph Tech.) The strings are secured with black plastic abalone-decorated bridge pins.

■ The guitar weighs a medium 5.25lb (2.38kg), heavier than some Dreadnoughts.

■ The fully-bound ebony fingerboard has tasteful pearl leaf markers. The frets are 2mm light gauge and beautifully dressed and polished. There are 20 complete frets giving us top C. The fingerboard radius is a flattish 15in (38.1cm).

■ The headstock carries the Taylor logo in pearl on a veneer of ebony. The 44.6mm nut is a beautifully cut piece of Tusq.

■ The screwed and bolted machine heads are Taylor gold-plated with matching knobs.

> 'It's an "acoustic" electric guitar neck – as an acoustic guitar maker I had always been jealous of electric makers because their neck didn't end at the 14th fret with sort of a floppy fretboard glued to a drum head of a guitar top!

Bob Taylor on the NT neck

The Taylor NT neck

The Taylor line of acoustic guitars has expanded the idea of the bolt-on neck originally tried by the Italian Luigi Mozzani of Cento and patented in 1912. A similar but much less sophisticated system was used by Fender in the 1970s and Bob Taylor tells me he first saw the idea on his own '70s Italian EKO guitar.

The Taylor system, however, has the advantage of modern CNC computer accuracy of cut and has the flexibility of interchangeable precision shims or spacers. Bob Taylor told me: 'You can't make an NT neck by hand – the accuracy required is integral to the CNC construction process.'

The neck spacers are available for specialist fitting at Taylor service centres and come in varying increments of two thousandths of an inch.

There are two shapes of spacer designed to fit perfectly in the top or side cavities for the utmost versatility of adjusted neck pitch to a tolerance of .039° from one shim to another.

Bob continued: 'This is a difficult neck to make because of the extreme tolerances. The spacer fitting and alignment is *not* intended as a DIY operation, as the finer detail of the neck-fit involves some putty-like caulking which Taylor dealers are trained in applying in very frugal amounts. Unless you're a trained repairman the area of acoustic neck pitch is probably best left to an expert.

'The virtuous aspect of this accuracy is to get the perfect neck angle *from the factory*!'

If problems arise all Taylor dealers are geared up to adjust the NT neck, so this shouldn't present an issue.

Specific routine maintenance

Setting the action: With a capo at the first fret to take the nut out of the equation and the string stopped at the last fret, check the neck relief with your feeler gauges. The neck should have some relief, perhaps .010 at the seventh fret sixth string for light fingerpicking, slightly more for hard bluegrass flatpicking. The Taylor is set quite low at .010. If the neck relief does need adjustment the Taylor requires a ¼in truss rod wrench (the Stewmac types are easier to handle than a bodged spanner – see *Useful contacts* appendix).

Follow the nut and saddle set-up guides on pages 64 and 70 for any saddle height and nut adjustment.

The strings on this guitar are Elixir Light Gauge with 'Nanoweb' coating. Bob Taylor says: 'Keep in mind that although the string gauges we factory-install at Taylor are optimised for a range of uses, there's room to adjust to suit your playing approach. We put light gauge strings on our Grand Concert and Grand Auditorium models, but you can use mediums (although we don't recommend it for models with cedar tops).'

When changing strings it's worth checking the machine head fixing screws, which tend to work loose. On the Taylor this requires a 10mm socket for the front locking nuts. Do not overtighten – just enough to stop the machine head moving in normal use. Due to wood shrinkage all the screws and nuts on this guitar were slightly loose.

The closed Taylor machines are tensionable and should be loosened for string changes and retightened for a comfortable working setting. This requires a No.1 Phillips.

A little graphite from a pencil tip will keep the strings moving at the nut when tuning. Planet Waves' Lubrikit is another solution.

A little ebony wax on the fingerboard will help avoid any drying shrinkage.

Always examine the string retaining pins for wear – good tone depends on a correct fit and the correct break angle at the bridge. Excessive wear at the bridge string contact point needs professional attention. The current set-up on this guitar is excellent as expected. A jammed pin needs careful extraction; the tool found on the end of many string winders is perfect – this coupled with pushing the old string into the hole usually works!

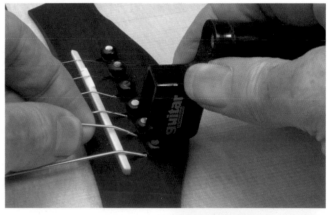

Whilst you have the tools out it's worth checking the end pin – this is integral to the battery compartment in a very neat arrangement. There's not much to go wrong here other than checking the Phillips No.1 retaining screws haven't worked loose. However, a neglected battery can cause havoc, so I recommend keeping the battery out of the guitar if the instrument is being left unused for any length of time.

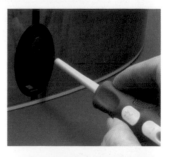

Under the hood

■ The truss rod access is at the headstock. Once the shield is removed with a No.1 Phillips the rod itself requires a ¼in wrench for any relief adjustment. See page 62 for more on neck relief and adjustment.

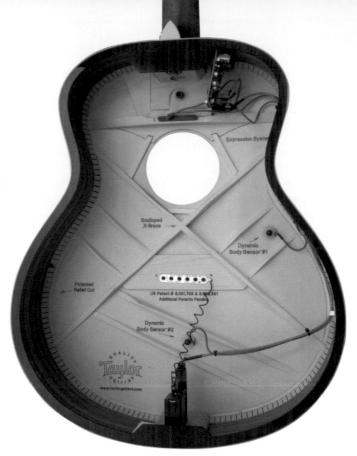

The Taylor story

Bob is unusual in that he came to luthiery not through an apprenticeship but simply as a young man who wanted a guitar and was practical enough to build one. 'I did it and felt "chosen" or driven to do that very thing!' This approach has the uninhibited freshness of radio repairman Leo Fender. Bob eventually evolved his own company in the mid-1970s in California – as Chris Martin puts it 'Every Coca Cola must have its Pepsi!'

Bob says: 'As any serious player will tell you, his or her acoustic guitar sounds different when it's amplified, and most would like for it to sound the same. I considered this a fundamental problem of the amplified acoustic guitar, and decided to focus on solving it.'

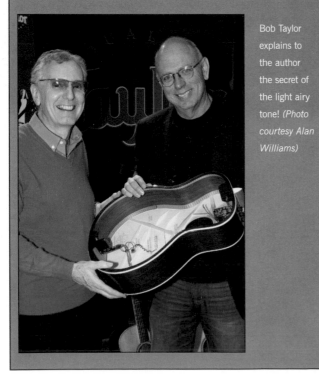

Bob Taylor explains to the author the secret of the light airy tone! *(Photo courtesy Alan Williams)*

■ The 614CE has what Taylor call Standard II ('Forward shifted pattern w/relief rout'). This means heavily scalloped X-bracing with an extra upper bout parallel strut and two top soundhole braces. There are also extra 'belly' struts behind the bridge, a small neck block and the Taylor NT neck joint. (**NB:** For practical reasons the shown guitar is a rosewood version but the bracing system is almost identical.)

■ The back of the guitar has centre splice and four lightweight (9.9mm wide) end scalloped ladder braces, all of which are visible through the soundhole (these are similar dimensions to the Yamaha 310 Dreadnought braces). The kerfed side supports are 14mm wide but slim and tapered.

■ All the interior woodwork is wisely left unfinished.

■ It's worth checking occasionally for any loose braces; with time and humidity changes these can come unglued, resulting in warping of the top – an expensive fault to repair. Loose braces often produce a rattle that's easily detected. However, it's not always this obvious. Another symptom is a loss of bass response – the guitar sounds inexplicably 'thin'. A gentle check once in a while can save an expensive repair.

Three simple, unobtrusive onboard control knobs preserve the aesthetic beauty of the Taylor, yet allow easy adjustment of the volume, bass and treble to suit personal preferences and performance environment. When set flat, the tone controls add no colouration and produce the most natural sound.

Players also have the ability to turn off one or both body sensors and rely on the neck pickup. This gives the player the ability to voice their guitar to suit the performance environment.

An on/off switch for each body sensor is easily accessible on the preamp circuit board inside the soundhole, so a player can make adjustments on the fly.

This Expression System is available exclusively on Taylor guitars in the 300 Series and above.

Electrics

This guitar has Taylor's own 'Expression System' transducer electrics. The Expression System incorporates three discreet moving coil sensors: two strategically placed 'Dynamic Body Sensors' affixed to the underside of the soundboard capture the complex nuances of the top's vibration, and a Dynamic String Sensor mounted beneath the fretboard extension registers string and neck vibration.

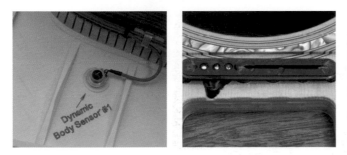

The preamp, developed with collaborative input from pro audio pioneer Rupert Neve, boosts the pickup signal cleanly, without the need for artificial EQ 'colouration'. The balanced, low-impedance signal thus produced can run direct into a mixer or PA in most situations, and can be distortion free at almost any volume.

Signed off

This is a fascinating guitar – beautifully finished materials that result in a wonderfully responsive modern-sounding instrument. The intonation is accurate throughout. A guitar that makes you want to play!

For his innovative NT neck, Expression System electrics and unmannered genius I consider Bob Taylor to be the Leo Fender of the acoustic guitar. As Leo would say, 'It isn't a radically different thing that becomes a success, it's the thing that offers an improvement on an already proven item.'

1953 'L5 Professional Special Grand Concert Model' Gibson archtop

In 1922 the L5 was the world's first production F-hole or cello-type guitar. Our case study instrument represents a fascinating musical crossroad. The carved archtop concept – introduced from the violin-making tradition by Orville Gibson and developed by Lloyd Loar – had flourished in the pre-electric period, with a peak in manufacture in 1937 of 251 L5s.

However, by 1953 Leo Fender and Les Paul were establishing a bold new path with the solid-body electric. In the '40s many 'acoustic' archtops had 'pressed' rather than carved tops and often came with magnetic pickups – the 'semi acoustic' era was well established. From the late '50s on the purely acoustic archtop was left to a small following of enthusiastic aficionados; Gibson only shipped 15 L5s in 1953 and discontinued the line in 1958 after having sold just three!

Having no serial number as such the 'factory order number' is useful in dating this period of Gibsons. I provide more on this in the appendix on page 197.

Condition on arrival

The guitar arrived a little forlorn, with roundwound .009–.042 rock'n'roll strings, a plain third and a mispositioned bridge. With encouragement from then owner Mick Bott, I have since experimented with flatwound medium gauge 'Jazz strings' and for this case study will try Martin bronze-wound .013–.056.

Interestingly Ivor Mairants, the great British L5 player, once examined Eddie Lang's L5 and was astonished to observe his strings were gauged .085–.020, including a wound second! For the L5's most famous player, these heavy strings were an essential part of being heard in pre-electric jazz, providing the tension and power to really pump that substantially braced carved top.

Ideal for

Strong rhythmic chordal accompaniment that will cut through any Gypsy Jazz jam or authentic early jazz horns.

Signature tone woods

Introduced at $275, this was Gibson's most expensive model. L5s were machine-carved, with some hand-finishing. Originally the top was carved from two-piece spruce, with initially a birch then in 1925 a maple back and maple sides. The top thickness is graduated – thicker in the centre and tapered at the edges – and 'tap tuned', a practice adopted from the great era of Italian violin making. Carved-top instruments are considered superior to 'pressed' in both strength and tone. This top appears to be one-piece and age and lacquer crazing make the grain very difficult to determine.

General description

Interestingly this classic non-cutaway L5 has a 41.9cm lower bout top. This sits somewhere between the original 1922 16in (40.6cm) and the 17in (43.2cm) guitar of 1934. The upper bout is 29.8cm with a 23.8cm waist. The replacement tortoise-effect plastic scratchplate 'floats', leaving the carved top free to vibrate.

■ The two 6¼in (15.9cm) unbound F holes are a significant feature, as the L5 was the first 20th-century guitar to have them. These are 1in (25mm) across at their widest point. F holes were originally introduced on violin family instruments to intercept transverse soundwaves in the table of a bowed instrument, on which 'sustain' is controlled by the bow. By design, F holes on a *plucked* instrument can cause a very steep loss of resonance if placed close to the bridge. This can conversely be thought of a way of heightening transient 'attack' rather than sustain – potentially a desirable feature on a predominantly 'rhythm' guitar. Decorating F holes with purfling can also interfere with their sound properties, and on the classic L5 they are left plain.

■ The one-piece 50.8cm maple back is machine carved.

■ The sides are bound and appear to be rosewood, which is surprising for an L5, though at this late stage in production Kalamazoo would be using lots of rosewood on its flat-tops.

■ The violin-like movable bridge is made from rosewood and has two overlarge metal adjustment thumbscrews. The mass of these metal parts absorbs acoustic energy and smaller wheels would be beneficial. This bridge may not be original. The integrated rosewood saddle is heavily pitch compensated, though it is not yet clear for what gauge strings. The break angle is only 13°, though the 'action' at the fingerboard is high, which may explain the current relatively poor sound projection.

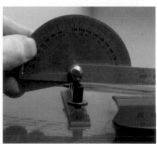

■ The guitar weighs a very light 4.75lb (2.16kg) and has a consistent 8.6cm depth.

■ The one-piece unbound neck seems to be mahogany under the thick and aged lacquer and has Gibson's oval shape and 14 frets to the body, the L5 being the first carved-top to have a neck with 14 frets clear of the body. The scale length is approximately 63.2cm.

■ There is no headstock joint and consequently no obstructing volute and the effective headstock angle is a reasonable 15°. The headstock has two cosmetic side wing laminations.

■ There are position dots on the front of the rosewood fingerboard and small dots on the fingerboard edge at III / V / VII / IX / XII. The frets are very slim 1.7mm gauge and fairly polished with very little wear; the fingerboard also has little wear. There are 19 frets – top B reasonably accessible on the first string. The fingerboard width at the 12th fret is 5cm and the virtual radius is a very 'modern' 10in (25.4cm).

 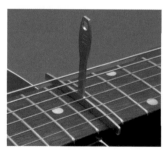

■ The headstock carries the 1950s Gibson script and the 42.7mm nut is made of yellowing bone.

■ The machine heads are '50s Kluson Deluxe type in a pair of three-asides. These are most likely replacements.

■ The L5 was one of the first guitars to have an adjustable truss rod; the neck-saving rod was a Gibson patent attributed to Thaddeus McHugh in 1921. On the '53 this is adjusted at the headstock and requires a '1' point Phillips for the shield removal and a 5⁄16in truss rod wrench.

Specific routine maintenance

Setting the action: With a capo at the first fret to take the nut out of the equation and the string stopped at the last fret, check the neck relief with your feeler gauges. The neck should have some relief, perhaps .008–.010 at the eighth fret sixth string for light strumming, considerably more for a hard swing groove. The neck on this guitar has currently settled slightly concave and requires a little expert attention beyond a simple truss rod adjust. An adjustment of the neck break angle and a replacement lighter mass bridge are all worth considering on a guitar built to perform. Take care to retain the older parts for dating provenance.

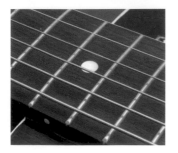

See the nut and saddle work guides on pages 64 and 70 for any saddle height and nut adjustment.

The strings on this guitar were stylistically incorrect .009–.042 but I've tried Medium .012–.053 flatwounds to *some* effect and will now try Martin .013–.056 bronze acoustics on the recommendation of luthier John Vickers of Belleville Guitars.

When changing strings it's worth checking the machine head fixing screws, which tend to work loose. On the L5 this requires a Phillips No.1. Do not overtighten – just enough to stop the machine head moving in normal use. Due to wood shrinkage all the screws on this old guitar were very loose!

A little graphite from a pencil tip will keep the strings moving at the nut when tuning. Graphite dust mixed with ChapStick or Vaseline is another solution.

The straight edge reveals the concave neck – solved with a half-turn on the completely loose truss rod.

All the frets should be of an equal height, and the fret rocker revealed several 'proud' frets in need of attention. See section entitled 'A little fret dressing' on page 96 for guidance.

Clearing 57 years of debris from the fret edges is made easy with a cocktail stick. Then give the frets a light polish with a Planet Waves abrasive paper. Finally a little lemon oil will clean the fingerboard.

Always examine the tailpiece – good tone depends on stability and the correct break angle at the bridge. Any excessive wear at the bridge string contact point needs professional attention. The current set-up on this guitar is robbing it of tone and power.

Whilst you have the tools out it's worth tightening the tailpiece. In this case this requires a No.1 Phillips. The neck-mounted strap retainer, a modern addition, also tends to work loose and likewise needs a No.1 Phillips.

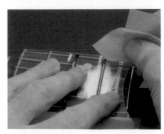

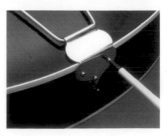

Under the hood

■ The truss rod requires a ⁵⁄₁₆in wrench for any relief adjustment. See page 62 for more on neck relief and adjustment.

■ L5 tops are supported by two nearly parallel braces – a treble bar and a bass bar. The accompanying picture shows the internal view, looking up at the two F holes and the twin full-length centre braces.

In 1934, as the top size increased, Gibson experimented briefly with Martin-style X-bracing. Originally the Loar L5 also featured a Virzi Tone Producer, a small wooden disc mounted inside the body directly under the bridge, designed to increase power and improve the guitar's tone. The device was dropped after Lloyd Loar left the company.

There are substantial kerfed side supports front and back. The right-hand picture below shows the view towards the neck block from the lower F hole.

The carved back of the guitar has no extra bracing. The left-hand picture shows the internal perspective from the top F hole.

■ It's worth checking occasionally for any loose braces; with time and humidity changes these can come unglued, resulting in warping of the top – an expensive fault to repair. Loose braces often produce a rattle that's easily detected. However, it's not always this obvious. Another symptom is a loss of bass response – the guitar sounds inexplicably 'thin'. A gentle check once in a while can save an expensive repair.

The Orville Gibson concept

'Front and back made in swelled shape by being carved, leaving the layer grain of the wood in the same shape as its natural growth, thus ensuring strength, free vibration and unusual sympathetic vibration.' – From the first Gibson catalogue, 1903.

A fascinating guitar with a very different sound.

Signed off

The installation of the medium gauge .013–.056
strings, some truss rod adjustment and the raising
of the bridge via the thumbwheels resulted in a break
angle at the bridge of 15° and a transformed resonance
in this guitar. It's still hard to play by comparison with
any modern jazz guitar but it does sound very loud in
the mid range and would sit very nicely with acoustic
bass and a tasteful drummer.

The guitar responds well to a very hard pick and
embarrassingly I have a very substantial 'tortoiseshell'
pick given to me as a gift in Japan, where such trade is still
tolerated. These picks were very common in the 1950s but are
naturally banned these days as a threat to endangered turtles.

Like many older glued-neck guitars, the L5 suffers from
a 'kick' (raised area) at the 14th fret. This is probably the

result of the top of the guitar
shrinking (witness the cracked
lacquer), causing a 'hingeing'
effect as the glued fingerboard
is pulled out of position by
the shrinking top to which
it is attached. The neck
has stayed put but the
fingerboard has moved
where it joins the

top. This may be solved by some fret levelling but
often requires a neck reset – a big job! However, the
guitar works fine before the 14th fret, where most of
the action takes place on a jazz rhythm guitar.

The archtop guitar has a special place in the hearts
of New York-centred jazz enthusiasts and master guitar
makers like Bob Benedetto, who revere the L5 for its bold
originality. The acoustic cello guitar is also in 2010 enjoying
a quiet renaissance in the hands of David Rawlings, who
plays a 1925 Epiphone Olympic with acclaimed singer
Gillian Welch of *Oh Brother Where Art Thou*. A tribute
'Loar' guitar is even available to custom order.

Ironically guitarist Les Paul had two L5s
that he treasured, and the carved top of his
eponymous revolution has its genesis in this
largely forgotten instrument.

Our case study guitar has a distinctive sound that
is gradually revealing its secrets, and I thank new owner
Andy Fairweather Low for making this rare bird available.

Kind Hearted Woman – The Author plays
Judy Collins's 12-fret Dreadnought and
Andy plays his '53 L5, July 2010.

Spanish-made Ramírez 1A 'Traditional' Classic

Signed by Amalia Ramírez and manufactured at No 8 Calle de La Paz, Madrid, this particular instrument is their standard Classic guitar made in the tradition of Antonio de Torres, with modern machine heads and a red cedar top.

All Ramírez professional guitars are built in the Ramírez's small artisan-style workshop under the supervision and participation of Amalia Ramírez, who also inspects each completed instrument.

Ideal for
Launching a professional career in classic guitar or adding a real Spanish flavour to some studio overdubs.

Signature tone woods
The combination of Indian rosewood and red cedar gives this instrument its classic sound – more robust than the flamenco type with increased low frequency resonance. José Ramírez III was a fervent proponent of the red cedar top, declaring that even Antonio Stradivarius would have been drawn to its acoustic properties.

Condition on arrival

This is a new example of the current 'Traditional' as manufactured by Ramírez from a design by Amalia's father José Ramírez III. It comes in a custom hardshell Hiscox case with the Ramírez logo. The guitar is also available with a German spruce top – the other popular choice for classic Spanish guitars; both have their own tonal characteristics.

General description

The guitar has the classic mid-20th century shape and size, specifically 37cm lower bout, 28cm upper bout, with a 23.5cm waist (a fraction slimmer than the Ramírez flamenco). The small 8.25cm soundhole is decorated with an elaborate set of inlays.

■ The beautiful two-piece 49cm back is matched from Indian rosewood with an elegant double centre inlay and a slight tension arch.

■ The 10cm deep sides enlarge to 10.5cm at the lower bout, a contrast to the Ramírez flamenco with its parallel back. The sides are crafted from rosewood with an unusual complete cypress interior double side. The guitar has inlayed edge binding front and back.

■ The rosewood bridge has an unusual rear extension. The saddle is a simple piece of uncompensated bone. The strings are secured traditionally in a knot known as the timber hitch or bowyer's hitch depending on geography!

■ There is a separate headstock joint, resulting in a headstock angle of only 9° (compared to 15° on my Peterson Classic and 12.5° on the Yamaha NCX), with the fingerboard set traditionally below the headstock veneer.

■ The three-piece neck has a traditional U profile with a separate heel sculptured both outside and inside and the usual 12 frets to the body. The scale length is approx 65cm, with 18 full frets and a 19th part fret giving top B on the first and sixth strings. A version with Segovia's longer 66.4cm scale is also available.

■ The traditional flat ebony fingerboard has no inlays or position markers and the frets are medium 2.1mm gauge, shaped to a high crown and in need of a finishing polish.

■ The guitar weighs a light 3.75lb (1.7kg).

■ The slotted headstock carries the distinctive Ramírez shape and a rosewood cap. The 53mm nut is a well-cut piece of bone.

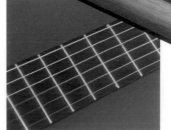

■ The three-a-side machine heads are beautifully made Exagons, gold-finished, with Ramírez crested buttons and nylon bushings. The gearing ratio is 18:1.

> **This is a wonderful world full of artists making beautiful different guitars for everybody, and for every taste, and I love that.**
>
> *Amalia Ramírez*

Specific routine maintenance

Setting the action: The action on a Classic guitar is traditionally set quite high to facilitate a heavy dynamic without fret rattle. This new guitar has sensibly been set a little over-high, allowing the player to decide his preference on delivery.

With a capo at the first fret to take the nut out of the equation and the string stopped at the last fret, check the neck relief with your feeler gauges. The neck should have some relief, for acoustic volume perhaps .011–.012 at the seventh fret sixth string, but this is a matter of personal taste. Naturally the guitar has no truss rod.

See the nut and saddle work guides on pages 64 and 70 for any saddle height and nut adjustment.

The strings on this guitar are .029–.045 medium tension monofilament one to three and wound-on nylon four to six.

When changing strings it's worth checking the machine head fixing screws, which tend to work loose. On the Ramírez this requires a very thin-bladed 4mm straight-slot. The bushing cogs require a very slim-bladed 5mm straight-slot Do not overtighten – just enough to stop the machine head moving in normal use.

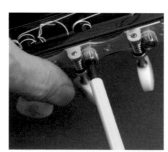

A little graphite from a pencil tip will keep the strings moving at the nut when tuning, and a little lemon oil will clean the fingerboard, preventing shrinkage.

Periodically examine the saddle – good tone depends on a correct fit and avoiding any gaps between bridge and saddle. Also the intonation will be upset by any tendency to 'lean' from the vertical. The current set-up on this guitar is excellent. A good secure string knot is essential if the guitar is to hold its pitch.

Under the hood

The top has a variant of traditional Torres non-scalloped fan strutting with a sculpted neck block and a 'Spanish foot' joint. Note the 'unbroken' back supports without traditional kerfing and the kerfed top supports.

■ It's worth checking occasionally for any loose braces; with time and humidity changes these can come unglued, resulting in warping of the top – an expensive fault to repair. Loose braces often produce a rattle that's easily detected. However, it's not always this obvious. Another symptom is a loss of bass response – the guitar sounds inexplicably 'thin'. A gentle check once in a while can save an expensive repair.

■ This traditional-type guitar has no transducer electrics.

Signed off

This is testament to the Ramírez heritage – beautifully finished A1 materials, which result in a responsive instrument. The guitar is new and needs 'playing in' before achieving its full tonal potential. As is often the case the guitar also needs a little minor setting up, including some fretwork. A professional player would instruct his own luthier to set the guitar up to suit his own playing style.

The intonation is accurate throughout.

■ Amalia Ramírez was understandably reluctant to give me a technical diagram of the precise brace and tone bar measurements due to rampant plagiarism. The back of the guitar has *three* parallel 7.4mm wide 'end-scalloped braces' and an ellipse centre splice, all of which are visible through the soundhole (*four* rear braces are often found on bigger-bodied Dreadnought-type guitars).

NB: Ramírez also offer a 'Classico Especial' model in the style of José Ramírez IV. This is lighter and omits the cypress double sides. This is also offered in eight- and ten-string versions.

USA-made National 'Reso Phonic' Style 3

Serial No 15070
Prod No 1917

Signed off in San Luis Obispo, California, on 17 June 2009, this is a modern and improved reproduction of a guitar first made famous by jazz and bluesmen in the 1920s in a pre-electric strive for volume

In 1927 John Dopyera patented his solution to the problem of the guitar being heard on an increasingly noisy stage. Whilst Gibson and Loar experimented with the violin technology of a carved table, Dopyera opted to innovate by the adaption of speaker cone technology, driven not yet by electricity but by the mechanical energy of the guitar's strings.

Ideal for
Bottleneck blues, in the studio or discreetly miked on stage – one glissandi chord and you can *smell* the Delta.

Signature materials
This guitar exudes plated brass but in fact has a lot of wooden ingredients contributing to its distinctive tone. The neck is figured maple, the fingerboard ebony, and under the hood the considerable braces and wedges are all timber.

Condition on arrival
The guitar arrived beautifully set up from Dave King Guitars UK. It comes with heavy .013–.056 strings ideal for bottleneck slide, and enclosed in a traditional fabric finish 'Ameritage' case.

General description

Has a version of the distinctive curvaceous National shape, specifically 36, 24, 26 (centimetres!) lower bout, waist and upper bout, with a flattish top sculpted by the 2cm rise around the cone and bridge cover. The single cone Style 3 is hand-engraved with a 'Lily of the Valley' design.

■ There are two 'conventional' F holes, each actually comprising six individual apertures; and the cone itself has 369 holes arranged in a series of nine diamonds. So the holy grail of blues slide guitars has a holey total of 381!

■ The bridge is covered with a metal hand rest. Removing the cover with a 1.5cm Allen reveals the simple wooden bridge attached directly to the centre cone of the resonator 'biscuit style'. The biscuit has a natural sympathetic resonance at B flat. Note the neat V cut to the bridge for an accurate intonation point at the front.

■ The 50cm back is also lavishly decorated and has a gentle pliage that resonates like an expensive Trinidad steel pan.

■ The neck is made of highly figured maple, a deep V to the seventh fret and more oval to the 12th fret to the body. The scale length is 63.5cm on 19 frets and the fingerboard radius is 16in (40.6cm), not reflected at the bridge where the low E and A are currently set higher.

■ There are mother of pearl position diamonds on the front of the ebony fingerboard and small dots on the fingerboard edge at V / VII / IX / XII / XV / XVII / XIX.

■ There is no headstock joint and consequently no obstructing volute. The slotted headstock has a relatively gentle 12° angle. An engraved shield and double-cut border adorn the headstock, which has a bone 46.7mm nut.

■ The frets are substantial 2.75mm gauge and polished. The fingerboard width at the 12th fret is 58mm. The fretboard binding, heel cap and headstock overlay are made of ivoroid.

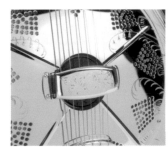

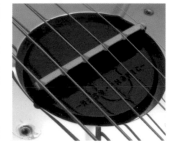

■ Some intonation adjustment could be had by carefully filing this saddle, which has a very flat radius of approximately 20in (50.8cm).

■ The guitar weighs a substantial 9lb (4.09kg) and is definitely a 'sitting on the porch at sundown' instrument.

■ The truss rod is accessed via an ivoroid shield accessed with '1' point Phillips and requires a 3mm Allen wrench for any adjustment.

■ The three-a-side slotted Waverley machine heads are made from a tastefully decorated brass, with traditional untensionable buttons.

Specific routine maintenance

Setting the action: With a capo at the first fret to take the nut out of the equation and the string stopped at the last fret, check the neck relief with your feeler gauges. The neck should have some relief, perhaps .010–.015 at the eighth fret sixth string for fingerpicking, slightly more for hard bottleneck playing. The neck on this guitar has been set generously concave to suit loud and raucous blues.

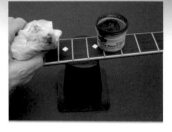

The ebony board may benefit from a little KGB board wax.

The strings are set in a metal tailpiece 'over the top' – National aren't keen on players trying to improve the break angle by going under!

Whilst you have the tools out it's worth tightening the end pin, which tends to work loose and needs a No.2 Phillips.

See the nut and saddle work guides on pages 64 and 70 for any saddle height and nut adjustment.

The strings on this guitar are heavy .013–.056, which work well in triggering the guitar's resonator.

When changing strings it's worth checking the machine head fixing screws, which tend to work loose. On the National this requires a 3.5 straight-slot for the securing screws and a 4mm for the bushings. Do not overtighten – just enough to stop the machine head moving in normal use. As expected, due to wood shrinkage all the securing screws on this headstock were slightly loose.

A little graphite from a pencil tip will keep the strings moving at the nut when tuning.

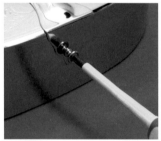

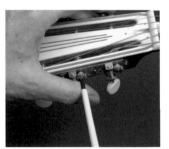

Under the hood
■ The tailpiece is retained by the end pin/ strap button and the top of the resonator is protected by a strip of felt.

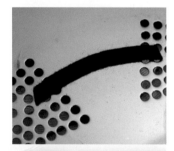

National Reso-phonic Inc

The 'new' National Reso-phonic Inc was established in San Luis Obispo, 200 miles north of Los Angeles, California, circa 1988 by Don Young and McGregor Gaines. Both partners had worked previously for the Dopyera brothers' company OMI. The Dopyera brothers had migrated to the USA from the Austro-Hungarian Empire and had become famous for their banjos before taking on the acoustic amplification of the guitar.

■ Removing the nine resonator screws with a No.1 Phillips reveals the incredibly light 40gm 23cm cone and the neck brace. The cone vibrates freely in its cavity like a drumhead, only held in place by the downward string pressure; hence the distinctive pump action sound quality – up and down like an archtop guitar but with an inherent metallic resonance. The biscuit needs to be securely attached to the cone. This requires a No.1 Phillips.

Signed off

This guitar has a wonderfully distinctive voice, adding character to a gentle *Romeo and Juliet* and energy to *Death Letter Blues*. For me it works best with a metal 'bottleneck', when the whole metal superstructure sings like a haunted wolf at the Devil's crossroads.

The guitar's resonator has a fundamental resonance at B flat, an unusual key for a guitar but one very prevalent in the context of brass-based jazz at the time of the National guitar's peak popularity. B flat is unlikely territory for a solo bluesman so the resonance sits comfortably away from the open guitar keys of C, G, E, A and D, a good arrangement.

So acoustically, how many decibels louder than an L5 or a 12-fret Dreadnought is the National? An experiment, with a AKG capacitor microphone at 20cm from resonator or table (an averaged downstrum of a first position E chord):

The resonator is 8dB louder than the other '20s guitar, the Gibson L5!

And 4dB louder than the other contemporary, a 12 frets to the body Dreadnought. This would have been a significant advantage in the acoustic era and still gives the guitar a distinctive voice these days, even when 'unplugged' usually means plugged into the PA!

■ A 9in (23cm) cone would have a fundamental frequency range of 80Hz–1Khz, which explains the distinctive mid-frequency tone and the volume; 1KHz is where our ears are at their most sensitive – the key speech frequency.

For correct intonation the replaced cone needs to be very carefully aligned, as it is directly attached to the bridge.

■ A videoscope inspection through the top F hole towards the resonator shows the substantial wooden brace running the length of the body, and underneath the replaced resonator. A shim prevents any 'wood to metal' rattle. A pair of crude but effective wedges keep the neck joint solid – it's obviously essential that nothing rattles inside this resonant chamber.

■ National seem to endorse Flitz metal polish for their instruments, as supplied with this guitar.

USA-made Ovation electro-acoustic LX series J1778LX 5SM

Serial No 615182

As long ago as 1966 – long before MTV's *Unplugged* renewed interest in acoustic guitar sounds – Ovation introduced their radical 'Balladeer', an acoustic guitar with a 'plastic' Lyrachord bowlback and, eventually, innovative built-in electronics – at that time an acoustic guitarist's dream and very unusual. This particular guitar, made in New Hartford, Connecticut, is steel-strung, though Ovation also offer nylon-strung and 12-string models.

Ideal for
No-hassle amplified 'acoustic-like' sounds. In the 21st century the Ovation has stiff competition and some very flattering emulation, but this original remains distinctive and still very futuristic, with a sound all its own.

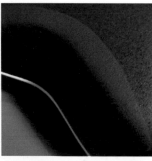

Signature materials
An unusual combination – solid Sitka spruce top and a hard composite Lyrachord GS body, which Ovation claim improves projection and reflects top vibrations better than wood and is now lighter and stronger than ever.

Condition on arrival

Set up ready to play, the guitar comes in a custom-shaped Hiscox-like case built to accommodate the unusual bowlback.

General description

This guitar has the distinctive signature Ovation shape and size, specifically 40cm lower bout, 28.5cm upper bout, with a 26cm waist.

■ There is no scratchplate and the solid Sitka spruce top is 4mm thick at the soundholes.

■ The distinctive array of 11 round soundholes vary in size, with one at 1½in, two at 1in, seven at ½in and one at ⅜in. On this model they're all single-layered, though other Ovations are seen with 3D multi-layered soundhole arrays and also conventional single soundholes.

■ The back is moulded from Lyrachord. For the LX Series, Ovation has refined and improved the original 1960s composition by the addition of glass 'microspheres', which reduce the weight of the new Lyracord GSTM bowl by up to 30% whilst maintaining its stability. The lighter structure vibrates more freely and allegedly produces a louder, more dynamic sound. A special 'non-slip' section on the bowl in the area of the leg rest prevents the guitar from slipping around during playing.

■ There are *no* sides – just a continuous bowl.

■ The bridge appears to be ebony with a very complex custom-filed compensated saddle with six individual piezo loaded segments – one per string. The strings are unusually secured directly through the bridge.

■ The guitar weighs a medium 5.5lb (2.5kg), slightly heavier than the average modern Dreadnought though the new Lyrachord GS bowl weighs half a pound less than the original. An integrated platform, moulded in the bowl at the neck-joining area, is the start of a stable structure that helps support the neck. See below for an interior shot of this.

■ The unbound maple neck is a two-piece longitudinal laminate and has a gentle V profile not dissimilar to a 'Clapton' Strat, with a tapered capped heel. There is good high fret access due to the 14 frets to the body and the deep cutaway. The scale length is approximately 64cm – slightly shorter than a Dreadnought. The overall feel is more akin to an electric guitar. There's a small strengthening volute at the neck/headstock junction, which doesn't get in the way.

■ The neck has a lightweight dual-action truss rod and carbon fibre stabilisers that assist in keeping the fingerboard aligned at the bolt-on neck/body joint.

■ The rosewood fingerboard has no front markers – a minimalist classical approach – but simple dots at III / V / VII / IX / XII / XV / XVII are located on the player's side of the fingerboard. The frets are a generous 2.4mm gauge and quite well dressed. There are 22 frets extended to the first three strings, with top D a tone below the second octave on the first string and top A on the second – this means you can comfortably play a D major scale at the 19th position (if you're so inclined the high frets will need a little work). The fingerboard radius is a modern Strat-like 9.5in (24.1cm).

■ The very distinctive headstock carries the classic Ovation logo embossed on to what I suspect is Lyrachord. The narrow 42.85mm nut is a well-cut piece of black Tusq.

■ The screwed and bolted machine heads seem like black Ovation-branded Schallers.

Specific routine maintenance

Setting the action: With a capo at the first fret to take the nut out of the equation and the string stopped at the last fret, check the neck relief with your feeler gauges. The neck should have some relief, perhaps .010–.015 at the seventh fret sixth string for light fingerpicking slightly more for hard flat picking. If the neck relief does need adjustment the Ovation requires a 3/16in truss rod wrench (the Fender type is easier to handle than a hardware-store Allen – see *Useful contacts* appendix).

Follow the nut and saddle set-up guides on pages 64 and 70 for any saddle height and nut adjustment.

The strings on this guitar are D'Addario EXP16 (.012–.053) Phosphor Bronze. However, Ovation are happy with any gauge, with the proviso that some relief adjustment may be required. I would, however, suggest sticking to these gauges as the intonation will otherwise drift and need compensation at the saddle.

When changing strings it's worth checking the machine head fixing screws, which tend to work loose. On the Ovation this requires a No.1 Phillips at the back and a 10mm socket for the front locking nuts. Do not overtighten. Due to wood shrinkage all the screws and nuts on this guitar were slightly loose.

The machines are tensionable and should be loosened for string changes and retightened for a comfortable working setting. This requires a No.1 Phillips.

A little lubricant from the Planet Waves Lubrikit will keep the strings from binding in the nut. A little lemon oil will clean the fingerboard.

The current set-up on this guitar is pretty good as supplied, but if you wish to experiment Ovation recommend removing an undersaddle shim for

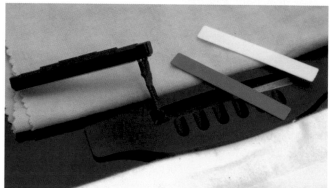

lowering the action and adding the same for raising it. The two supplied shims are designed to give increments of 1/64in at the 12th fret – they are in fact 1mm and 0.8mm thick, with both in place as a factory setting. Caution is required here to avoid damaging the undersaddle transducers and output cable!

Whilst you have the tools out it's worth tightening the strap pins. These require a No.1 Phillips. The output jack often works loose, but a Stewmac 'Jack The Gripper' and a 1/2in spanner wrench will do the job.

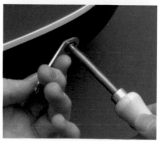

Under the hood

■ Truss rod access is via the shield located on the headstock. You need a No.1 Phillips to remove this and a ³⁄₁₆in hex wrench for any relief adjustment. See page 62 for more on neck relief and adjustment.

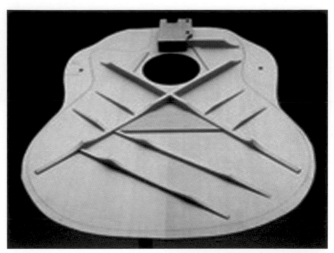

■ Removing the access cover at the back of the guitar with an 8mm straight-slot reveals the main X braces to be 8.13mm and heavily tapered. There are no conventional wooden kerfed supports for the top but a specially moulded plastic beading instead.

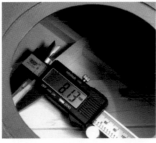

■ Though the bracing diagram above shows a conventional soundhole, the LX uses an almost identical bracing system.

■ All the top woodwork is wisely left unfinished, but watch out for splinters!

■ The unusually thick 4mm top has heavily scalloped LX bracing, with an extra supporting brace at the neck and two 'fan-like' tone bars behind the bridge. There is also a mahogany neck block and a complex neck joint.

■ If necessary the whole neck can be removed from inside with a ³⁄₁₆in Allen.

■ It's worth checking occasionally for any loose braces; with time and humidity changes these can come unglued, resulting in warping of the top – an expensive fault to repair. Loose braces often produce a rattle that's easily detected. However, it's not always this obvious. Another symptom is a loss of bass response – the guitar sounds inexplicably 'thin'. A gentle check once in a while can save an expensive repair.

■ The rear access cover is held in place with a tensioned 'spider' that needs careful alignment for replacement.

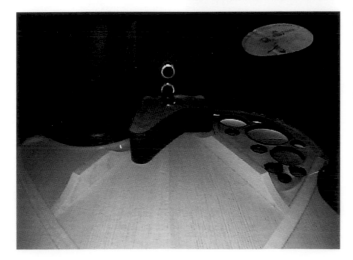

Charles and Bill Kaman

Though a guitarist, Charles Kaman's expertise was in designing helicopters! Wanting to diversify his business he first tried to buy Martin and Harmony, and when that didn't work out he designed his own guitars instead. The prototypes appeared around 1964 and the Ovation company was founded in 1966. Son Bill eventually took over as CEO. 'In the beginning only about 15% of the guitars we built had pickups,' Bill says. 'Ten years later, 90% of our guitars were acoustic/electric. The truly amazing thing is that it also took about ten years before any of our competition began to offer acoustic/electric models as standard in their line.'

Piezo pickups have a very high electrical impedance, which means that the frequency response or 'tone' is prone to change over long cable runs. In order to prevent this, Ovation have designed a buffered preamp that lowers the impedance, stabilising the tone at the output stage.

Bill Kaman recalls: 'Our first preamp was a very clean design. It had two contour filters to enhance the "acousticness" of the sound, and combined with bringing the impedance into the right range the guitar sounded very rich and full. The first preamps were volume only. Later we added a tone control to the circuit, as well as offering a stereo preamp.'

The whole preamp unit is a removable module for easy servicing.

Electrics

As industry innovators in the area of the acoustic electric guitar you'd expect some refinement of the original piezo concept, and that expectation is fulfilled. The LX series currently has OP-PRO/Studio preamp coupled to a sophisticated undersaddle pickup.

Few manufacturers go to the length of *individual* undersaddle piezos. The aim here is a more even string to string balance.

It has the usual low, mid and high EQ but also has a tuner and a compressor, the full functions of which are described below. Battery replacement is easy.

Extreme care is required on replacing the preamp module, as without care the multi-way connector pins can be damaged.

Preamp spec

Characteristic	OP-Pro studio preamp
Battery voltage	9VDC
Idle current	17mA (approx 25 hours' battery life)
Tuner on	20mA (max)
Sleep current	38uA (approx 1½ years' battery life)
Battery LED turn-on V	7V
LED flash rate	≈25/minute
Max input (1kHz)	16VP-P
Max output (unbalanced)	9VP-P (47K load/flat/ volume max)
Max output (balanced)	16VP-P
THD @ 1VP-P input	<0.1%
S/N ratio	≈80dB
Flat response (+/–3dB)	10Hz–8kHz
Preshape EQ	-7dB @ 500Hz +3dB @ 780Hz
Low EQ response	+8dB @ 80Hz
Middle EQ response	±11dB @ 550Hz
High EQ response	+8.5dB @ 12kHz
Tuner accuracy	<1%
Tuner auto-off	1 minute

The other controls on the preamp

■ **Drive:** This increases or decreases the depth of harmonic enhancement from the 'exciter' circuit. Turning this control clockwise emphasise the harmonics in the range of open-string fundamentals as well as the guitar top frequencies. This may enhance chord work and provide a more 'woody' timbre to upper register solo performance. This control is used in conjunction with the 'Expressor' slider (see below), which regulates the amount of the harmonic content mixed with the direct piezo signal.

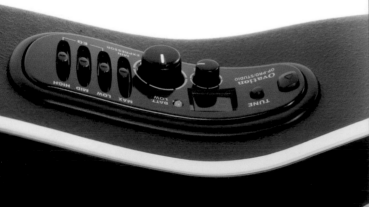

■ **Expressor:** This simultaneously controls the mix of the 'exciter' circuit and sets the threshold of the inbuilt compressor/limiter. The slider allows the player to set the playing level at which the compressor/limiter circuit engages.

Once set, playing louder will mean the output of the preamp output is compressed (a common studio technique for enhancing acoustic guitar sounds). Ovation say this feature allows the performer 'a greater dynamic playing range' without negative effects on the mix or creating headroom issues for mixers or amps.

Once the threshold setting of this control is established, the Drive control can be set to achieve the desired harmonic enhancement to suit the compressor/limiter setting. 'Now remind me, what key were we in?'

Interior view of the electronics.

Signed off

Many guitarists have been put off the Ovation concept, preferring more traditional materials, construction and sound. However, this guitar has plenty of character and a very electric guitarist-friendly neck. This is the perfect acoustic guitar for when your drummer is too loud!

An early and devoted advocate of the Ovation – Joan Armatrading.

Appendices, glossary and contacts

Further notes on guitar tuning, materials, and serial numbers.

LEFT Reso Phonic 'biscuit' bridge.

RIGHT Gibson SJ200.

■ Appendix 1
Understanding Martin 'type' classifications

The initial letter(s) usually stand for the body size/type.
00 = 00
000 = Auditorium
0000 = Grand Auditorium
5 = Size 5 Terz
B = Acoustic Bass
D = Dreadnought
J = Jumbo
M = Grand Auditorium
OM = Orchestra

Other style options include:
12 = Twelve-string
C = Cutaway
H = Herringbone
HP = Herringbone pearl
V = Vintage

Note: a hyphen (-) separates the size prefix from
the style prefix.

Ornamentation
The number after the letter designates the ornamentation
or series styling. The higher that number, the fancier the
guitar. Ornamentation styles of Martin Standard and Vintage
Series models are: 18-28-35-40-41-42-45-50-100.
Other styles run: X-Road-1-15-16-17.

Special features
The letter after the number denotes a special feature:
A = Thin body
DB = Deep body
E = Electronics
GT = Gloss top
LS = Large soundhole
N = Nylon strings (Classical)
S = 12-fret neck to body juncture

■ Appendix 2
Martin serial numbers

Year	Last serial number	Year	Last serial number	Year	Last serial number
1898	8348	1936	65176	1974	353387
1899	8716	1937	68865	1975	371828
1900	9128	1938	71866	1976	388800
1901	9310	1939	74061	1977	399625
1902	9528	1940	76734	1978	407800
1903	9810	1941	80013	1979	419900
1904	9988	1942	83107	1980	430300
1905	10120	1943	86724	1981	436474
1906	10329	1944	90149	1982	439627
1907	10727	1945	93623	1983	446101
1908	10883	1946	98158	1984	453300
1909	11018	1947	103468	1985	460575
1910	11203	1948	108269	1986	468175
1911	11413	1949	112961	1987	476216
1912	11565	1950	117961	1988	483952
1913	11821	1951	122799	1989	493279
1914	12047	1952	128436	1990	503309
1915	12209	1953	134501	1991	512487
1916	12390	1954	141345	1992	522655
1917	12988	1955	147328	1993	535223
1918	13450	1956	153225	1994	551696
1919	14512	1957	159061	1995	570434
1920	15848	1958	165576	1996	592930
1921	16758	1959	171047	1997	624799
1922	17839	1960	175689	1998	668796
1923	19891	1961	181297	1999	724077
1924	22008	1962	187384	2000	780500
1925	24116	1963	193327	2001	845644
1926	28689	1964	199626	2002	916759*
1927	34435	1965	207030	2003	978706
1928	37568	1966	217215	2004	1042558
1929	40843	1967	230095	2005	1115862
1930	45317	1968	241925	2006	1197799
1931	49589	1969	256003	2007	1268091
1932	52590	1970	271633	2008	1337042
1933	55084	1971	294270	2009	1406715
1934	58679	1972	313302		
1935	61947	1973	333873		

* Serial numbers 900001 to
902908 were used on Sigma-
Martins in 1981 and 1982.

NB: The above serial numbers do not include Little Martin and
Backpacker instruments. Production totals are not published.

■ **Appendix 3**

Gibson factory order numbers

The sheer volume of data involved in addressing Gibson serial numbers and factory order numbers means that I must refer the reader to *Gibson Acoustic Serialization* from the *Blue Book of Acoustic Guitars* by Zachary R. Fjestad, available online in 11th-edition form on the Gibson website at:

http://www.gibson.com/Files/downloads/bluebook/ GibsonAcoustics.pdf

– or in up-to-date 12th edition (2009) form from:

Blue Book Publications Inc
8009 34th Avenue South, Suite 175
Minneapolis
MN 55425
USA.

■ **Appendix 4**

Leadbelly 12-string gauges

For the authentic sound of early 12-string blues;

Leadbelly tuned his ladder-braced Stella down to C. The lower pitch, coupled with very heavy gauges, gave the guitar his rich, booming tone. Another great 12-string blues veteran, John Pearson, tells me that when they found Leadbelly's last Stella it was strung;

| Low octave | .064 | .046 | .036 | .025 | .018 | .014 |
| High Octave | .014 | .019 | .016 | .025 | .018 | .014 |

Now that is HEAVY!

Ball-end – Conventional type of guitar string end.

Biscuit – The wooden disc often attached to the bridge of a resonator guitar.

Bout – Term used in describing a guitar's body – upper bout, lower bout etc.

Bracing – The back and sides of acoustic guitars are usually braced for strength, and also for the 'tuning' of inherent resonance.

Capo – Abbreviation of 'Capodastro', originally a Spanish device. A clamp across the strings of a guitar, shortening the effective sounding length for musical transposition.

Cone – The audio lens used in a resonator guitar, similar to a loudspeaker cone.

Equal temperament – Or ET, the name given to a system of dividing the chromatic scale into 12 mathematically equal half-steps.

F hole – A functional aperture found either side of the bridge on many archtop guitars.

Feeler gauge – A gauge consisting of several thin blades, used to measure narrow spaces.

Gotoh – Manufacturer of guitar machine heads.

Grovers – As above.

HPL – High pressure laminate.

Kerfing – The technique of part-indenting side supports to facilitate curvature.

Kluson – Type of machine head commonly found on vintage guitars and now reintroduced.

NT neck – New technology neck patented to Taylor Guitar Company.

PA – Public address system.

Purfling – Binding ornamentation on a guitar, serving both aesthetic and functional purposes, its principal purpose generally being to protect and cover any exposed endgrain.

Shimming – Adjusting the pitch of a guitar neck by inserting thin wooden shims or wedges in the neck cavity.

Spanish foot – The traditional Spanish neck joint.

Tone woods – Woods prized for their acoustic resonance.

Useful contacts and suppliers

- Peter Cook's Guitars, Hanwell, London (www.petercooks.co.uk), a great source of guitars, amps and advice.
- Stewmac in the USA (www.stewmac.com), the world's best source of luthiers' parts and tools.
- www.jawbonepress.com, a great source of books and music biographies.
- Draper tools, for all the general tools you'll need for guitar repair and maintenance.
- www.wdmusic.co.uk, for parts.
- Seymour Duncan (www.seymourduncan.com), for pickups.
- Schaller (www.schaller-guitarparts.de), for parts.
- Hipshot (www.hipshotproducts.com), for parts.
- Jaydee (www.jaydeecustomguitars.co.uk), for custom guitars.
- Luthier's Corner, Denmark Street, for instruments and equipment (www.luthierscorner.co.uk).
- Dr Junger Company (www.dr-junger-saiten.de).
- David Dyke (www.luthierssupplies.co.uk), for select woods, tools, equipment and books.
- D'Addario strings (www.daddario.com)

Bibliography

Brad Bechtel, *Hawaiian Guitar History* (www.well.com/~wellvis/mymusic.html).

Paul Brett, *Introducing Blues Guitar* (Koala Publications, 2004).

Walter Carter, *Gibson Guitars: 100 Years of an American Icon* (Gollehon Press, 1996).

— *The Martin Guitar: 170 Years of Fine Guitar-making* (Backbeat Books, 2006).

Dan Erlewine and Todd Sams, *Building an Acoustic Guitar Kit* (Stewmac two-DVD pack).

Mo Foster, *British Rock Guitar – The Guide* (Northumbria Press, 2011).

Nick Freeth and Charles Alexander, *The Acoustic Guitar* (Bramley Books, 1999).

Al Handa, *The National Steel Guitar, Part Three: Tampa Red and Son House* (National Steel Guitars website, 1998).

Neil Harpe, *The Stella Guitar Book: The Guitars of the Oscar Schmidt Company* (http://www.stellaguitars.com/guitar%20book.htm).

The Hawaiian Steel Guitar Association, *The Hawaiian Steel Guitar* (Centerstream Publications, 1996).

Adrian Ingram, *The Gibson L5* (Centerstream Publications, 2008).

Franz Jahnel, *Manual of Guitar Technology* (Verlag Das Musikinstrument, 1981).

Richard Johnston, Dick Boak and Mike Longworth, *The Martin Guitar: A Technical Reference* (two volumes) (Hal Leonard, 2009).

Hal Leonard Corporation, *Acoustic Guitar Owner's Manual: The Complete Guide* (Hal Leonard, 2000).

Ivor Mairants, *My Fifty Fretting Years: A Personal History of the Twentieth Century Guitar Explosion* (Ashley Mark Publishing, 1980).

John Morrish (editor), *The Classical Guitar: A Complete History* (Backbeat Books, 2002).

Mike Read, *The Story of the Shadows* (Elm Tree Books, 1983).

Jeffrey Pepper Rodgers – *Pete Seeger guitar info* (www.jeffreypepperrodgers.com).

Larry Sandberg, *The Acoustic Guitar Guide: Everything You Need to Know to Buy and Maintain a New or Used Guitar* (Cappella Books, 2000).

Christian Seguret and Matthieu Prier, *The World of Guitars* (Greenwich Editions, 1999).

Roger H. Siminoff, *The Luthier's Handbook: A Guide to Building Great Tone in Acoustic Stringed Instruments* (Hal Leonard, 2007).

Michael Simmons, 'The Origins of Twelve String Power' *Acoustic Guitar magazine*, November 1997 (http://www.frets.com/fretspages/history/12string/12storigins.html).

James Tyler, *The Early Guitar: A History and Handbook* (Oxford University Press 1980).

Graham Wade, *The Classical Guitar: A Concise History* (Mel Bay Publications).

Brian Whitehouse, *The Ramírez Collection: History and Romance of the Spanish Guitar* (ASG Music, 2009).

Robert Benedetto, *Archtop Guitar Design and Construction* (Stewmac.com).

Acknowledgements

Many thanks to:

- Judy Collins, Andy Fairweather Low and Joan Armatrading for their time and interviews.

My thanks to:

- Bob Taylor and Chris Martin IV for taking the time to talk and being so candid and open.
- The great luthier John Diggins and his son Andy of Jaydee Custom Guitars (www.jaydeecustomguitars.co.uk), who give me the run of their workshop and put right my errors!
- Peter Cook's Guitar World, who make most of the guitars available, and particularly Paul White who knows his Taylors, makes a fine cup of tea and is quick on the wit; also Richard Chong, Rob West, and Trevor Newman – together they keep alive the spirit of the great guitar shop.
- John Vickers for advice and diagrams on Belleville guitars (www.bellevilleguitarcompany.com).
- Celine Camerlynck of Luthier's Corner, Denmark Street, London W1 for Kalamazoo repairs and advice.
- JHS@JHS.co.uk
- Fishman pickups – particular thanks to Catherine Willis.
- Rod Matheson at Olympus Remote Visual Inspection for use of Videoscope.
- L.R. Baggs – especially Michael Newsom, marketing director.
- Sir Graham Wade, the world's foremost authority on classical guitar, for Antonio de Torres info and much more.
- D'Addario strings, especially marketing manager Elaine Smith, managing director Simon Turnbull, and Angela Magliocca, marketing specialist USA.
- Matthew Speed, Bill Lewington Ltd.
- O-Port – distributed by Planet Waves.
- Chuck Kirschling, Grover tuners.
- Roberto Margaritella, Exagon tuners.
- guitarplayernails.com.
- Mbrace of Tucson.
- Dave King of Dave King guitars.
- National Reso Phonic Guitars and Martin advice.
- Sandy Trach, C.F. Martin & Co Inc customer service.
- Taylor Guitars – Bob Taylor CEO for much help with technical matters, Chalise E. Zolezzi, public relations manager, and David Hosler, vice president of customer service and repair.
- Gibson guitars' Jeremy Singer for Roy Orbison 12-string.
- Roger Bucknall of Fylde Guitars.
- Darryl West for the loan of his excellent J200.
- Russell North, Fender Great Britain & Ireland Marketing & AR, for Taylor info and advice.
- Ron Casella of WD Music for tuner advice.
- Bruce Coyle, Fender GBI service coordinator.
- Hercules Stands.
- George Gruhn for L5 info.
- 'Rare Bird' – www.vintageguitar.com.
- *Guitar Player* magazine, September 1984.
- Amalia Ramírez.
- Bruce Falconer of Elixir Strings.
- Brian Whitehouse of Anglo Spanish Guitar Company Ltd (www.spanishguitar.co.uk), exclusive distributor for José Ramírez instruments in the UK.
- Josef's Pianos, Rothwell – John for the Ramírez and Strunel guitars.

- Judy Caine for Music On Earth management and photo research.
- Karl David Balmer for putting up with Daddy making a noise, and taking some photographs!
- The late great Brendan McCormack for 43 years of inspiration and endless patience. The beat goes on!
- Stewmac.com for many specialist guitar tools, excellent advice and luthiery, especially Jay Hostetler, Jayme Arnett and Erick Coleman.
- Bose Ltd – Andy Rigler for L1 information and loan.
- Jack Duarte and Peter Sensier.
- Charles Chilton for a Josh White guitar and Black Diamond information.
- David Guptill, Fingertone Picks.
- Peter Einhorn, CEO of Creative Tunings, for Spider capos.
- Stephen Green, marketing executive of Clarke International, for bench grinder.
- Ian McWee Bottlenecks & Slides (www.diamondbottlenecks.co.uk).
- John Callaghan of *Guitar and Bass* magazine.
- Mick Taylor of *Guitarist* magazine.
- Peter Goalby of Hiscox Cases.
- David Vincent, Artist Relations, KMC Music.
- Rob Smith and Emily Cooper of the International Guitar Festival of Great Britain (www.bestguitarfest.com).
- Ben Cooper of *Acoustic Guitar* magazine.
- David Greeves of *Guitar Buyer*.
- Dick Boak of Martin Guitars.
- Jim Cavanaugh of Black Diamond Strings.
- Paul Brett of Stellaguitar.

Credits

Author – Paul Balmer

Editor – Steve Rendle

Design – Richard Parsons

Copy editor – Ian Heath

Studio photography – John Colley

Technical photography – Paul Balmer

Photo research – Judy Caine

Library photos:

Andy Fairweather Low
Anglo Spanish Guitar Company
Ashmolean Museum, University of Oxford
Bose UK
C.F. Martin Archives
Classical Guitar Magazine Archives
Collections/Brian Shuel
Delta Haze Corporation
Fender UK

Frith McCormack and Ana Chong
Getty Images
Gibson UK
KMC Music
Musée du Musique, Paris
Music on Earth Productions
Paul Brett
Taylor Guitars
Yamaha Music Europe G.m.b.H. (UK)

Index